ONE SIGNAL
PUBLISHERS

ATRIA

THE WHITE WALL

HOW BIG FINANCE BANKRUPTS BLACK AMERICA

EMILY FLITTER

ONE SIGNAL
PUBLISHERS

ATRIA

NEW YORK • LONDON • TORONTO • SYDNEY • NEW DELHI

ATRIA

An Imprint of Simon & Schuster, LLC
1230 Avenue of the Americas
New York, NY 10020

Some names have been changed.

First One Signal Publishers/Atria Paperback edition April 2024

ONE SIGNAL PUBLISHERS / ATRIA PAPERBACK and colophon are
trademarks of Simon & Schuster, LLC

Simon & Schuster: Celebrating 100 Years of Publishing in 2024

For information about special discounts for bulk purchases,
please contact Simon & Schuster Special Sales at 1-866-506-1949 or
business@simonandschuster.com.

The Simon & Schuster Speakers Bureau can bring authors to your live
event. For more information or to book an event, contact the
Simon & Schuster Speakers Bureau at 1-866-248-3049 or visit our
website at www.simonspeakers.com.

Interior design by Dana Sloan

Manufactured in the United States of America

1 3 5 7 9 10 8 6 4 2

Library of Congress Cataloging-in-Publication Data has been applied for.

ISBN 978-1-9821-8324-0
ISBN 978-1-9821-8325-7 (pbk)
ISBN 978-1-9821-8326-4 (ebook)

This book is dedicated to the memory of my grandfather Rabbi Milton Richman.

CONTENTS

2024 FOREWORD

Late in 2022, a few weeks after this book was first published, I received a note from a man who had been listening to the audiobook while driving.

"I pulled over to a parking lot because I just finished your book and had to say thank you," he wrote.

He described himself: He was a Black man who had been working in finance for twenty years.

"This book validated my feelings and views. I'm not alone," he wrote. "I imagine this is how victims of sexual assault must feel when others speak of their truth."

In the years I spent writing this book and since its publication, America has gone through ripples of reckoning with its racist past in various sectors, from education to healthcare, with little meaningful change to show for it. Despite its leaders' pledges, the financial industry has been largely unmoved. This is particularly frustrating given its ubiquity: It intersects with every element of our daily lives, from employment to home ownership, and its biased systems continue to deny Black people the capital and dignity they deserve.

But even as institutions and the people in control of them continue to look away, individual readers are taking notice. At first, I was simply glad to hear that the book had resonated with the people closest to its subject. But his message was followed by other similar ones from Black readers, and together they revealed the contours of a reality that I had not considered while writing the book. Seeing stories of present-day racial discrimination and abuse assembled in one place was traumatizing to many Black readers. More precisely, the act of reading those stories was retraumatizing.

"I have been in a lot of situations similar or similar enough to bring up fears I have when banking, dealing with buying large ticket items with a credit card, not being believed that I have an excellent credit score, being questioned on how could I afford big ticket items," one woman wrote to me, adding that she had started listening to my book while walking on her treadmill. After about twenty minutes, she said she had to stop.

"I became so triggered," she wrote.

For white readers, the stories collected in this book are likely to create feelings of surprise and bewilderment. Could things really be this bad, even now? The answer is yes. Banks are still actively trying to avoid lending to Black borrowers. We know this because regulators continue to bring new redlining and discrimination cases against them. New research is demonstrating just how differently insurers continue to treat Black claimants. Black job applicants are still routinely gaslighted and passed over while contending for positions in banking and finance. As a finance reporter for the *New York Times*, I've continued to cover those stories. Examples of racism in finance that have taken place too recently to be included in this book are piling up.

For Black readers, though, additional powerful feelings may arise. In this latest edition of the book, I wanted to offer a bit of guidance to all readers for how they can prepare themselves.

I needed advice myself, so I turned to Professor Koritha Mitchell of Ohio State University, who teaches English literature and has done landmark research on depictions of violence in the literary and dramatic arts throughout the history of the United States. Mitchell's first book, *Living with Lynching: African American Lynching Plays, Performance and Citizenship, 1890–1930*, explored how communities terrorized by lynchings used dramatizations to process their pain and trauma. I suspected that, in dealing with some of the most horrifying material the U.S. experience has contained, Mitchell had likely had similar interactions with her readers and students. And as a Black woman, she had her own pain to process as she faced the heartbreaking facts so often obscured and distorted by dominant public narratives.

Step one, as Mitchell framed it, was confronting the gaslighting that so much of the public discourse includes. In finance, that gaslighting often takes the form of blaming victims of discrimination for their own misfortunes. As one reader who wrote to me put it: "Of course EVERYONE is treated the same . . . racism is over . . ." and: "Who would not give a person with an 824 TransUnion credit score a lower interest or mortgage rate, there MUST be another reason, and not racism." While many may think we've made progress, Mitchell described it like this: "If I believe this country, then I believe it's always my fault."

Calling out the gaslighting is painful in itself. And then there is the heart of the matter, the actual details of mistreatment and abuse motivated by conscious racism or unconscious bias. Mitchell said she knows that these descriptions will cause readers pain. It is to be expected and embraced. When dealing with the reactions of people encountering her own work, Mitchell said she saw the pain expressed by readers and students as a recognition of the humanity honored in the woeful stories she was recounting. She saw the reader mail I was getting in a similar way.

"When people are walking around with these experiences, it's affecting them at all times, whether it's acknowledged or not," she told me. Having those experiences recognized at all can be soothing to those at the center of them. By connecting others' experiences to their own, Mitchell said, "they can take charge of the story of what they have gone through."

Part of her message, then, which has also been a personal journey for her as she explores the history of racist abuse in the United States, is that confronting these painful episodes can help readers reclaim reality itself.

"When I have given someone the tools to face what we as Black people in this country have never been able to escape—we have never been able to escape unjust attack—that doesn't mean it stops there. My being human includes the fact that I have some choices about how I move forward," Mitchell said. "I can deliberately work toward recognizing when I'm simply accepting the dominant discourse and when I'm marching toward something more closely resembling the truth."

Making these connections is one way—but not the only way—*The White Wall* can actively serve the purpose of repairing the injustices done to Black Americans.

This idea also helps answer a question I get almost every time I talk about *The White Wall* with an audience, which boils down to: "This is really eye-opening, but now what can I *do* about it?" According to Mitchell, witnessing, reading, listening, absorbing—that is *doing* in a very important sense. The stories gathered here are wrenching. Reader, allow them to take hold of you. Once in their grip, you can start to contemplate the urgency of the need to bring about change, and the scale of the steps I am calling for the financial industry to take to bring about that change.

During our conversation, Mitchell pointed out that she and I are in different positions. She has experienced pain and trauma along with the subjects of her work and Black readers and students. I, as a white woman, have not had those same experiences. In suggesting how I might respond in the future to messages from readers like the ones described above, Mitchell recommended words to me, which I will repeat here just as she said them, representing a sentiment that I seek to embody fully:

"I'm so glad that you saw that *I* saw the pain of this, and the injustice of this, and I am honored by the fact that you saw it."

INTRODUCTION

A PROBLEM OVERLOOKED

It started with a name.

A tip came in to me about a man, John Lockette, who was suing Morgan Stanley. Other reporters had glanced at the case and deemed it too small and singular to pursue. As the banking reporter for the *New York Times*, however, I felt a duty to make sure I wasn't overlooking an important coverage area on my beat. Even though I doubted this would lead to a story—people sue banks all the time and very few of those cases merit a headline in the *Times*—I decided to check it out.

On paper, it was the story of a Black man who had been fired by the bank despite having performed well in his job for years and even being promoted and who now claimed to be a victim of racial discrimination. The bank's position was that nothing unfair had happened—that his firing was justified because he had actually *not* been performing that well. It was a classic he-said-she-said situation, and I could see why the others had passed. To find a worthwhile story in the Lockette case, I would have to unearth some larger truth that the case served to illustrate.

Morgan Stanley, unsurprisingly, did not want to talk about it at all. But Linda Friedman, Lockette's lawyer, was all too eager to set up a phone call for me with her client.

His voice on the phone was quiet, its tone full of resignation. Lockette seemed exhausted. It was early 2019 and he had been out of a job for almost three years by then. The struggle to attract widespread attention to his story was no help, either. He walked me through what had happened, from his hiring and promotion early on, to the vague criticisms his managers had made of him toward the end. Critiques that made no sense, such as the idea that his direct reports felt uncomfortable meeting with him, and that he was difficult to communicate with. No one had any specific examples to back up these claims, but that did not save him from being dismissed.

Lockette's case, it turned out, would never even make it to trial. It was quickly diverted away from public view through a process called arbitration, a common tactic among Wall Street banks to corner disgruntled employees. This is a system in which complaints are heard behind closed doors, by a panel of old, often semiretired (overwhelmingly white, overwhelmingly male) judges hired by private arbitration companies and paid by the corporate clients they're charged to rule on. A study published in 2015 found that, once in arbitration, employees won cases against their employers just 21 percent of the time, compared with a win rate of 36 percent in cases decided in federal court and 57 percent in cases heard in state court. A dramatic public confrontation with Morgan Stanley was, therefore, impossible. That also meant that there would be fewer details available for me to write about.

Another problem with Lockette's story was that it did not contain any cinema-worthy examples of racism. No one had called him the N-word, as far as he knew. No one had made any jokes about slaves or plantations, and no one had explicitly said that they disliked him because he was Black.

I, like the others, decided not to write about the Lockette case.

Then I learned that it was not the only one.

By early 2019, there were Black former employees of Morgan Stanley all over the country, from Maryland to Hawaii, reporting treatment similar to that which Lockette had experienced: exclusion, isolation, even name-calling and absurd prohibitions on behaviors that their white peers were freely allowed to do. Lockette's lawyer was in touch with all of them, and she had been trying to convince a judge to allow them to form a class to pursue a discrimination case all together against Morgan Stanley. Some of them ran up against the same wall that Lockette had hit—mandatory arbitration—but they had not yet given up. Friedman argued that if enough of them could be shown to have employment agreements with the bank that did *not* require arbitration, then the rest should be allowed to join them in open court. The chances for success were slim.

Even after learning about the other Morgan Stanley complaints, I did not view the issue of racism on Wall Street to be a top priority. I had joined the *Times* late in 2017, when the #MeToo movement was at its height and powerful sexual abusers in Hollywood and the TV news media were being exposed. One of the top goals of the finance team at the *Times* was to try to do the same for sexual harassment and abuse on Wall Street. We knew it would be tricky, since most harassment complaints met the same fate as Lockette's discrimination case: They were quickly diverted to private arbitration panels and settled with strict confidentiality agreements. A year in, we still had not found any accusations that would break the issue wide open in the financial industry.

One of my early conversations with Friedman, in fact, had drifted into the matter of sexual harassment. I had told her that what I was *really* dying to find was evidence of a #MeToo-style cover-up on Wall Street, and I asked her whether she had any good cases to share.

She swiftly swatted the idea away.

"Sexual harassment was a problem thirty years ago, and of course it still happens, but the racial discrimination is so bad," she said. "I tell this to every reporter I talk to and no one wants to listen."

"I'll listen," I said. "So which firm is the worst? Which one should I go after?"

"It's not like that," Friedman said. "You're missing the point."

I thought she might choose a name if I pressed her harder.

"Is Morgan Stanley the poster child? Are they particularly evil?" I asked.

"No!" she said, getting frustrated. "It's not about one bank."

That was one of many talks I would have with Friedman over a period of more than two years. It is hard for me to believe now that she and I have still never met in person. During many hours of phone conversations, I came to understand her motivations, her defenses, and her passions. Not quite a cynic, she was certainly a realist about what she—or anyone advocating for the rights of a minority group—could expect from a large American company. Her speech was practical, not political. Her secret weapons were details, things other people overlooked. They were all-important to her and they were both the substance and style of her messages. She did not rely on rhetoric.

I grew accustomed to her slightly raspy voice and her staccato speaking style—so quick and unrelenting that I often despaired of keeping up with her during our interviews—twined with the long, flat vowels of her Chicago accent. She packed a multitude of facts into every opinion she offered me but never any spare sentiments, nary an illusion. She presented herself both as a historian of the whiteness of Wall Street and an organizer against it. Her Chicago-based firm, Stowell & Friedman, was not the only one working on big racial discrimination cases against financial firms, but it was one of the most prominent. Friedman seemed to be everywhere, and as a result her view of the issue was both broad and deep. She had been working on racial discrimination cases for years, and had sued almost every one of the major banks—in some cases multiple times.

One of Friedman's favorite stories was a courtroom scene from 1998 in which she'd appeared in court before her idol, Constance Baker Motley, the first Black woman ever to become a federal judge. Friedman was representing a class of female stockbrokers at the firm Smith Barney who had been subjected to absurd mistreatment by their male bosses. Some were even forced into what was called "the boom-boom room," a chamber in the firm's Garden City, New York, offices where male bosses groped and assaulted the women.

Motley had asked Friedman: "You've done a lot for women, but what have you done for African American men? I wasn't born yesterday; I know that there's racial discrimination on Wall Street in addition to gender discrimination."

Friedman had replied: "We've done nothing."

"Why?" Motley had asked.

Friedman had responded that there weren't enough Black men employed at Smith Barney to form a class.

Her point in telling the story—which I heard at least three times—was a surprisingly hopeful one, considering how grim its components were. In Friedman's eyes, progress toward equality could be measured by the difference between there being any notable number of Black employees at all on Wall Street and there being none, or next to none. Big brokerage houses in the mid- and late twentieth century simply did not hire or promote Black workers. Today, in the early twenty-first century, some Wall Street firms—but not all—employ enough Black executives that, when they seek to take collective action against mistreatment, they are able to reach the class action status's forty-person threshold.

Once she had my attention, Friedman was relentless. Over and over again, she nudged me back to the problem of racism on Wall Street and in the financial industry at large. Slowly, painstakingly, she peeled my attention away from #MeToo issues and pressed it onto the matter of anti-Black discrimination at big banks, brokerages, and other financial companies. And that, it turned out, was only the start.

THE RACIAL WEALTH GAP

In 2017, not long before I began to focus on the troubles Black Wall Street employees were having, a group of researchers at Yale published the results of a curious study: They had recently asked a large, broadly representative group of Americans for their views about the difference between the amount of wealth white people in the United States had compared to Black people. They were not asking these survey subjects what they thought might be causing the gap, nor were they seeking suggestions on how to close it. Instead, they wanted to know whether most Americans were even aware there was a problem. Their findings revealed an astonishing ignorance of reality: Most Americans they surveyed did not think there *was* a racial wealth gap at all.

They were wrong, of course. The racial wealth gap in the United States, which has existed in an extreme form ever since the country's founding, is alive and yawning. White Americans hold, on average, almost $1 million in family wealth compared with an average of just $143,000 for Black American families—less than 15 percent of white families' totals. The size of this gap was largely the same in 1968, just as some of the civil rights era's landmark antidiscrimination laws were going into effect. That massive difference in net worth reflects not just unevenness in the earning power Black Americans possess compared to white Americans; it is also caused by different homeownership rates, debt loads, and wealth transfers from one generation to the next.

White people find it easier to raise significant sums of money from wealthy relatives through informal loans or gifts. They are likely to have richer, better-educated parents. The homes they own are generally worth more money on the market. And they are more likely to have retirement savings accounts. The sociologist Thomas M. Shapiro points out that not only do Black families inherit money less frequently; they're actually more likely to have to provide financial support to struggling relatives. Put simply, even when Black Americans do acquire wealth, holding on to it is harder.

On a large scale, the racial wealth gap has barely budged over the last seventy years, since the U.S. Census began collecting income data by demographics. Closer up, it has actually grown over certain periods: Most notably, in the years just after the 2008 financial crisis, Black families' fortunes shrank by 50 percent, while those of white families stopped shrinking and stabilized after a 30 percent drop. The crisis hurt Black families more than white families in part because, when they were trying to originate and sell as many home loans as possible to satisfy an ever-hungrier group of Wall Street bond investors, banks targeted Black communities, convincing people who had no need to refinance their homes to swap their sturdy thirty-year fixed mortgages out for loans with exploding interest rates and other predatory terms.

The Yale study found that virtually all the survey's participants were unaware of the wealth gap. In their search for an explanation for this obliviousness, the researchers identified several contributing factors: Rich white Americans wanted to feel like they hadn't accumulated their wealth by accident, which would suggest they might not deserve it. Black Americans were determined not to admit defeat. They did not want to live in a society that openly barred them from all hope of improving their economic standing. Poorer people wanted to feel like there were no obstacles to getting ahead in the world. In general, it had to be true that things were moving in the right direction.

The Yale researchers later found in an expanded study that America had her arms wrapped tightly around a myth of equality and prosperity that was founded on something they called the "racial progress narrative": the idea that while things had been bad for Black people living in the United States in earlier times, they had gotten better recently. Why? Because now that slavery had been outlawed and the Civil War was over, now that segregation had been deemed unconstitutional, America had developed into a true meritocracy. Hard work and dedication would pay off. But this view of their fellow citizens' experiences was *making reality worse* for Black Americans, the researchers found, since it justified pushback against programs that had been put in place to try to help level the playing field. People who thought that an evenness had already been achieved would no longer support those special programs.

The consequences of ignoring the racial wealth gap are widespread and dire. Economists estimate its presence will sap the U.S. economy of between $1 trillion and $1.5 trillion over the next ten years, thanks to lost consumption and investment. The Yale group recognized this threat and concluded that the general public's perception of the issue needed to change—pronto. They also knew it would take a Herculean effort to bring about that change. As they put it: "The observed gaps between perception and reality, particularly with regard to the Black–White wealth gap, are among the largest effects we have collectively observed in our combined experience in the field of social psychology."

NONE OF IT IS IN THE PAST

The collective blindness to the racial wealth gap has a parallel in the perception of racism itself in America. When most Americans think about the issue of racism, especially in the present-day corporate world, they are likely willing to admit that there are still instances of discrimination here and there but are also apt to say that the biggest issues are mostly structural, which means, in their minds, that they are nobody's fault in particular. This is the "*I* didn't practice slavery, so why should *I* feel guilt about it?" argument. But we know, through undeniable data, that Black Americans start out in life with disadvantages that are directly correlated with economic and professional setbacks. The "Not I" brand of denialism allows some to feel comfortable avoiding close examinations of whether any ongoing action is responsible for these disadvantages.

Bound up in the idea of structural racism is the belief, slyly embraced by corporate America over decades and solidified in the public discussion that followed the election of Barack Obama as U.S. president, that active racism has come to an end. Of course, this does not preclude discussions of "diversity," nor does it make marketing departments trying to target various racial and ethnic groups think twice about what they are doing. It simply serves to ease the minds of corporate and government power brokers about whether the mistreatment of Black Americans by companies and people based on hateful or biased motives is still a problem. Since American voters selected a Black man to lead them as president of the United States, this view says, clearly there is no longer a problem.

This is the idea of "post-racialism" as defined by law professor Sumi Cho of DePaul University College of Law. In a 2009 article in the *Iowa Law Review*, Cho described the term as "a twenty-first century ideology that reflects a belief that due to racial progress the state need not engage in race-based decision-making or adopt race-based remedies, and that civil society should eschew race as a central organizing principle of social action." If racism is "over," and all that's left behind is a bit of catching up that Black Americans have to do now that they have the same opportunities as white Americans, then the world can carry on with business and not worry about having to make any inconvenient accommodations.

Tell all that to Ricardo Peters, a former JPMorgan Chase employee whose story shoved me the rest of the way toward writing this book.

I met Ricardo in the summer of 2019 when he did what dozens of witnesses of brutality against Black Americans have done in recent years: force a reckoning with unacknowledged injustice. When Peters pulled out his iPhone and hit "record," he swept away the ambiguities that normally plague cases like his, the kind that abounded in John Lockette's story. And, like the terrified witnesses watching police beat, shoot, and strangle Black people, Ricardo made history. The story I wrote about him in December of 2019 attracted a million and a half readers and set me on a path to discovering other, similar cases— scores of them.

I never did write about John Lockette, but each subsequent story of discrimination I have encountered has made me reflect on his struggle. There are countless others like him whose perhaps too "subtle" or "quiet" stories are no less awful than his or Ricardo's.

My work on Ricardo's story led me to perceive the scope of the effects of active, ongoing racism in the financial industry, and once that door opened, the truth came rolling in. Racism in banking and finance is a devastating force—in our capitalist society, perhaps *the* devastating force—that prevents Black Americans from gaining equal footing in the United States. And as I learned, finance's role in that story is no secret to the financial firms that determine who wins and loses in this country.

THE SCREAM

In 1991, while excavating a lot in Lower Manhattan near Wall Street in preparation to build a new skyscraper that would house various federal government offices, construction crews discovered a giant unmarked grave. Archaeologists determined it to be a site where African slaves brought to New York for trade or labor during the 1600s and 1700s were buried when they died. Hundreds of people's remains filled the grave, including children who had died of malnutrition and adults whose bones showed signs of injury from strenuous labor. The discovery was a reminder that slavery had not been confined to the American South—that northerners had exploited and tortured human beings kidnapped from another continent as well. As the federal government, which owned the site, tried to decide what to do with it, Black community groups started to organize a response to the discovery to highlight the site's importance and protect it from being sloppily dismantled and then entirely covered up by an office building, as plans for the site, at 290 Broadway, dictated.

As excavation continued apace, the gruesome details of Wall Street's past became less and less avoidable. The remains spoke of enslaved persons who died in bondage if not agony. Some were bunched together as if they had all been buried at the same time, the victims, perhaps, of an epidemic. One skull in particular lay with its jaws wide open, as if frozen in a scream.

The resident archaeologist explained that the posture of a decomposing body changed as its muscles and tendons fell away, but Deadria Farmer-Paellmann could not get the vision of its tortured pose out of her head. Deadria, a multidisciplinary artist working for the New York City Health Department, soon joined the fight to see this site treated with respect. Watching the project continue despite the sensitivity of the location was a wrenching experience for her.

At one end of the carefully dug-out trench, some of the workers had set up an altar where they regularly left fresh fruit and water, an attempt to show respect for the dead and to protect the living. The colorful altar, too, fixed itself in Deadria's consciousness.

And she was impressed by the power of the demonstrators— clergy members, artists, politicians, actors, scholars—who came to the site to pay their respects and give voice to their grievances over how it was being treated. Beginning on August 9, 1992, for twenty-six hours, through periods of wind and drizzle, hundreds of people stood watch to call attention to injustice present and past.

When it was over, Deadria felt that something, for her, was unfinished. Protest and spirit alone were not going to heal this wound. She decided to make this her life's work. She quit her day job at the health department and enrolled in law school, setting her sights on the concept of reparations, an idea she had earlier explored at various points as a college and graduate school student.

It would not be easy. Just as Deadria was gathering evidence and gaming out strategies, other efforts to seek justice for the memories of the people enslaved for centuries in the United States and for their descendants were running into dead ends. In 1995 a federal appeals court decision focused on the sovereign immunity of the United States government appeared to bar anyone from making claims against the federal government for its role in slavery. But Deadria had another idea in mind: Thinking of how close the mass grave lay to Wall Street, she reasoned that some of the country's longest-lasting private companies might have stains on their records similar to the federal government's.

There was no public accounting of American companies' roles in slavery, so Deadria combed through various archives on the East Coast, looking for clues. More than five years after the discovery of the grave in Lower Manhattan, she found her first connection. The health insurer Aetna had, during the first half of the nineteenth century, insured the lives of slaves. This was significant, but Deadria knew it was just the tip of the iceberg. Huge swaths of the financial system during the American colonial era and the early decades of the United States were awash in money from slavery, whether it was in the form of deposits of the proceeds from the slave trade at a bank or collateral notes backed by slaves that their enslavers used to obtain loans. These records weren't things any company made it easy to find; they existed in the annals of ports in New England and in the archives of various local historical societies. Deadria painstakingly collected them, venturing to Providence, Rhode Island, with her young daughter, a babysitter, and the babysitter's daughter in tow, and even traveling to London to conduct research at the British Museum.

The total absence of any public admissions about their contributions to slavery by the companies whose names Deadria was turning up in her research, including certain members of the ever-growing consolidation of regional banks that would become the present-day Bank of America, left her aghast.

How could these businesses pretend like nothing bad had happened?

How can we?

FACING THE WALL

The White Wall is my attempt to face, head-on, the issues financial industry executives have ignored. The people whose stories I highlight have known for most of their lives that this was what the world was really like. Although they, too, might be inclined to underestimate the size of the wealth gap, they will make no mistake in their assessments of the daily toils of being Black in America and trying to go to a bank, get a job in finance or another realm of the corporate world, or access the seamless consumer experiences white people around them take for granted. They have stared down enormous disappointments. Repeated setbacks. Endless frustrations, humiliations, slights, the memories of which keep them awake at night and make them feel exhausted and ill. Yet they have carried on with their lives.

In the three years I have spent exploring this topic, I have certainly not reached its limits. Fifty different books could be written about racism in the financial industry and there would still be plenty more to say about it after that. In my own effort, I have made false starts. I have discovered the deficiencies in my own knowledge and understanding of Black Americans' experiences along the way. I am neither a social scientist nor a historian, neither an anti-racism authority nor a public intellectual. I want readers of this book to see the many ways in which my perception is limited by my own shortcomings. That is why I have decided to weave some of my personal experiences into the mix of stories that I collected for this book. There was no way for me to write about this without also documenting my own process of learning and discovery.

PART ONE

ONE

BANKING WHILE BLACK

"PLEASE USE CAUTION . . ."

The email blasts went to a wide audience. Hundreds of employees working in the same region of JPMorgan Chase's national branch network in the suburbs north of New York City in New York and Connecticut—a part of the country where its branches were most numerous—received each message. At the top, in the subject line, there was always the same warning: "Please Use Caution . . ."

They were never meant to be seen by the public.

The messages were a way for Chase branch employees to alert each other of suspicious activity at their branches. Each cluster of Chase branches across the country had its own system for alerting employees to potential fraudsters on a regular basis, with new alerts popping up almost daily. The warning systems were not all the same; it was up to area managers to decide how to structure them. Here in the dense northeastern suburbs, if a customer came to a branch and tried to fool employees into giving out money, a message with the words "Please Use Caution . . ." in its subject line would go out to nearby branches, so the suspicious person would not be able to succeed at a second location after failing at the first.

Some of the messages that circulated in this region described blatantly bad behavior by people attempting to use stolen account information to get their hands on money that wasn't theirs. Others described situations that were decidedly more ambiguous, in which a person seeking to complete a transaction in a Chase branch didn't seem legitimate but was not unmistakably in the wrong. Someone may have been lying—or perhaps not—and a banker had decided to err on the side of caution.

One message, from March of 2020, read:

African American man, tried to cash a check from a business from Texas.

Another, from February of 2020:

I had a young gentleman come in African American with dread locks around 21 years old. The account was recently opened and a transfer was made into the account for $17,000 the client wanted to withdraw $6500 but had already made a $7000 withdraw at another branch. I declined the transaction and he went to our ATM to withdraw $1000. The client had a debit card and pin number, he also had a CT drivers license. Joinda is calling fraud dept now to get the account restricted.

A few days after that:

Young black man about 6' wearing a red jacket came in and attempted to withdraw $9500 from account. We called fraud and they said that the account is being restricted however the account is still open. He left saying that he lives in New Rochelle and will be going to a branch there. Please be cautious in doing any transactions.

And another:

An older looking African-American male, Chad J.*, attempted to cash a 14,448.93 Chase Cashiers Check. His ID looked fake and he definitely looked older than the date of birth on his license. He said Chase recently closed his accounts and sent him this check. I looked up the name, and that much was true ([account number]). I told him I couldn't cash the check and he would have to deposit it at another bank.

Thus went the chatter between tellers and other bank branch employees over how to spot and deal with potential fraudsters. Messages like these are not an exclusive creation of JPMorgan Chase. Every big bank has a way for branch employees to communicate with each other about suspicious characters they encounter. While the formats of each bank's warning systems may differ, the core activity is the same. Bankers are constantly assessing the trustworthiness of customers, almost all of whom are strangers to them, and using their assessments to decide whether to do business with those customers.

There was another feature of the JPMorgan Chase "Please Use Caution . . ." emails that highlighted the difference between the way bank branch employees see Black customers and white customers: In the case of white customers, race did not seem to merit a mention.

Often, the people described in the "Please Use Caution . . ." emails had had their driver's licenses scanned by bank employees, and in those cases images of their identification documents were attached to the warning emails so that anyone reading them could see exactly what the potential fraudsters looked like. This made it even stranger that the Black customers among them were described as such. Why

---

* Author's note: The customers' last names have been replaced with initials to protect their privacy.

bother providing a description of someone whose photo was attached anyway? It was something that seemed to happen to Black customers more often than white customers, at least in the cache of emails I reviewed, which were secretly provided to me by a Chase employee who felt uncomfortable with the way other employees seemed to routinely profile Black customers.

One such email included a photocopy of a customer's driver's license showing that he was a white man. But the description of him did not include that detail. The banker had simply called him an "older male."

In another case from mid-2020, a man whose attached driver's license photo also showed that he was not Black, was described only by his last name, "Mr. G.," and the account of his suspicious behavior was limited to what he actually sought from the bank—$25,000 in cash from an account that had recently received a $159,900 deposit from the Small Business Administration—and not what he looked like.

A woman, also clearly not Black according to the attached copy of her ID, who came to a drive-through window and tried to withdraw cash from an account that had recently received a large deposit that had aroused the bank's suspicions, was described only by the color and make of the car she was driving.

And yet a man who tried to take $2,200 out of an account under the name Chris V. got an extra kick of racial pigeonholing when the banker describing his case concluded her email with: "He was a black African American, wearing a black jacket & black hat, please be careful."

The emails provide a rare window into the minds of bank employees as they gaze out from behind their reinforced glass partitions at customers, always on the lookout for someone who might be trying to scam them. The words of these employees and the mindset they reveal could help explain the behavior of a group of bankers at a Wells Fargo branch in Wilmington, Delaware, when, in March of 2019, a thirty-six-year-old Black man named Jabari Bennett walked into their location seeking to withdraw several thousand dollars in cash to buy a used car.

NO WITHDRAWAL

Jabari was a recent transplant to the area, having just moved to Wilmington from Atlanta, where he had lived for the past several years. He had come to Delaware to take care of his mother. Before moving north a month earlier, he had sold his house in Georgia and had pocketed $71,000 in the deal, a sum that was now sitting in a Wells Fargo bank account he had recently opened.

He was still trying to get important pieces of his new life in order, and he needed to buy a car. His current set of wheels was a gas-guzzler, an old Lincoln Town Car. He wanted something smaller and more fuel efficient. He had just started a new job training program and needed to economize.

He was not in a fancy part of town. Perched in an empty corner of a shopping complex at the busy intersection of two highways in suburban Wilmington, the building housing the Wells Fargo branch was a stone-clad, one-story structure with a row of picture windows that made it look as though it could just as easily have been a Waffle House as a bank. As Jabari walked through its front entrance, his heart was already beating fast: He was excited about the car he had just picked out from a dealership down the street. It was a sensible choice, a Toyota Camry, and with a price tag of just $6,400, it was an economical one, too. And since Jabari expected the purchase to be an all-cash deal, he was already picturing himself driving away, radio on, his business done for the day.

He expected to be in and out of the bank and back to the dealership in a matter of minutes. It was fortunate, really, that he was going to the bank today, since he had been meaning to move some money from his own account into his mother's anyway. He intended to take care of both things at once.

Jabari wasn't dressed in a suit. Since car buying was his main activity for the day, he was dressed exactly the way he wanted to be, in baggy pants, with a cloth tied over his hair. Comfortable, relaxed, casual. But to the bank branch employees his look said something else.

Tall African American male in baggy white pants and a durag... Would that have been the "Please Use Caution . . ." version of Jabari's figure? We'll never know. But there is no doubt that the Wells Fargo employees were suspicious of him.

"I'd like to withdraw some money," he said to a teller, explaining that he wanted to move $10,000 into his mother's account and take out $6,400 in cash for himself. At first the teller—a white man—who took Jabari's driver's license from him in preparation for processing his request showed little enthusiasm for helping him. He walked away with Jabari's license, was gone for a minute, returned to the window, and handed Jabari the license.

"We're unable to complete this transaction at this time," he said.

"What?" Jabari said in disbelief.

"There was an issue with your license."

"What issue?"

"Your license is from another state, it doesn't match up with your information," the Wells Fargo employee said.

"I can explain," Jabari said. He knew it was a little bit complicated: He had gotten his driver's license in Missouri while studying for a commercial trucker's certification. He had not yet changed it to reflect his new Delaware address, since he'd only arrived in the state a couple of weeks earlier. But the banker didn't want to hear it.

"I'm sorry," he said. "We can't verify your identity. This transaction cannot be completed."

"But I can answer questions, take me in a back room, away from the other customers, ask me what my last transaction was. When did I get that amount of money put into my account. Ask me—"

"Sir, I'm going to have to ask you to leave the bank," the employee said.

Stunned, Jabari walked back out the front door empty-handed. But on the street, in the cold March air, it made even less sense. He called his mother from his cell phone and told her what had happened. She provided him with her account number. If he couldn't withdraw the money in cash, he could transfer it to her, and *she* would withdraw it, they decided. He turned around and marched back into the bank.

"Sir, we can't help you here," the employee called out to him. But he approached the counter anyway. Another man came scooting out to meet him, introducing himself as the branch manager. Jabari repeated to this new interlocutor the purpose of his visit.

"The problem is," the branch manager said, "your driver's license is off. It's from Missouri."

"Yeah, I know, but what's the story? Did you decide it's fraudulent? Did you decide there is a fraud? Because if there's not a fraud, then why can't I complete my transaction?" Jabari asked. His voice was rising; he felt like he was close to begging.

"We have some new policies in place, and I'm afraid that we can't help you at this time," the branch manager said. "You'll have to leave."

Jabari explained that he had given up on getting the cash and just wanted to transfer some money from his own account to his mother's.

"It's a new policy," the branch manager said. "We don't let you put money into someone else's account if that person isn't here."

Exasperated, Jabari exclaimed: "I just want my money!"

"Leave now or I'll call the police," the branch manager said.

"But I want my money!" Jabari said again. The man turned away from him and started to walk quickly over to a phone while looking over his shoulder at Jabari, who stayed where he was. The man picked up the phone. Jabari saw him dial 911.

That was when he turned and left.

• • •

Even though Jabari's experience occurred at a Wells Fargo, JPMorgan Chase's "Please Use Caution" thread offered an internal perspective on what had happened to him. Some of the incidents described by JPMorgan employees sounded similar, either because they involved employees refusing to withdraw money at a Black customer's request or because they focused on employees' unwillingness to accept the idea that a Black customer's check was legitimate. In one "Please Use Caution . . ." email, a teller described a November 2018 incident:

> *Very young African American male with blonde dreds came in and presented this check for cashing, I told him I had to verify the check and got very upset and confrontational. I called the maker and they said they did issue that check. He took it with him.*

From 2019:

> *We had an African American man with a grey t shirt and khaki pants with glasses try to cash a check for 910 from the account of James F. V., which we think may have been stolen. The guy's name is Drequan J. He didn't have a car, as he came walked to the branch.*

Early 2020:

> *An account was opened for a tall African American Male with dreadlocks and facial hair. After fraud was called, the account was restricted. Attached is copy of payroll check.*

In July of 2020, a banker became suspicious when a young Black man tried to withdraw money from his account that had been deposited there by the Small Business Administration as part of a program to help businesses survive the coronavirus pandemic.

I had a young African American guy with a red hoodie who wanted to withdraw $1750 from his College Checking account. He recently had a $10,000.00 deposit from SBAD TREAS 310 MISC PAY EI

I asked him if he had a business and he said yes and it controlled through his tax guy. I asked him if he had any proof of the business and he said he will be back with it. He also stated that he already spoke to someone about this and they confirmed it was not fraudulent. There are no notes on the account. I refused the withdraw and he may or may not be back with proof.

These descriptions show how subjective a determination of potential fraud can be. The banker who refused to deal with the young Black man who had received an SBA loan wielded a significant amount of power over the man's access to what may have been his own money.

Of course, it's possible that some of the people described in the "Please Use Caution . . ." thread may have indeed been trying to commit fraud. Some of the emails I saw recounted incidents where police were called and the would-be customer was arrested after bankers were able to present convincing evidence of wrongdoing. When I asked Trish Wexler, a JPMorgan Chase spokeswoman, about it, she pointed out that the bank's employees did need to "alert each other of potential fraud attempts to help protect our customers' money." In an email to me, she seemed at first to be condemning the general concept of identifying people by their race. She reminded me that people in other industries do it too. "This is an example of what we unfortunately see across society—and in the press in particular—where arbitrary use of a race descriptor perpetuates unfair biases," she wrote.

But further along in the email, she delivered this carefully worded message: "Unnecessary use of race descriptors not in service to stopping illegal activity reinforces unfair stereotypes."

My mind first translated her statement into simpler terms as this: *Using race in descriptions of suspicious people doing suspicious things reinforces unfair stereotypes.*

But that's not actually what the sentence means.

"Unnecessary use of race descriptors" can be rephrased like this:

If *a person is described by their race* and *there is no need to identify them in that way* . . .

Add the phrase "not in service to stopping illegal activity" and you get this:

If *a person is described by their race* and *there is no need to identify them in that way,* since *it is not actually helping to stop illegal activity* . . .

Well, *that* is what reinforces unfair stereotypes.

Embedded in this sentence, unspoken yet precisely shaped by the qualifiers in its structure, is the idea that if someone is described by their race and it *is* part of a process of trying to stop illegal activity, then it does not necessarily reinforce unfair stereotypes.

In other words, this is a legally buttoned-up way of saying, *Yes, our employees sent these emails, and as long as they were doing it in the service of stopping illegal activity, it's okay.* But that wasn't the end of Wexler's statement. She added: "We're continuing to educate our employees on unconscious bias and reinforce behaviors that contribute to an inclusive culture."

But how can employees know beforehand whether they really are stopping illegal activity? As Jabari Bennett's story shows, not even a call to the police supports the idea that an employee has found clear evidence of fraud. Sometimes, calling the police can be an intimidation tactic. And sometimes a call to the police is what finally serves to sort out a dispute between a Black bank customer and an obstinate teller, a terrifying prospect for Black Americans, who have suffered grave injustices at the hands of police officers.

QUESTIONING A CHECK

Clarice Middleton, an Atlanta resident who in December of 2018 was working as an Uber driver when she ducked into a Wells Fargo branch in Druid Hills, a wealthy (white) neighborhood, endured just such terror while trying to cash a $200 check.

The check had been issued from a Wells Fargo account by Clarice's landlord, an Atlanta-based property manager. Having worked as a bank teller herself, Clarice felt confident that she understood how things worked when a stranger walked into a bank branch needing a check cashed. She reasoned that the fact that the check had come from Wells Fargo meant it would be easier for Wells Fargo's branch employees to cash it on the spot than it would be for employees at a bank that had not issued the check. She brought two forms of identification with her, so there could be no doubt about who she was and whether she was the rightful recipient of the money. It wasn't that she had any doubts that she could get this simple little piece of banking business done; it was that she was a belt-and-suspenders sort of person and always wanted to be extra sure that she was following the rules. She was confident that she would have no problem at the bank.

Things did not go as she had expected.

The teller who took Clarice's check, a woman, was silent and still for a long time.

"Is there a problem?" Clarice asked her.

The woman did not respond. Clarice thought: *That's rude.* She watched as the woman got up from her window and walked away with

Clarice's check. She walked over to a man in the back of the room who looked like he might be the branch manager. They spoke too quietly for Clarice to hear, and she wanted to know what was happening with the check, so she called out: "Is everything okay?"

The man took Clarice's check and walked back toward her.

"I have the check stub, I have another form of ID, whatever you need to see," Clarice said as he approached.

"We don't need any of that," the man said. Clarice started to argue.

"Why not?" she asked. "Why can't you look at what I've brought with me? Why can't you cash my check?" She felt herself getting agitated, her voice rising. It was unfair. It made no sense.

Just then, a door in the back opened and another man stuck his head through it. The first man looked over his shoulder. "Call the police," he said to the second man.

Panic, like icy water, washed over Clarice's whole body. She wondered whether to run. They were calling the police on her! It was shocking. A voice in her head started saying, on repeat: *I don't want to die. I don't want to die.*

"Call the police? Why?" she asked the man. She was nearly in tears.

"This is a fraudulent check," he said.

"No it's not!" she argued. "It's not fraudulent!"

"It's fraudulent," he said.

Before Clarice knew what had happened, she was wailing. Tears were running down her face and she was begging the tellers to return her $200 check. They would not. They told her the police were coming and that she was disturbing the other customers. One of them walked over to Clarice, stopping within inches of her as if to use his presence to make her move. "You need to leave," he said.

The man guided Clarice out of the bank but kept her check. On the sidewalk out front, she wasn't sure what to do. She couldn't leave—the Wells Fargo employees had her check—but she was terrified of what would happen when the police arrived. She realized that she was shaking.

(In 2020, a Wells Fargo spokeswoman told me that Clarice had been ejected from the bank and that the police had been called because she was yelling "abusive and profane language" at the bank employees. Clarice's lawyer disputed that claim.)

After a wait in which Clarice could focus on little besides her own panic, a patrol car pulled up. An officer got out. He marched right past Clarice, ignoring her attempt to make eye contact with him, and walked up to where the two male branch supervisors were waiting, right outside the entrance to the branch. The three of them conferred. Clarice hung back at a safe distance until they were finished, and the officer came over to her and asked her for her side of the story. She gave it. The two Wells Fargo employees disappeared inside.

To Clarice's surprise, the officer left after listening to her story, offering little comment on the situation beyond a brief suggestion that Clarice ought to have been more understanding of the Wells Fargo employees' suspicions. One of the Wells Fargo managers stuck his head out of the doorway to the bank branch and held up Clarice's check. She saw that someone had written all over the back of it in pen.

"We'll cash this," the manager said to Clarice. "If you still want us to."

Some part of Clarice wanted to swipe the check from his hand and march away with her head up, but she knew that with all the pen marks on it the check would be even harder to cash somewhere else. She lowered her eyes to the ground.

"All right," she said.

THE RIGHT TO PROFILE

The Civil Rights Act of 1964 lists specific businesses that may not treat Black customers differently: movie theaters, hotels, restaurants, and performance and sports venues. Federal courts in some parts of the country have held that because the law identifies the kinds of businesses to which it applies, those not on the list, such as banks, cannot be held to it. That loophole makes it hard for victims of racial profiling to win in court.

There is an additional limitation. In 1866, just after the Civil War had ended and the Thirteenth Amendment abolishing slavery in the United States was passed, Congress created new laws to establish rights for Black Americans, including one giving them the right to enter into agreements to buy goods or services and have those contracts enforced. Some courts have since ruled that the law requires only that service be granted eventually, even if there is a delay or an extra difficulty. According to these rulings, the 1866 law does not guarantee equal treatment for everyone in the course of doing business.

In 2012, for instance, a federal appeals court ruled that a Hispanic man who had been turned away by a white cashier at a Target big-box store in Florida did not have a case against Target because he was able to complete his purchases with a different cashier. This was especially relevant to Clarice's case. When she sued Wells Fargo over the Druid Hills incident, the bank tried to fight the suit by arguing that because she was eventually able to cash her check, a judge should dismiss it.

Clarice and Jabari both decided to do something about the way they were treated. And they both hired the same lawyer, Yechezkel Rodal, a Florida-based attorney who went by the nickname Chezky and who had made a name for himself representing Black people mistreated by banks. His career was still fairly new in 2021—he had run a restaurant in Broward County before two hurricanes knocked him out of business in 2008—but Chezky had already handled a dozen different lawsuits against banks for racially profiling their customers and had taken on close to fifty other cases of the same kind that had been settled in secret, before any lawsuit was filed. He had become so well-known that he'd had to adopt a policy of turning down any case that was not severe enough to involve police. And he had seen some severe ones. In one case, bankers had sicced an entire SWAT team on a Black woman.

By the time he met Clarice and Jabari, Chezky had begun to see his work as part of a larger cause. He focused his attention on closing the serious loophole in federal law in which courts have sometimes maintained that it is not illegal for some businesses to racially profile their customers.

Others are aware of this loophole. After I wrote a *New York Times* story in June of 2020 about the paucity of protections for Black bank customers in state and federal laws, Democrats in the United States Senate drafted a bill to strengthen protections for Black customers trying to do business at banks and other financial firms. It was called the Fair Access to Financial Services Act, and it was introduced into the Senate Banking Committee in late 2020 but was never passed.

Chezky, meanwhile, began to craft legal arguments to try to close the loophole illustrated by the 2012 Target case. Clarice's lawsuit looked like a great opportunity to pursue this particular goal. Chezky expected the case to be dismissed by the federal judge who first over-saw it, specifically because the Wells Fargo bankers did, in the end, cash Clarice's check. If the judge did dismiss the case, he would appeal the dismissal and try to get the same federal appeals court that issued the Target ruling to revisit that 2012 case and agree to view it in a narrower fashion so that cases like Clarice's could proceed.

His argument: Rosa Parks, the civil rights icon who refused to move to the back of a public bus in the segregated South, also got to her destination, despite being humiliated along the way. Should that really have cut her off from all recourse to justice? Chezky also hoped to point out that, in contrast to the Target cashier who was alone in refusing to serve the Hispanic customer, bank branch employees in cases like Clarice's act in concert with each other once they have decided to treat a Black customer with suspicion. The customer cannot simply go to the next window at the bank and get service.

I never got a chance to meet Chezky in person. The COVID-19 lockdowns kept us in our separate cities—New York and Fort Lauderdale—but over the course of a couple of years, beginning in late 2019, we talked fairly regularly on the phone and I learned a few things about his day-to-day life. He was a Hasidic Jew who talked a mile a minute and once, deep in the pandemic, described to me in meticulous detail his sister's Zoom wedding in Brooklyn; I had interrupted his virtual attendance of the event by calling to talk about a story I was working on. Whenever Chezky got going talking about one of his discrimination cases, his voice would take on a burning urgency. I felt I could hear what was in his imagination: Chezky Rodal, finally making headway on a matter of fairness for Black Americans, bringing his passion to the somber setting of an appeals court. But he was also a realist. He knew the chances of getting the federal appeals court to narrow its Target decision were not good. He knew, as lawyers around the country know, that it is best to rely on states to pick up the slack in the federal government's antidiscrimination protections.

The strength of various states' antidiscrimination laws is quite uneven. On the day Clarice walked into the Wells Fargo branch in Atlanta's Druid Hills neighborhood, the state of Georgia did not have a law prohibiting businesses from refusing to serve customers based on their race. As of the writing of this book, this is still true. In 2016, some of the state's lawmakers tried to enact one. It was called the Georgia Civil Rights in Public Accommodations Act (Georgia House Bill 849). Georgia's legislature voted it down. A conservative group, Concerned Women for America, celebrated the bill's demise because it would have prohibited businesses from turning away gay or transgender people. And besides, it was "not necessary," the Concerned Women said, because of the federal antidiscrimination laws already in place. The group called the death of the bill "a victory for the privacy and safety of women and children."

It was a good thing for Sauntore Thomas that he did not try to do his banking in Georgia. He had enough trouble as it was in Michigan, where he lived, and where a robust labor movement had, over decades, created some of the strongest state antidiscrimination laws anywhere.

Sauntore took three checks, amounting to almost $100,000, to the Detroit-area bank where he had held an account for two years. The money was for a settlement in a race discrimination case against his former employer, Enterprise Rent-A-Car. (Sauntore did not disclose the settlement amount; a bank official told the *Detroit Free Press* how much the checks were worth.) The bank accused Sauntore of forging the checks and called the police. Sauntore, meanwhile, called Deborah Gordon, his lawyer in the Enterprise case, and, with her help, used Michigan's state laws to sue the bank, TCF Bank. The parties quickly reached a confidential settlement. What happened to him is pretty much the best-case scenario for a Black bank customer who is denied service. The bank's leadership even apologized publicly.

The phenomenon of mistrust and poor treatment of Black customers knows no financial bounds. In October of 2020, Ernst Valery, a Haitian-born real estate developer in Baltimore, took a $3 million check issued to him by the state of Maryland—a tax credit he had received for work he had done to revitalize an abandoned church property—to a local Wells Fargo branch where he had been a customer for twenty years. A branch manager there simply refused to believe that the check was real and that it was for him. Ernst sued the bank in December of that year. (Chezky did not get this particular case; another law firm did.)

Chezky never got a chance to present Clarice's case to an appeals court. Wells Fargo agreed to a confidential settlement of the matter. The same sort of agreement concluded Jabari Bennett's case. Settlements can often bring needed financial relief to the people who filed the lawsuits in the first place, but they present a major drawback for any larger effort to change a pattern of behavior because their details are ever after deemed secret and they relieve the accused party—Wells Fargo in these cases—of having to admit to wrongdoing.

TWO

MYSTERY SHOPPERS

In September of 2012, a manager at BancorpSouth, one of the largest mortgage lenders in the U.S. Southeast, called a meeting of loan officers to order. Everyone in the room was white. The bank manager leading the meeting began by instructing officers not to linger over the applications of people who belonged to a "protected class" of borrowers, like racial and religious minorities. Sitting on them would expose the bank to potential legal and regulatory trouble, the manager warned, so it was best to hurry them through. He told the team that any applications submitted by people who qualified as members of a protected class had to be dispensed within twenty-one days.

Then he explained that this policy applied specifically to Black borrowers.

With $13 billion in assets at the time, the Mississippi-based bank had an especially strong presence in parts of the South, where megabanks like Bank of America and Wells Fargo offered minimal service. The bankers gathered for the meeting were in Memphis, Tennessee, where two-thirds of the population was Black and where BancorpSouth got the most requests for mortgages compared with any other market in which it operated.

Memphis's demographics might have suggested that the best way to do business would be to try to win over Black people who made up the majority of BancorpSouth's potential customers. But the bank did the opposite. Its leaders had located its branches in parts of the city where Black borrowers were not likely to venture. It had also directed its advertising to white potential customers, studiously avoiding reaching out to Black customers. And, as federal authorities would claim in a 2016 lawsuit, it had given its loan officers broad discretion about how much to charge mortgage borrowers in annual interest. These officers routinely charged the few Black borrowers who did manage to get loans from the bank higher interest rates than white borrowers. It was a practice that was supposed to be illegal, outlawed on paper in the late 1960s when Congress passed the Fair Housing Act. The act was part of a package of new laws designed to end the practice of redlining, by which city officials, banks, insurers, and other businesses forcibly segregated Black populations in cities by refusing to give them the same services that white populations were getting. BancorpSouth's unequal treatment of its Black and white customers was the perfect example of the limits of those new laws' impact on real-world conditions. Redlining might technically be illegal, but banks and other businesses still engage in it until they get caught, if they ever do.

One loan officer attending BancorpSouth's 2012 meeting joked that *they*—meaning Black borrowers—"need to get their credit up" and to "stop paying their damn bills late." Another loan officer observed that everyone in the meeting was white, to which the manager leading the meeting replied: "I'm sure I'll hear about that soon, too. I'm looking. I don't know where I'll put one, but I'm looking."

"Don't use the N-word!" someone called out.

"What's up, n*ggas!" someone else shouted.

The room erupted in laughter.

This scene, secretly recorded by someone in the room that day, came back to haunt BancorpSouth when the Consumer Financial Protection Bureau took it to court in 2016 over its treatment of Black bank customers. The bank paid nearly $11 million to settle allegations that it had engaged in widespread discrimination against Black customers not only in Memphis but in other areas where it had branches as well.

It turns out the CFPB's work to bolster its case against Bancorp-South did not stop there. Officials revealed that they had sent people posing as potential mortgage borrowers—"mystery shoppers"—to various branches of BancorpSouth to test whether the bank was discriminating against Black mortgage borrowers. The findings were grim. In one instance, two undercover investigators posing as customers visited the same loan officer at a branch in Madison, Alabama. One "customer" was white, the other Black. Both professed to be first-time home buyers, but the Black customer had a higher credit score and a higher salary than the white customer did. Nevertheless, the loan officer offered the Black customer a smaller loan with a higher interest rate.

The tendency to view Black customers with extra suspicion—or at least to include their Blackness explicitly in descriptions of suspicious behavior—is only one of the myriad ways in which Black customers get treated differently from the second they walk in the door of a bank.

Bankers make all kinds of private, race-based judgments of bank customers, and they extend far beyond a tendency to disbelieve customers' claims about their identities and the sources of their wealth. It's a fact that has been borne out time and again not just through individual anecdotes but in rigorous studies of how banks treat Black customers compared to white customers. In its regular surveys of consumer banking in the United States, the Federal Deposit Insurance Corporation has found a "substantial" difference between the number of white bank account holders and the number of minorities with bank accounts; as of 2019, less than 3 percent of white Americans lacked one, while the percentage of Black Americans with no bank account was closer to 14. The FDIC's 2019 survey also found that, among the households that did have bank accounts, Black people were less likely to make in-person visits to bank branches than white people were, and they were less likely to rely on loans from banks to conduct the day-to-day business of their lives.

One reason for this discrepancy that is captured particularly well by the mystery shopper method of research is the striking difference between the way bank employees often treat Black and white customers. Sending undercover researchers to see how bank employees behave when they think no one with regulatory authority over them is watching unearths soft, subtle, yet powerful obstructionist actions. Researchers are only just beginning to try to note and categorize these actions head-on.

In 2019, I spoke with a slew of Wells Fargo customers who were all living in the same nightmare: Wells Fargo had cut off access to their accounts in preparation for closing them. The customers never knew exactly why the bank had decided to do this; they'd all received letters informing them that the bank had made the decision to close their accounts with no explanation as to why. Inconvenience then turned to nightmare in the form of Wells Fargo's failure to actually stop all activity in the account. Automatic payments the account holders had set up were still going out months after the bank had declared their accounts closed, which meant that overdraft fees would pile up. The bank would then send these customers to its collections department. They received calls from Wells Fargo employees warning them that if they did not immediately pay the balances they owed as a result of these fees and automatic debits they would be reported to a national database that tracked deadbeat bank customers and barred them from the banking system.

Two years after my Wells Fargo story came out, I spoke with Susan Shin, legal director of the New Economy Project, a New York–based group that tries to help local residents navigate the financial system. The group had for years received a steady stream of calls from people describing the same sequence of events I had detailed in my story: Bank abruptly closes account, pursues customer for continually mounting overdraft fees, threatens customer with exile from the banking industry.

"When I read your story I felt like you'd been living in my head," Shin told me. "We see that all the time here." She added that *all* the people who had called New Economy for help had been non-white. Nothing they had tried could convince their banks to stop charging them more and more overdraft fees after closing their accounts. Shin said she had felt that race played a part in banks' willingness to stick to their positions and show no mercy by reducing or waiving the fees. "It's hard to quantify that, but that's been our experience," she said. A national survey of banks conducted in 2021 seemed to bear out her observations when it found that, across the industry, Black and Hispanic account holders paid more than twice as much in fees on their accounts as white account holders did.

Not all the mistreatment is as hard to quantify. For years a group of researchers working with the National Community Reinvestment Coalition, a nonprofit group that tries to get banks to do more business in low-income and minority-heavy communities where redlining was once rampant, have been conducting experiments similar to the CFPB's undercover operation, secretly sending visitors to banks across the country to test their employees' reactions to a wide variety of customers. Similar to the CFPB's design, these mystery shoppers are armed with financial profiles that all display at least the same level of wealth and stability. But the customers themselves look different. Some are men; others are women. Some are white; others are Black.

Sometimes, the non-white mystery shoppers actually have better profiles than the white shoppers. Time and again, it is the Black customers who are denied the same products or deals that the white customers get. Men, as a rule, get better service than women. Black women are at the bottom of the ladder.

In 2018 and 2019, NCRC researchers sent mystery shoppers to ninety different bank branches in Washington, DC, and Atlanta, sampling the service at fifty-four different institutions. They wanted to know whether banks were asking for the same information from all their customers, giving the customers the same information about what kinds of loans and services they could get, and providing the same quality of engagement for all customers—friendliness, encouragement, warmth. The mystery shoppers were all small-business owners. Again, they all had the same level of wealth and financial stability. But did they get the same treatment?

The answer was a resounding "No."

Black women in the Washington, DC, area were much more likely to be asked by bankers about the names of their businesses and how the businesses were registered, as if they might not be legitimate or desirable. They were far less likely to be offered help applying for a small-business loan. Overall, the survey found that Black women did not get the same encouragement or information as the other groups. The difference was so large that the researchers concluded that the way they were being treated by the banks—which were never identified by name in the published research—could violate the Equal Credit Opportunity Act of 1974, one of the federal laws that was enacted to outlaw redlining.

A separate survey by the same organization sent mystery shoppers to 160 different branches of 32 banks in the Los Angeles area and found that in almost every area of interaction the testers measured—

all the way down to the warmth of bank employees' greetings, the information they asked for in order to help customers, and the advice they gave—white men got preferential treatment. The bankers did a poor job in any case explaining what small-business loans were available to potential borrowers, but Black and Hispanic customers got the most muddled, least complete information.

Most crucially, bankers shared with white would-be borrowers important details about the small-business loans they could get, including what the interest rates were likely to be and what kinds of fees went along with the loan.

REDLINING IN ACTION

Redlining, or refusing to lend to people in communities of color, has appeared in subtler forms at the biggest banks. In 2019, Citigroup was ordered by the Office of the Comptroller of the Currency to refund $25 million to customers it had denied the benefit of one of its promotional programs, in which potential housing mortgage customers were offered discounted rates in exchange for the opening of a new checking account with the company. Return of the money satisfied the government regulatory action in place, but Citi still claimed to have already fixed the problem by the time the case inquiry was initiated. However, in 2020, I got a call to the contrary. Dr. Sierra Washington had a story to tell about her experience trying to get a mortgage with Citi that was far more recent than anything described in the OCC's regulatory action. It had just happened, but it was strangely familiar.

Sierra, a professor of medicine at State University of New York at Stony Brook, wanted to lower her mortgage rate after the Federal Reserve brought rates back to zero in response to the coronavirus pandemic. In April of 2020, she applied for a new mortgage with Citi after receiving reassurances from a broker that the operation would be a breeze. She was, after all, a high-earning professional with a solid, visible job. Her house was spacious and well built and located in a nice neighborhood. She was also a Black woman.

Days and weeks went by and each time she checked in with the loan officer she got the same response: The bank was still examining her application. Occasionally, Citi employees reached out to ask for more information: another month's pay stub, another statement proving Sierra was current on her mortgage payments.

At first, she chalked it all up to delays related to COVID-19. Bankers were working from home and many people were going through a great deal of personal strife in addition to having to keep up with their jobs. But the housing market was booming as people fled locked-down cities looking for more private spaces of their own. It was clear that, for mortgage borrowers across the country, the wait for a loan was not interminable. Deals were getting done, so what was the holdup?

By October, six months after she first applied, Citi had collected eight of Sierra's pay stubs and just as many mortgage payment confirmations and had still not decided whether to lend her any money. The loan officer who had been working on her application called her and said that in order for the deal to get done, she would have to open a checking account with Citi, deposit $50,000 into it, and give Citi permission to automatically take payments out of it.

"It wasn't offered like an option," Sierra said, describing the conversation she had with the Citi employee in an email to me several months later. "I was TOLD," she said. "I HAD to open the account in order to get the loan. Otherwise they said I couldn't refinance."

She did as he instructed, but still no approval came. Frustrated, she decided to stop trying to get answers from the low-level employees who had none to offer her. Instead, she composed an email to the bank's CEO, Michael Corbat.

"I am a physician, otherwise known as a frontline essential health worker, I am a first responder and like yourself I am a Harvard graduate. As such I am in the top 1–2% of earners in this nation. You should want my business," she wrote. "I am beginning to think you are discriminating against me based on either my race or gender."

The very next day, the Citi mortgage officer she had been dealing with called her. "I don't know what you did, but we need to get this done right away," he said. She did as he asked, and three weeks later the deal was done.

After I asked about Sierra's story, Rob Runyan, a Citi spokesman, told me that the bank had reviewed its treatment of her and found "no evidence of discrimination in connection with this loan." But, he added, "we did find areas of opportunity to improve the level of service that we seek to provide all of our customers and we apologize for the inconvenience that we caused Dr. Washington in the course of refinancing her mortgage."

Sierra's experience is yet another recent indicator that mistreatment of Black customers does not stop at a particular income level. Even the wealthiest Black customers can struggle. And I don't just mean wealthier customers. I mean *the wealthiest*.

In 2016, journalist Tanzina Vega chronicled the experiences of the "Black 1 percent," the tiny subsegment of the absolute wealthiest Americans who also happened to be Black. At the time of publication, qualification required roughly $7.9 million in wealth, a figure that meant just 1.7 percent of the 1 percent was Black. Among those interviewed was Sheila Johnson, a cofounder of the television network Black Entertainment Television. In 2005, years after she had successfully launched BET, with a fortune worth hundreds of millions of dollars, Johnson sought to start a luxury resort business, and she found she could not get a bank loan.

"There were people out there that said 'You don't know what you're doing. You're an African-American woman. You don't know about the hotel business. It isn't going to work. I've never seen anybody Black do anything that has excellence,'" Johnson said in an interview for Vega's piece, which aired on CNN.

Johnson went on to say, "The white kids that are out there, they got Daddy's law firm or whatever. They're taken care of and never have to worry about it."

THE COLOR OF ENTREPRENEURSHIP

Black bank customers have continued to face problems on a massive scale. Their strife has been especially visible since early 2020, when the coronavirus pandemic forced Americans into lockdown. In response to the economic shutdown the pandemic necessitated, the federal government designed an operation, the Paycheck Protection Program, to deliver aid to struggling Americans and small businesses by entrusting nearly $1 trillion to the country's banks and leaving it up to them to distribute it.

Congress designed the program so that the distribution process mimicked the steps of obtaining a bank loan. Business owners had to find a bank that would examine paperwork showing their employee head count, overhead costs, and other activities and make them a loan, knowing that the bank would then immediately submit the paperwork to the federal government's Small Business Administration, which would afterward give the bank the equivalent sum of money so that the business owners would never have to actually make any repayments as long as they met certain conditions for how the money was spent.

To the designers of the Paycheck Protection Program, requiring businesses to pretend they were getting bank loans made eminent sense. The process would help separate out fraudsters, they believed. Market forces would act in their rational manner, and those who had real need would see that need met. Banks' normal requirements for examining their customers' needs and their abilities to repay loans made them natural candidates to perform the vetting process for this unprecedented aid effort, Treasury Department officials and some elected leaders reasoned. (In the end, an audit found that $3.7 billion in aid had been given to people and businesses who were ineligible for it, so the benefit of structuring the aid disbursements like loans was questionable at best.) At first, they did not seem to give any consideration to the fact that banks weren't always fair.

In reality, the consequences of relying on the banks were dire for Black business owners across the country. Years of past encounters with banks suddenly took on new significance.

During the earliest days of the PPP's existence, I met a young woman, Yasmine Young, who owned her own hair salon in Baltimore. No one had called the cops on her or thrown her out of any bank branches, but in 2016, soon after opening her salon, she had tried to get a business credit card from Bank of America and had been discouraged from even submitting an application. Even though she had her business checking account at Bank of America, she had to get a business credit card from one of the bank's rivals, Capital One. That move had consequences she could never have foreseen. In April of 2020, when she asked Bank of America, where she still had her business checking account, to apply to the Small Business Administration for a PPP loan for her salon, the bank's representatives told her that only credit card customers or customers who had other outstanding loans from the bank could get that help. Bank of America was technically her bank—it held her money—but it turned her away when she sought help.

Minority-owned businesses often have weaker banking relationships than their white-owned counterparts—a legacy of redlining. Research shows that Black and Latino business owners are denied loans at higher rates.

Some minority business owners have avoided dealing with banks entirely. Carlos Swepson, a chef in New York, is one of them. When he wanted to start a restaurant, he borrowed $240,000 from his parents, who mortgaged their house to lend him the money. He later raised $400,000 from friends, one of whom also took out a mortgage while another borrowed against a retirement account to fund him. He did not feel comfortable dealing with banks; they'd made him feel "lost," he said.

He had a business checking account at Affinity Federal Credit Union, a small credit union based in New Jersey, and when the coronavirus pandemic forced him to close his Harlem restaurant, he went to Affinity for a PPP loan. The paperwork, while routine for banking customers, was complicated and unlike anything Carlos was accustomed to filling out. He sought help from a patron of his restaurant who happened to be a lawyer. This is how tenuous relationships with banks can seem at first to be no big deal but can later become a huge problem.

Carlos is no rebel, either; he was in broad company. A study published in 2016 by economists at the Stanford Institute for Economic Policy Research found that only 1 percent of Black business owners get a bank loan during their first year of business compared with 7 percent of white owners. Twice as many white business owners—30 percent of the total—use business credit cards during their inaugural year, compared with Black owners, among whom only 15 percent rely on a credit card. Black businesses also start out with far less capital—whether from investments or bank loans—than white businesses, the study found.

"Black-owned businesses continue to rely on family loans to a greater degree than white-owned firms in the three years following the firm's founding," the researchers found. "This suggests that access to formal debt channels remains limited for minorities."

The federal government has, for decades, maintained policies that are designed to try to combat some of these inequalities. The institutions that frequently lend to minority-owned businesses, especially those in low-income neighborhoods, are nonprofit organizations called community development financial institutions. They rely on government funding and charitable donations to make loans and grew out of earlier efforts to help Black Americans build wealth in the wake of slavery and segregation.

But in 2020, at the beginning of the coronavirus pandemic, only 78 of 950 such organizations were participating in the government program to give emergency loans to small businesses, the one Carlos and Yasmine sought to access. The majority of the community development financial institutions in the United States had not previously been approved by the Small Business Administration to make loans backed by the agency, so they did not get authorization to participate in the Paycheck Protection Program until much later—too late for some businesses operating on razor-thin margins to stay afloat.

In late April of 2020, as an initial round of funding for the PPP dwindled, the Business Leadership Council, a group of Black investors led by Mellody Hobson—co-CEO of the firm Ariel Investments and a JPMorgan Chase board member—proposed in a letter that more than a quarter of the $250 billion ($68 billion) in additional money for small businesses that Congress was considering adding to the program be set aside for Black businesses.

"By prioritizing clients that already have existing lines of credit, black businesses and nonprofits find themselves yet again excluded from life-saving relief," the investors wrote. "This roughly $68 billion will only begin to address the disparities within capitalism brought into relief by coronavirus."

It would have been an improvement, even if it was a small one. The bill that created the PPP set aside very little money to specifically help minorities. It allotted $10 million, for instance, to minority chambers of commerce, local organizations that could theoretically help their members overcome some of the hurdles to getting banks to deal with them. But despite the publicity the Black investor group's letter generated, it did not compel Congress or the Treasury Department to meet the needs that the letter described. A second aid package ended up setting aside $30 billion for minority- and women-owned businesses.

The need for extra help was clear. Soon after the Paycheck Protection Program was launched in April of 2020, the National Community Reinvestment Coalition and its academic research partners did a PPP-specific version of its earlier "mystery shoppers" study and found that Black business owners were more likely to be hindered in seeking coronavirus financial aid than their white peers. The study, conducted from late April to late May of 2020, looked at how more than a dozen Washington, DC–area banks handled requests for PPP loans.

The researchers sent pairs of would-be loan applicants to branches of seventeen banks. This time, to make the study more conservative, the researchers gave the Black borrowers slightly better financial profiles than their white counterparts.

The Black borrowers were offered different products and treated significantly worse by employees than white borrowers were treated in almost half of the tests, the study found. Of the seventeen banks, some of which were tested through multiple branches, thirteen had at least one test in which a white borrower was treated better than his or her Black counterpart.

Conditions may have been even worse than what the researchers found, but it was hard to measure the disparity during the first weeks of the program's existence because the government didn't begin collecting data on the race and gender of aid recipients at the outset, making it nearly impossible to use data released by the Treasury Department to determine whether Black business owners were approved for loans as often as white business owners.

During the first phase of the program, which took place entirely in April of 2020 and when competition for aid was fiercest, 75 percent of loans went to businesses in census tracts where a majority of residents are white. By comparison, 68 percent of the population lives in majority-white areas, according to a *New York Times* analysis of government data that was compiled by the Urban Institute. Another study, conducted after the PPP ended, found that Black business owners were much more likely to get PPP loans from online lenders. They had struggled noticeably at banks, especially smaller ones, where bank employees' bias was by far the biggest obstacle to their success.

Overall, the coronavirus pandemic acted like a hothouse, accelerating the effects of racism in the banking industry so that their economic impacts grew larger and at a more rapid pace. All those "Please Use Caution . . ." reactions were being amplified by the urgent need Black business owners suddenly had for help from banks. The data collected about who was getting PPP loans and who was not made it clear: The many forms of suspicion and mistreatment of Black customers, some subtle and others blatant, amounted to an oppressive force pressing down on Black Americans, backing many people further away from prosperity.

THREE

RICARDO AND JIMMY

Ricardo Peters still has the picture of himself with Jamie Dimon from when things were good, before he came to believe that Dimon was one of the biggest hypocrites of them all.

The two men, one Black and one white, both in dark suits, are standing side by side in the hallway of a fancy hotel with their bodies pressed together. It's clear from the position of his right shoulder that Ricardo has his arm around Dimon the way most people do when they're posing for photos. His grin is wide and his eyes are clear and confident. Dimon's mouth is closed, his smile dimmer. He looks calm but caught. Stiff.

When the picture was taken, in February 2015, at a conference in Orlando celebrating the top-performing bankers at JPMorgan's retail arm Chase, Ricardo was bursting with ambition and energy and directing all of it toward his career at the bank. He had started seven years earlier in as menial a position as anyone could get at the giant financial firm, working a customer service job inside one of Chase's massive call centers in Lake Mary, Florida. His mission there was to help Chase credit card customers with whatever they needed and, while he had them on the line, to try to sell them as many new options for their cards as possible. His ability to put callers at ease, make them smile, and seal new deals with them helped him stand out.

He advanced quickly and deliberately along his chosen career path. When he found that Chase did not have a branch network in Florida that would give him room to grow, he moved to Arizona. In just a few short years he was working in a Chase branch in the Phoenix area and regularly winning recognition and kudos for his sales numbers. The plaudits came in the form of trophies for standout performances on a yearly basis as well as little merit-marking cards, like miniature awards certificates handed out by managers documenting his monthly achievements: for example, in June 2014, "#1 in AZ South Market"; in July 2014, "'Top' Relationship Banker in the South Valley District." Ricardo saved them all.

Work was, for him as for millions of other Americans, his biggest source of pride and self-worth. He bought himself an apartment in Phoenix and paid for a condo in Florida for his mother, too. And he aimed high. He wanted to do more and more work and win better and better titles inside Chase.

The arc of Ricardo's career took him to a Chase branch in Sun City West, a wealthy Phoenix suburb. By mid-2016 he had passed the licensing exams he needed to advance from the role of a banker inside the branch to a financial advisor—someone who could help customers for regular business like checking and savings accounts get involved in more sophisticated relationships with Chase. This work involved hand-in-hand interactions with the other bankers at the branch, so Ricardo got to the task of developing relationships with his coworkers.

He grew particularly close with a Chase banker named Daniel Acosta, and the two often tag-teamed on clients. Acosta would pass wealthy customers on to Ricardo, who would then inquire about any need of further assistance in managing their savings. Patricia was one such customer. She had come to Daniel and Ricardo with a heartbreaking problem: She was married to a woman who was dying, and

Patricia was concerned about Chase's position on smoothly transitioning her wife's financial affairs after her death. To Acosta and Ricardo, there was a significant amount of money at stake.

Acosta assured the woman that Chase would make the process easy for her when the time came, and brought over Ricardo to further reassure her. Patricia explained her situation, and Ricardo told her that he would take care of whatever she needed. Patricia seemed satisfied with that answer, maintained the couple's relationship with Chase, and wouldn't be heard from again for nearly two years.

A CLASS ACTION

Ricardo continued to advance at Chase against a backdrop he hardly noticed but one that would come to define and eventually destroy his career for no other reason than the color of his skin.

To save money, Chase had tapered the services offered within its retail locations around the country. In 2019, for instance, the bank operated about 5,000 branches, but only around 3,200 of them offered a full suite of services on-site. That let the company cut down on labor costs by reducing the number of employees needed to staff each branch. In particular, a sub-brand, Chase Private Client, would now only be available to certain customers at certain branches.

Chase "Private Clients" had to have $250,000 or more. The status unlocked special perks: lower rates on mortgages, personal loans, and other Chase products; tickets to Chase-sponsored sports events and concerts; and access to entertainment booths at those events where Private Client customers could gather for refreshments and other special treatment. Private Clients also got discounts on travel services and enjoyed visible status symbols, like an especially weighty metal credit card.

Not merely wrapping paper for the wandering eyes of customers, Chase Private Clients also held weight behind the scenes at Chase.

Access to the wealthy Private Client customers was limited to a select group of bankers at the company, and if a particular banker hadn't been designated as "able" to deal with this group of elite clients, he or she was supposed to pass those clients on to someone higher up in the food chain who was.

To Chase's management, this all made sense. It was a way to keep costs down, create hierarchies inside the retail bank that would drive more sales by making bankers compete fiercely against each other for promotions, and firm up the boundaries of a brand. But there were also harmful consequences to this system, whether or not Chase intended it.

Customers who weren't Private Clients couldn't get access to the special perks the status offered—that was clear enough—but even customers who *did* have enough money to qualify for the status needed to go to certain Chase branches to get it. Those branches were in richer, almost invariably predominantly white neighborhoods; again, it was something that seemed to make sense from a business perspective but was not helpful for people living in not-so-rich neighborhoods who happened to have plenty of money themselves.

Chase's public line was that three-quarters of the branches that didn't offer the elite suite of services were within five miles of a branch that did, but that was of little help to those left to languish with sub-par service and potentially tens of thousands of dollars in unnecessary costs. Some customers who could have been designated as having an elevated status did not even know they qualified for such services. Others wanted to access the services but were left confused when they learned the people at Chase whom they knew and trusted already would not be the ones to help them through the process.

The secret was that, inside Chase, managers got to choose who was granted access to Private Client customers. In theory, this should have been a meritocracy, with the plumb positions of "Private Client advisor"—i.e., financial advisor to the wealthiest retail customers in the bank—going to the people who best fit the job: the best salespeople and the best money managers.

But this is not how it worked out in practice; slots were given to people who'd won personal favor with their managers even if they weren't the ones with the best sales records. And what was worse, the people who came up short for the positions were, by definition, cut off from dealing with Chase's most lucrative customers. The two-tiered system created a vicious cycle: Bankers needed rich clients in order to hit the sales goals required to win promotions, but only promotions (or the favor of managers) could grant permission to deal with those rich clients.

The Private Client system sounds problematic enough at its core—rife with off-book favor trading and employee dissatisfaction, and a potential PR nightmare bubbling just under the surface of public attention. What caused more problems was the fact that a huge contingent of people who were being shut out of the system internally by being denied promotions and branch placements that would allow them to deal with Chase's wealthiest customers were Black.

In 2016, a group of Black current and former Chase employees who suspected they had run afoul of the bank's two-tiered system because of their race got together and went to a lawyer who specialized in bringing large discrimination cases against big Wall Street firms. The lawyer on the case was none other than Linda Friedman, the preeminent veteran of big racial discrimination fights with Wall Street banks, and she knew Chase well. Not only that, she knew the entire world of wealth management, and she knew that every bank had exhibited basically the same pattern of bias against its Black employees.

JPMorgan Chase's leaders knew Friedman well, too. The two sides were so familiar with each other, in fact, that Friedman did not even have to drop a lawsuit on the bank immediately. Instead, she reached out to its legal team and began to outline the facts of the case and the scope of it, opening the door for the bank to figure out how to fix things and pay the wronged employees damages for their hardship.

The Black financial advisors claimed they were being held back from becoming "Private Client" advisors and that they were being shunted to branches in poor neighborhoods with smaller staffs and fewer financial products on offer. Often, one Black financial advisor had to cover several different branches of this type, splitting his or her time between them in a way that minimized the chances of meeting new clients—let alone significantly wealthy new clients—right off the bat.

The negotiations between Friedman's team and JPMorgan's lawyers lasted more than two years. The two sides had much to discuss, such as whether the bank would seek to fight the formation of a legal class that would allow all its Black financial advisors to access whatever eventual relief was provided in the settlement. JPMorgan agreed to let a class form without a fight, and it agreed eventually to a settlement worth tens of millions of dollars.

THE POWER OF PROOF

While all this was going on, Ricardo Peters's life was getting harder and harder. And since he wasn't part of the group who were actively pursuing a case against JPMorgan, Ricardo had no idea that what was happening to him was part of a larger story. He just knew that his bosses were making him feel terrible, and it wasn't right.

Ricardo felt he had to deal with two main antagonists: his boss, Frank Venniro, and another manager, Susan Kirchmeier. The slights he encountered were confusing but also blatant, like when Ricardo was assigned a three-letter identification code for use inside JPMorgan's computer systems, and the code was APE. *Seriously?* he thought.

This can't be happening. Other financial advisors who saw the code started teasing Ricardo about it, so he went to Frank and asked to be assigned a different three-letter code. Any. Other. Letters. No can do, Frank told him.

In general, whenever Ricardo wanted to talk about his career goals, Frank appeared to be most interested in placating him rather than advising him. Ricardo was laser focused on getting a promotion from financial advisor to Private Client advisor, because it meant he could deal with richer clients. Frank told him he needed to clock in more time as a regular advisor first. When Ricardo asked about the move in late 2016, Frank pointed out he hadn't even done a year as a regular advisor. "Wait till next spring," Frank said.

In the meantime, Ricardo had to deal with Kirchmeier, who appeared to be searching for things to nail him with. With increasing regularity, Frank started calling Ricardo into a secluded room to talk to him about how he was making Kirchmeier feel. If Ricardo failed to say hello to her, she complained about him to Frank. If he *did* say hello but she felt like he looked at her funny, she complained to Frank. The constant talking-tos started to undermine Ricardo's sense of reality. He knew he didn't deserve them; they weren't about his performance or his interactions with customers.

It was then that he started to record these private meetings.

Once, for instance, when he got stuck in traffic on the way to work, Kirchmeier berated him for coming in late, then complained to Frank that Ricardo had failed to speak to her in a meeting later that day. When Ricardo tried to give Frank his side of the story, Frank waved him away. "She's bothered by whatever you're doing or not doing," he told Ricardo.

Things only got worse for Ricardo with Kirchmeier. Annoyed by his very presence, she moved him away from where the other advisors sat in the branch and made him take a desk in a windowless room in the back of the building. At first it seemed like a temporary thing, but Ricardo watched as a prime spot opened up in the front and was promptly taken by a recent hire whom he far outranked. In a conversation by text with a coworker, Ricardo complained about being stuck in the back of the office. The coworker said that the woman who had taken the desk had confided in him that she knew it had been given to her because Kirchmeier had wanted to avoid letting it go to a "certain someone"—meaning Ricardo.

Ricardo had had it with Kirchmeier, but he was holding out hope that things would improve for him in spite of her interference. By then it was the spring of 2017, the season Ricardo had been waiting for, because Frank had promised him the promotion to Private Client advisor. In April he sat down with Frank and spoke of his unhappiness and also of his expectations.

Frank dashed them: "Things changed." He had no intention of giving Ricardo the promotion.

"Do I want you to be a PCA?" Frank said, using the acronym used internally for the "Private Client advisor" title. "I'd be happy to make you a PCA if I thought you would succeed. [But] I have a lot of concerns that you will not succeed as a PCA."

Ricardo didn't know it, but all across the country Black financial advisors were being told things like that. That they weren't a "good fit," that things weren't going to "work out," vague criticisms that did not leave much room for a response. But Ricardo wasn't having it. He had a shelf full of awards from the very institution whose representative was now telling him he wasn't good enough. He believed the trophies and the cards and the commendations. He didn't believe Frank Venniro.

Ever a champion of logic, Ricardo began offering Frank examples of the accomplishments he thought should propel him into Private Client advisor status. He raised the subject of a woman he'd recently made a connection with at the bank, a new client who had brought a significant amount of money to the branch.

Her circumstances were not happy. Her young son had died and she'd received a $372,000 settlement because of his death. She had signed up for basic banking services, but she obviously had enough money to become a Private Client, and he wanted to sign her up for that program as well. This client happened to be Black.

Frank would have none of it. He told Ricardo that the woman did not qualify to be in the Chase Private Client program, regardless of the fact that she had over a hundred thousand dollars more than what was required.

"She doesn't qualify for CPC," Frank said. "The dollars don't make you qualify."

Ricardo protested, but Frank pressed on. "You've got somebody who's coming from Section 8, never had a nickel to spend, and now she's got $400,000," he said. "This is not money she respects. She didn't earn it."

It's not clear whether the woman actually ever lived in subsidized housing. JPMorgan later said Frank didn't know the woman's race, but the "Section 8" comment was a giveaway. A reference to a federal housing voucher program heavily bound up in modern-day redlining—landlords had to be taken to court to accept the vouchers, and insurers are still reluctant to write policies on buildings where recipients of the subsidy live—it is closely associated with poor Black renters. It is indisputably a stand-in for a racial slur. What's more, Ricardo believed Frank knew for certain that the woman was Black.

Frank pressed on with his assessment of what the woman would do with her money. He said he expected her to have spent it all "within twelve to twenty-four months—I see it all the time."

"If there's nobody to intervene and show her how to do it," Ricardo countered. "I thought that's why we get involved."

"You're not investing a dime for this lady," Frank told him. He had no idea that Ricardo had recorded the entire exchange.

. . .

Early the next year, Ricardo was booted from Chase's upscale Sun City West branch and assigned to cover two branches in poorer areas of Phoenix. It was mostly a setback, with one exception: If it hadn't happened, Ricardo never would have met the other pioneer in the recording of racist activity at JPMorgan in Arizona, Jimmy Kennedy.

Jimmy, affectionately known as "GRIZZ," had earned $13 million during his nine-year career as a player in the National Football League and had won a Super Bowl playing defensive tackle with the New York Giants. Originally from Yonkers, New York, he had left the Northeast and a troubled childhood there far behind. He lived in a large house near Phoenix with his wife and three children and was happily ensconced in a role as a minor celebrity around town, promoting local charities and boosting a weekly spoken-word poetry night hosted by a Phoenix-based poet and activist, Qosmic Qadence.

He was the kind of person most banks would be happy to have as a client. He drove flashy cars and wore expensive watches, making it clear he was not afraid to spend money—and that he had a lot of it on hand. He had bought homes for relatives, including one for his mother-in-law in Los Angeles. He was studying finance himself at a local university and wanted to have an active hand in the management of his savings and investments.

Jimmy kept various sums in accounts at three of the four largest U.S. banks: Bank of America, Wells Fargo, and JPMorgan's retail arm, Chase. For several years he had no favorite among them. But he began to notice that whenever he visited his wife's family in Los Angeles and accompanied her mother to her local Chase branch to help with money matters, he found himself attracting a very specific sort of attention. His mother-in-law was technically their customer, but the Chase employees were fawning over Jimmy. Did he want extra perks? Was he interested in a more personal touch? The employees in L.A. had a proposition for him: Become a Chase Private Client and let Chase manage his investments.

Jimmy was wary. The offers did not make a great deal of sense. He lived in Arizona, not California. Why were they soliciting his business here? He assured the L.A. Chase employees that he would explore his options closer to home.

His reservations aside, the idea of becoming a Private Client was tempting to Jimmy. He was especially keen on getting the travel discounts Chase had advertised, as he often traveled between Phoenix and L.A. and particularly relished taking family vacations with his kids.

But Jimmy had also been put off by the JPMorgan financial advisors in Arizona. They seemed overeager and patronizing. Each time a new advisor reached out to him, he felt unsettled. Until, in the spring of 2018, he met Ricardo.

"The chemistry was just so real because he knew exactly what I needed to do," Jimmy told me when we talked about what he saw in Ricardo.

The feeling was mutual. Ricardo was just as happy to land Jimmy as a client. It was a professional win that he hoped would finally propel him into the role he had been pushing Frank to give him.

The two quickly bonded, and Jimmy moved more money into his Chase account. He was excited to finally get the perks that came with Private Client status, and he was excited to have found in Ricardo Peters a financial advisor he trusted. He liked going to visit Ricardo in his office. (He barely noticed it was windowless and in the back of the Chase branch.) The two sometimes talked for hours.

Jimmy's presence was one of the few bright spots left in Ricardo's work life. Other wealthy clients Ricardo had landed had been taken away from him and given to people with "Private Client advisor" titles. This felt unjust. Why should Ricardo have to give up people he'd built relationships with simply because they were wealthy enough to qualify for a program in which his bosses would not let him participate?

The sting had been especially keen when one of Ricardo's old clients, a white man, had asked him for tickets to Phoenix's marquee golf tournament of the year, the Waste Management Phoenix Open. Held in February when the weather was just right, the grass on the course was always a perfect green and the light was soft and beautiful. Ricardo had wanted to take his client to the golf tournament himself. He felt he deserved to be able to escort a customer he had cultivated for many months and worked diligently to keep with Chase. But Frank had told him no. Only Private Client advisors were allowed to take guests to the tournament. Ricardo's client would be chaperoned by someone else.

In a text message conversation with another banker who *was* going to the tournament, Ricardo tried to laugh off the slight. "I need a new boss haha," he'd written, after the other banker had bragged about getting to go.

There was another prospect Ricardo had going: Patricia, the woman with the terminally ill wife, had reappeared. Her wife had passed, and she was looking for Ricardo, as promised.

RICARDO RAISES HIS HAND

Patricia came into the Sun City West branch and asked for Ricardo, and even though he wasn't there anymore, the banker she spoke to directed her to Ricardo's new location. But that banker was not Daniel Acosta, who had originally made the connection between Ricardo and Patricia. This banker's name was Jacqueline. She just happened to be the person who was available to talk to Patricia when she walked in.

Jacqueline helped Patricia, and afterward she emailed Ricardo and told him that she had done so. She thought that, since she had spoken to the client, she should get credit for directing the client's business to Ricardo. It's not clear whether she knew Acosta had introduced Ricardo and Patricia two years earlier. Ricardo ignored Jacqueline's email. It seemed irrelevant. He already knew who had set him up with Patricia, and it was Acosta, not Jacqueline.

Patricia and Ricardo began to do business. As part of his normal paperwork, Ricardo had to fill out a form on JPMorgan's internal computer system reporting who had brought this new client into the business. This sales credit system was how the bank tracked its employees' performances and decided, in theory, whom to promote and whom to reward. It had served Ricardo well in the past. Some of the professional commendations he had earned were based on the number of credits Ricardo had racked up in the system. Ricardo was now in a position to help other bankers, and he dutifully did so. In this case, he gave credit to Daniel Acosta, who had first connected him to Patricia. Acosta was, after all, the banker who had made the initial introduction to this valuable client.

By this point, things had only gotten worse for Ricardo with his boss, Frank Venniro. Frustrated by Frank's backtracking on the Private Client advisor promotion, Ricardo had stopped trusting him and was mostly trying to avoid him. Which is why, when Acosta told him that the sales credit Ricardo had assigned to him over Patricia had been reassigned to Jacqueline, he wasn't particularly surprised. But he was angry.

Acosta, who was also not white, was Ricardo's friend, and the two felt they had each other's backs. Ricardo was upset on his behalf and also because Frank had gone into the JPMorgan system and changed the sales credit without even talking to him first, which appeared to be a breach of the bank's rules. It was then that the dam holding back all his feelings of frustration and confusion and hopelessness burst. He was giving everything he had to his job and it wasn't working—and it wasn't his fault.

It was the middle of a night in late August of 2018 when Ricardo finally decided to do something about his frustrations. He had been working late, at home, completing a mandatory antidiscrimination training session on his laptop. The course emphasized the importance of reporting mistreatment to the bank's human resources department so any wrongdoing that was occurring could be put to a stop and made right. It felt like the message on the screen was addressed directly to one person—himself—out of the 170,000 employees of Chase. He was supposed to speak up when he witnessed wrongdoing or experienced discrimination. So when directions popped up on his computer screen for filing a report, Ricardo followed them. In a little comment window on a web page, he poured forth his feelings and experiences.

His report, filed at 2:33 a.m. on Friday, August 24, summarized his feelings. His bosses, he said, had "always treated me unfairly." He told the story of the sales credit switch with Patricia in great detail and added other evidence, such as the fact that he had been moved to a windowless office in the back of a Chase branch, to support his claim that the unequal treatment he was experiencing was tied to the color of his skin. He added that even when he had gone to Frank for help, he had gotten nowhere. Frank, he said, had refused to escalate his discrimination complaint to human resources officials, claiming he was not allowed to do so. It did not make sense. "I have been with this company for 10 [years] and in corporate America for more than 2 decades and I know for a fact that's false," Ricardo concluded.

To any human resources official, two key points should have stood out. The first was that Ricardo felt he was experiencing racial discrimination, a declaration that, according to JPMorgan's human resources procedures, should have immediately triggered a serious, regimented response. Officials should have immediately opened an investigation while also taking steps to make sure Ricardo's bosses weren't retaliating against him.

But that was not all: Ricardo's claim that he had tried to report the discrimination already to his manager and that his manager, Frank, had said he could not help him transmit the claim to Human Resources should have been seen as a major red flag according to JPMorgan's written policies.

Ricardo's claim seemed at first to have been ignored. The day that dawned after he'd hit "send" on it was a regular workday, and he'd gone into the office as usual and seen no signs that anyone he knew, including Frank, was aware of the complaint he'd made.

He tried to focus on his work. He did not notice when, two weeks later, on September 5, lawyers for JPMorgan reached an agreement with Linda Friedman to settle the class-action discrimination lawsuit Friedman had drafted on behalf of Black JPMorgan financial advisors. The bank would pay $24 million as part of the deal, which would be distributed among hundreds of financial advisors as a way to make up for income that they had lost because of the bank's unfair and abusive treatment. Ricardo was still not connected with any sort of community of other Black financial advisors taking action. He was still trying to get through his ordeal alone. He did not realize he had a choice.

He was caught completely by surprise when, on Monday, September 10, just over two weeks after he filed his complaint, Ricardo pulled into the parking lot of his branch early in the morning and noticed Frank's car in the parking lot.

This was strange. It was not a day on which Ricardo expected to see Frank in that branch at all—he split his time between several locations—and he knew something was up. As he walked toward the front door, Ricardo pulled out his phone, opened the "voice memos" app and hit "record," then casually slipped the phone back into his pocket.

As soon as he stepped inside, Frank sprang out from a corner. "Follow me," he told Ricardo, leading him to an elevator.

Their stilted conversation during the short ride to the basement is all on tape, in Ricardo's possession. So is the meeting that followed. Waiting in the basement for Ricardo were Travis and Christina, two members of JPMorgan's Global Security & Investigations team.

"I'll let you guys chat," Frank said, propelling Ricardo into a room with a table and some chairs. Then he was gone. He had shut the door behind him.

Travis and Christina introduced themselves by their first names only. They offered no business cards. They said they wanted Ricardo to tell them about the complaint he'd filed, but not about the discrimination part of it. Before beginning the interview, Travis told Ricardo to sign a form saying he was telling the truth. When he asked if the form covered things he was afraid to talk about for fear of retaliation, Travis said that wasn't its purpose.

"This is about lying, sending us on a wild-goose chase," Travis said. "To deflect away from maybe the main issue. Unfortunately we've had employees try that."

He told Ricardo that his report had been taken very seriously.

"The reason why we're out here today focuses about what you'd reported about the whole thing about the credit: You felt that there was something that was done with a credit that was evidently for Daniel that got taken away," he said.

Christina chimed in, seeming to want to soften the mood: "I know there was a lot more in there regarding other issues with management," she said. "That is being addressed with HR. I just want to make it clear that we don't handle personnel-type issues. I just want to make sure that you know that that hasn't been overlooked."

For more than an hour, the two investigators grilled Ricardo about the sales credit he'd given to Acosta for bringing in the wealthy widow

Patricia. They acknowledged that someone had changed the sales credit without talking to Ricardo about it. But they appeared to fault Ricardo for failing to talk to the other banker, Jacqueline, and explain to her why he believed Acosta deserved the credit.

"Why didn't you let her know right away and just say. 'Hey, I don't know what's going on, if you're trying to get credit, but this is Daniel's'?"

Their questions, at first, exasperated Ricardo. "This is bigger than just this sales credit," he said. "I feel like you guys are trying to make the victim turn into the bad guy."

But a pivotal moment came when Ricardo took a deep breath, lowered his voice, and explained his side of the story. He explained that Patricia had visited much earlier and that Acosta had introduced the two of them. He even admitted that maybe he should have been clearer to Jacqueline about it, but the fact remained that he had determined that Acosta, rather than she, deserved the credit.

To his surprise, Travis and Christina appeared to be satisfied with his explanation.

But Travis also asked whether Ricardo wanted to write out his version of the events in a statement that Travis and Christina could give to human resources officials.

"The statement is voluntary. This is your voice to the HR rep. To kind of explain your piece to this," he said, warning Ricardo that he himself would only give his superiors a "high-level summary" of what had happened. He also acknowledged that Ricardo had already explained himself in detail. The statement, he said, would be the chance to put in writing "exactly what you've done for the last hour and a half."

Ricardo said that if he had had more time, he would have been happy to write a statement. As it was, he had a meeting at the other branch where he also worked, with a potential new client he hoped would bring $2.5 million over to Chase.

When he thought about it later, he realized that Travis's offer had been a warning that his story would not be recorded or shared in any sort of detail. He would eventually learn that what Travis and Christina put into writing had very little to do with what he had told them and what they had seemed to understand.

A week later, while Ricardo and Jimmy Kennedy were meeting in Ricardo's office, Acosta called Ricardo's cell phone.

"They fired me," he said.

"Oh, God," Ricardo said aloud to Jimmy. "I'm next."

• • •

Over the three weeks that followed, several people from JPMorgan's human resources department, many of whom were based in New York, called and emailed Ricardo seeking to talk to him about his discrimination claim. He refused to talk. With Acosta gone, he knew he had no chance. And besides, the women—they were all women— who were trying to get Ricardo to talk kept inaccurately referring to his complaint as having been filed in mid-September.

Ricardo kept trying to correct them. In one email he explained that he'd filed his claim on August 24. The woman replied and said that she had learned of his concerns about discrimination from the global security investigators, Travis and Christina, who had brought them "to our attention" on September 14.

"GSI does not handle discrimination cases, but when you brought it up in their meeting with you, they escalated it to Employee Relations as per the correct protocol," she wrote.

Brought it up? Ricardo hadn't brought it up in that meeting. Christina had, when she had explained that she and Travis weren't there to deal with it.

"At this time I do not feel comfortable nor secure answering any questions or speaking to my claim based on how it has played out over the past several weeks," Ricardo wrote back.

He felt it would be impossible to cooperate with these people, who appeared to be creating a case against him before his very eyes.

The situation grew more and more absurd. On the morning of October 4, 2018, shortly after Ricardo arrived at work, he was told to go into a room where the shades were drawn and the door was closed. Frank was inside. A speakerphone was already carrying an open call from Rosemary Ruggieri, a JPMorgan human resources employee in New York. Frank told Ricardo to sit down, then he turned on his heel, swept himself out of the room, and closed the door behind him.

Ruggieri said that she felt she needed to get Frank to force Ricardo to sit down for a phone call after he did not respond to an email she'd sent him. She told him not to worry: Frank was handling the task of rescheduling the meetings Ricardo had set up with his clients. When Ricardo said that that made him uncomfortable, along with the fact that Frank was standing outside the door to the room he was in like some kind of security guard, Ruggieri replied: "We also have a no-retaliation policy, so regardless of whether you're in the branch and the manager that you're complaining about is in the branch, that's irrelevant."

The recording shows Ruggieri and Ricardo spent most of the rest of the twenty-four-minute call arguing over whether Ricardo had followed proper procedure for scheduling an appointment using Microsoft Outlook. Ruggieri kept insisting that it was Ricardo's fault that they had not been able to agree on a better time to meet; Ricardo said repeatedly that he had suggested alternative times using the Outlook calendar function and that they had been ignored.

The next morning, October 5, Ricardo again arrived at work and noticed Frank's car in the lot at an unusual hour, and he knew his time was up. Again Frank met him at the door and again he marched him into a room. This time he told Ricardo he was fired.

"Why?" Ricardo asked.

"They determined there was a code of conduct violation and be-cause of that code of conduct violation we're terminating your employment," Frank said.

"What violation?" Ricardo asked.

Frank said he didn't know. "I'm just given marching orders."

"THEY DON'T SEE PEOPLE LIKE YOU A LOT"

Ricardo's sudden departure left Jimmy Kennedy in the lurch. The two had been in the middle of rearranging Jimmy's investments, and Jimmy realized that, at least in the short term, he had to keep dealing with JPMorgan no matter how he felt about the way the bank had treated Ricardo.

On top of everything else, Jimmy still did not have the Private Client status that he had been promised, a process that had supposedly been in motion for months. How could it possibly take that long to run a credit check or review of accounts? And now he no longer had a financial advisor he trusted, either.

A new advisor was assigned to Jimmy, a man named Charles Belton. He, too, was Black.

"He's trying to be, like, 'cool Black guy,' like, 'What's up, bro?'" Jimmy said, describing his early interactions with Charles. "I'm, like, do they feel like to keep my business they need to assign another Black advisor to me? I didn't go with Chase bank because Ricardo was Black."

The relationship between Jimmy and Charles soured even more when Jimmy discovered that some of the investment decisions he had agreed on with Ricardo had either been reversed or had not been executed. In one case, $92,000 of Jimmy's money that was supposed to go into a new investment product ended up in a holding account that was inaccessible to Jimmy.

Charles explained that Ricardo's abrupt departure had left certain paperwork in limbo. Then he started suggesting investments that

Ricardo had distinctly guarded against. It wasn't clear why his approach was so drastically different, but Jimmy suspected he was no longer getting the straight talk he had come to appreciate so much from Ricardo.

That, and not a belief that he had become the victim of racial discrimination, was what first gave Jimmy the idea to make secret recordings of his own.

Jimmy had kept in touch with Ricardo and figured he could run whatever Charles said past his old, trusted advisor. He started secretly recording Charles with the aim to play the recordings for Ricardo and get a second opinion on Charles's investment advice. He'd turn his video camera on before walking into his Chase branch and leave his phone out on the desk during their meetings. Most of what Jimmy got was audio: The camera was usually pointed either straight down against the desk or straight up, fixed on the Styrofoam drop ceiling and the fluorescent lights.

One of the early results of this practice was that Ricardo was able to catch Charles in the act of trying to sell Jimmy a product with higher fees than necessary. Armed with Ricardo's criticism, Jimmy questioned Charles's advice and asked him why he had been pushing that particular product. He eventually admitted that he hadn't given Jimmy the best deal possible.

But throughout his negotiations with Charles, Jimmy got nowhere with his attempts to finally get Private Client status. By his account, he had more than $800,000 tied up with Chase in various ways. (Chase later disputed this claim, saying Jimmy had far less in his accounts.) Yet he had nothing to show for it. Not the metal bank card he had been looking forward to holding; not the exclusive travel deals; and, most significantly, not the special loan rates. He tried every way he could think of to get things moving, including talking to Charles's boss, the branch manager, Frank Venniro, who offered no more than vague assurances that the bank was working on his account and "things would get better soon."

One day, a fed-up Jimmy drove to the Chase branch where Charles worked. Secretly recording again, he asked Charles point-blank why he had not been made a Private Client. The response shocked him.

"You're bigger than the average person, period. And you're also an African American," Charles told Jimmy, who at six foot four had once clocked his weight in at 320 pounds.

"We're in Arizona," Charles said. "I don't have to tell you about what the demographics are in Arizona. They don't see people like you a lot."

Charles went on to warn Jimmy not to try to go above his head to pursue the Private Client issue.

"Come to me," Charles said. "Don't talk to Frank."

He asked Jimmy to think about the impression he left on people at the bank. He said that Frank had been afraid to tell Jimmy that his application to become a Private Client had been deleted when Ricardo was fired.

"You sit in front of him, you're like three times his size—you feel what I'm saying?—he already probably has his perception of how these interactions could go," Charles explained.

"We've seen people that are not of your stature get irate, and it's, like, 'Well, if this dude gets upset, like what's going to happen to me?'"

Charles made it sound like he was doing Jimmy a favor by spelling out that the white JPMorgan employees he had spoken to were afraid of him.

"They're not going to say this, but I don't have the same level of intimidation that they have, you know what I'm saying? Not only being a former athlete but also being two Black men," Charles said.

Charles's words made it eminently clear the disadvantages faced by Black customers trying to get simple things done at a bank were not just lingering side effects of a bygone era. These were not reflections of stubborn socioeconomic imbalances in society as a whole. What Charles described was racism, pure and simple, present and powerful. When Jimmy asked if he was saying that Frank was racist, he replied: "I don't think any person at that level is dumb enough for it to be that blatant.

"I don't have any reason to believe blatantly that he's that way. You feel what I'm saying? Now, whether there's some covert action? To be honest? I always err on the side of thinking that. You know, people that are not us probably have some form of prejudice toward us."

In other words, Charles was trying to assure Jimmy that banks and the people running them weren't racist even though bankers might sometimes feel uncomfortable around large Black men. Jimmy didn't buy it. He pulled most of his money out and filed grievances with an industry watchdog and with the Arizona attorney general's office describing what had occurred.

JPMorgan's written responses to both Jimmy's and Ricardo's discrimination complaints simply denied all wrongdoing. In Ricardo's case, a lawyer said that Ricardo had been an "abrasive" coworker and had made "unreasonable" demands of his bosses, and that his firing was justified by his bad behavior and his violation of bank rules. In Jimmy's case, a JPMorgan lawyer said the bank had simply found "no evidence" of discrimination.

The Arizona attorney general's office had fielded the bank's side of the story without examining the evidence that—in Ricardo's case, at least—had been carefully laid out to back up each claim. The cursory treatment brought both Jimmy's and Ricardo's cases swiftly to failure.

But that wasn't all. In Ricardo's case, JPMorgan submitted information that was flat-out false. Central to its argument against Ricardo was that he had not raised discrimination as an issue until after he learned he was being investigated for misconduct—for wrongly assigning that sales credit to Acosta—and that Acosta had agreed that he did not deserve the sales credit.

This was not true.

Reality, which Ricardo could back with audiotape, would show he had filed his internal discrimination complaint on August 24 and weeks later, on September 10, JPMorgan's global security investigators made reference to it when they interviewed him.

JPMorgan's letter also said that the bank had found "no evidence" that Ricardo had been discriminated against. It faulted Ricardo for being uncooperative with investigators trying to look into his discrimination claims. While it was true that Ricardo had refused to deal with human resources officials who were asking him about his complaint, JPMorgan's characterization of his refusal did not capture the reality of the situation. The bank's letter made no mention of the fact that, each time one of the human resources officials had contacted Ricardo, the central premise of their questions was that he had just recently complained after being interviewed by the global security team.

When Jimmy and Ricardo realized they were getting nowhere with the authorities who could help them get justice on their own, they turned to the press, to the *New York Times*, where an intermediary directed them to me. My story about their experiences, headlined "This Is What Racism Sounds Like in the Banking Industry," attracted more than 1.4 million internet page views. JPMorgan was forced to respond.

Soon after I reached out to JPMorgan representatives for comment, and before my story went public, the bank put Venniro on leave. He resigned soon afterward, guessing—correctly, according to my reporting—that he was about to be fired.

"Our employee used extraordinarily bad judgment and was wrong to suggest we couldn't help a customer," JPMorgan spokeswoman Patricia Wexler said in a statement that I included in my story. But Wexler also insisted that Venniro had not known that Ricardo's potential client was Black when he described her as being "from Section 8."

The bank also, at first, held on to its position that it was justified in firing Ricardo. Its authorities had made public the fact that Ricardo had been fired for misconduct by sending a report of his firing to a regulator overseeing financial advisors. The report, which anyone could view by searching Ricardo's name in a database, effectively cut Ricardo off from getting another job as a financial advisor.

By now Ricardo was wise to the existence of the broad settlement between JPMorgan and its class of Black financial advisors. And he had connected personally with Linda Friedman, who had agreed to represent him in a separate case against the bank. When Friedman, the same lawyer handling the discrimination class-action suit against the firm, confronted JPMorgan's lawyers about the discrepancies between the record Ricardo had preserved and the one they had submitted to Arizona officials, the bank's lawyers admitted to having made false representations to the state investigators and they agreed to inform Arizona officials accordingly. The lawyers said that JPMorgan officials had found the record of Ricardo's August 24 discrimination claim and that a clerical error had led to the claim being marked as having been filed in mid-September rather than late August. The bank lawyers offered no explanation for why, since the corrected record confirmed investigators had seen the complaint on the day Ricardo filed it, no one had done anything to address it for three weeks. Arizona authorities acknowledged receipt of JPMorgan's latest letter without asking any more questions or taking any further action.

It took months and months, but Ricardo eventually reached a settlement with his former employer. Part of the agreement forbade

Ricardo from ever revealing its details. There would be no public apology, no statement put out over the newswire or on the bank's website, but a change did take place after the two sides reached an agreement. In 2020, the public report JPMorgan had filed claiming that Ricardo deserved to be fired was expunged from Ricardo's regulatory record. Now a search of Ricardo's name turns up a spotless record for his career as a financial advisor.

PART TWO

FOUR

THE TRUTH ABOUT HR

Bill Winters was a former JPMorgan man. He had almost reached the top of the largest bank in the United States, but Jamie Dimon, JPMorgan's CEO, had pushed him out in 2009 amid rumors that Winters had eyes on Dimon's job. If he couldn't climb to the top of the heap among the American banks, he was determined to conquer Britain's banking empire. After leaving JPMorgan, he set about raising his profile in London, where he'd first made his name while working for JPMorgan's investment bank. He pumped up his profile by landing a spot on a parliamentary commission to improve the country's banking system in 2010, and took part in fame-making events like a London charity gala where, appearing on video, he stripped to the waist and, as one journalist had put it, sang a "decent" falsetto solo. Winters's efforts were rewarded when he was chosen to run Standard Chartered, the UK's fifth-largest bank, in 2015.

Winters had lost the battle to become JPMorgan's CEO, but this wasn't such a terrible consolation prize. He had gotten the chance to lead a bank with truly global scope, whose operations stretched from Hong Kong across Asia and the Middle East, down throughout Africa and into Europe and even the United States. Everywhere. He had taken charge at a time when the London-based bank needed a clean man of order. It had run afoul of anti–money laundering laws, lagged behind competitors, and drawn repeated fines for violations of economic sanctions by doing business in Iran.

On November 3, 2020, Winters received a note from Kayode Odeleye, a Nigerian banker who had spent thirteen years at Standard Chartered and risen to the rank of director on the bank's leveraged finance team in Africa. His job was to help Nigerian companies raise cash by underwriting bond deals and securing other kinds of loans and, as he described in his note to Winters, he had been very good at it. He was writing to let Winters know why—despite all of the above—he was now on his way out.

Kayode had been fastidious in his work for the leveraged finance team; now he had applied the same care to his note to Winters. He'd used the software that his team relied on to create deal pitches to clients to work up a graph of his own performance review history and had pasted an image of the graph into his email. The line plotting his performance rating over the progression of his years at the bank started out near the top of the graph and stayed there until his latest three years, and then it plummeted. In Kayode's telling, his last boss had been determined to push him out using any means she could, and bad performance reviews were just the beginning of her campaign.

"I have been the victim of sustained bullying," he wrote. "I believe this has to do with systemic racism, not an isolated case as there have been formal complaints by others."

Kayode detailed the alleged abuse: His manager had moved him off the Nigeria desk and made him take over South Africa, where the bank had already begun a formal retreat after a series of bad deals and had little interest in expanding operations. His existing Nigerian clients, with whom he had developed close relationships over years, were all handed to someone else, no questions asked.

(Standard Chartered does not deny that this happened, but officials called it a reorganization and characterized it as something that happens from time to time under normal circumstances. Maybe it was just a coincidence that the results of this restructuring were that all the Black people on the Africa leveraged finance team had been pushed out?)

Kayode described to Winters a particularly troubling moment in his relations with his antagonistic boss. He had, he said, a reputation for nurturing recent hires, yet was penalized for going against his boss's recommendation to make a bad report to human resources of-ficials about a junior banker who had just joined his team. His boss had wanted him to recommend that the young man be fired, but, Kayode explained to Winters, he had personally found the young banker to be competent, pleasant, and effective. Kayode also recognized a legal peril in trying to fire the young man, since he was Emirati and the group, based in Dubai, had an obligation to hire and retain a certain number of Emirati nationals each year.

And on top of all that, Kayode explained to Winters, he was the last Black employee standing on his boss's team. Everyone else had already left, either pushed out or offered resignation just ahead of termination. Several had complained of discrimination, and one of them, a banker more senior than Kayode, had even raised the issue to executives at such a high level that his report resulted in the abusive boss receiving a coaching session, a verbal talking-to from human resources representatives who had found her to have treated the Black employee unfairly due to "unconscious bias."

This was the thrust of Kayode's report to Winters: It was too late for him, he said, but he wanted to leave Winters with the tools to make sure other Black employees did not suffer the same fate.

Winters replied: "Thank you for your note, Kayodeodeleye [sic]. I will ask the team to look into your complaints. Given your comments, I expect I will hear that your case has been thoroughly reviewed but I will confirm. I can clearly confirm that we have no tolerance for bullying nor discrimination."

THE POWER OF A POLICY

Winters's email was one of many examples I have come across of a financial firm asserting that an employee's claim of discrimination could not be true because the firm had a policy of not tolerating discrimination. I assumed that this circular argument was formed from a combination of laziness and dedication to an impenetrable public relations veneer above all else.

But I was wrong. The truth is even more sinister. It is more than casual corporate gaslighting. America's courts have given legal weight to the claim that, because there are policies and procedures in place to prevent discrimination, no discrimination can possibly have occurred. More precisely, from the corporate perspective, that weight allows employers to argue that discrimination could not possibly have occurred *in a way in which the company ought to be held liable for it.* Since the late 1990s, companies all across America have used similar language to get federal judges to rule in their favor in discrimination cases.

In 1998, two cases dealing with the federal law that makes it illegal for employers to discriminate against their employees, Title VII of the Civil Rights Act of 1964, came up before the Supreme Court. Neither dealt specifically with race discrimination. In one, a woman who had worked as a lifeguard for the city of Boca Raton, Florida, had been sexually harassed to such an extent that her managers' behavior had created a "hostile work environment." In the other, a woman working a sales job in a textile company had been stalked by her boss and punished for refusing his sexual advances.

The question was whether the employers in either case, both of which dealt with hostile work environments, could claim that they had an "affirmative defense" against the accusation that they should have done more to stop the harassment or help its victims. An "affirmative defense" is basically a pass given to a person or entity (like a company) by the court that says even if the bad actions at the heart of the case occurred, that entity or person is not liable for them.

Industry leaders of all kinds and sizes very much wanted this pass. A trade group representing corporate human resource departments, the Society for Human Resources Management, filed an amicus brief in both of the cases, arguing that the court should spell out how much protection companies could reasonably expect when disgruntled employees filed suit against them with claims of discrimination or sexual harassment. The SHRM wanted the court to give companies credit simply for having policies and procedures in place.

The court agreed. It ruled that employers were protected from liability as long as it could be proven they had taken "reasonable care" to prevent or stop harassment from occurring and that the employee claiming harassment had failed to sufficiently utilize the employer's resources to stop it—a vague, nearly inarguable standard in the hands of a well-staffed and -funded legal defense. The mere presence of anti-discrimination policies and reporting procedures—written evidence of a "zero tolerance" policy on racism and the maintenance of a hotline for employees seeking to report instances of discrimination—was one way an employer could demonstrate that it had taken that "reasonable care."

As Lauren B. Edelman, a law professor at the University of California, Berkeley, put it in a 2018 article for the *Harvard Business Review*: "Having a policy became a proxy for companies actually doing something to prevent sexual harassment . . . [I]t has become almost impossible for an employee to win a hostile work environment case about sex or race harassment."

This was why, during Ricardo Peters's call with JPMorgan Chase human resources official Rosemary Ruggieri, the bank's "no-retaliation policy" came up as a reason why Ricardo should drop complaints about the possibility his abusive boss might overhear his descriptions of the abuse.

Some of these written policies do translate into actual activity inside a bank. For instance, at Standard Chartered it is not uncommon for managers to be assigned unconscious bias training after one of their employees complains about discrimination, even if an investigation does not find any evidence of misconduct. This is, at least in part, another way to reduce the company's legal exposure. In the case of Kayode's boss, for example, she really was ordered to take a training course on unconscious bias.

Along with this protective shield, Standard Chartered employed another very common defensive tactic in Kayode's case: the orientation of its human resources department's priorities. When Kayode complained to Human Resources, he thought he was seeking justice. What he had actually done was alert the company to a problem that needed to be dealt with: Kayode, the employee making the complaint.

"NO EVIDENCE"

Essma Bengabsia was a savvy young woman employee at BlackRock, the world's largest asset manager. Even though her job as an analyst on the company's trading floor was entry-level, she was already equipped with the awareness it took to recognize when something wasn't right and to document it, so when she reported to Human Resources her senior colleagues' misconduct, Essma arrived with evidence. Every time a coworker bullied her—ridiculing her Muslim faith, harassing her for failing to wear a Christmas sweater to a holiday function or for greeting her parents in Arabic on the phone—she would take out her personal phone and text a friend or relative a description of what had happened. The texts were time-stamped and offered her a way to back up some of her specific claims.

When she made her report about discrimination to BlackRock officials, Essma offered to supply the texts in support of her case, but she never explained in detail where she was keeping them. "I verified this through my text messages," she said periodically in the report, as she described what had happened to her. She filed it and waited for a response.

Less than a week later, Essma's work-issued cell phone stopped working. It didn't appear broken; it was just locked. Something was happening to it. For several days—an eternity in the go-go environment of the finance industry—Essma could not use her phone at all—for anything. She showed it to one of her bosses. "Look," she told her, "I can't get into my phone." Shrugging, her boss replied: "It's probably just doing some kind of update."

After a few days, Essma's phone came back online. But it had been wiped clean. All her texts, call log, apps—everything she had put on the phone since it had been given to her at the beginning of her job—had been erased.

A few weeks later, Essma took a short-term disability leave. The oppressive atmosphere in which her colleagues and bosses all insisted that *she* was the source of all her problems, not they, had become too much to handle. She was at home when a human resources representative called to tell her that the department had found "no evidence" to back up her claims. No one had ever asked to see her text messages.

"THIS IS NOT WHO WE ARE"

The captains of industry never seem to shy away from confidently offering to justify their self-love to the public. Ask them who they are, and they will tell you they are wonderful people doing amazing things.

Thanks to them, businesses grow, deals are made, homes are purchased, family savings pile up, and the world advances. Lloyd Blankfein, the former CEO of Goldman Sachs, told a journalist after the 2008 financial crisis that he and his colleagues were "doing God's work," explaining that Goldman was at the heart of a "virtuous cycle" in which its activities helped companies grow, which created wealth for them, which allowed them to employ more people who could build up their own wealth. He faced an avalanche of criticism for his comments, which were still circulating two years later when "Occupy Wall Street" protestors took over a park in downtown Manhattan to highlight the massive economic inequality the financial system was perpetuating.

Bankers learned from the backlash Blankfein's words generated. Most don't say things like that in public anymore, although they do still say them in more polite tones of voice, even to us journalists after we have agreed to their requests to speak candidly "off the record." But there are plenty of other ways bankers continue to publicly demonstrate their sense of importance. Some of the best and most consistent examples have been found in the contents of Jamie Dimon's annual letter to shareholders.

Each April, Dimon, the CEO of JPMorgan Chase, publishes an address to JPMorgan's shareholders on the bank's website. He emails it personally to bank regulators. His spokespeople send it directly to the crew of financial journalists on the JPMorgan beat. It is much more than a commentary on the company's financial performance over the past year. It contains a summary of Dimon's expectations for the U.S. economy's performance in the year to come and serves as a not-so-subtle nudge to government officials and other business leaders on what the great JPMorgan (aka Jamie Dimon) wishes to see prioritized in the coming year.

In April of 2018, for instance, as President Donald J. Trump's appointees carried out his directives to separate migrant children from their parents at the U.S. border and make it as difficult as possible for them to enter and remain in the United States, Dimon wrote: "We need to resolve immigration—it is tearing apart our body politic and damaging our economy." He went on to opine that immigrants to the U.S. "should be taught American history, our language and our principles." He did not explain how suggesting that immigrants should be required to study English fit into his purview as a bank CEO. It was one of many illustrations of Dimon's confidence in his ability to identify pressing political and social problems, frame them, and offer solutions.

By 2021, he had turned his attention to economic inequality and the racial wealth gap. In his view, Black Americans, along with other minorities, were being held back by a failure of state and federal officials to provide them with a suitable education. Overall, American leaders had "failed to design effective policies" for governing the country, Dimon added, before offering a long list of reasons why, including political partisanship, "short-termism," "bureaucratic plaque," and "media hype." Although Dimon's gaze in his annual letters is sweeping, it has never rested on his own institution or those of his financial industry peers as part of his quest to identify America's problems and suggest ways to fix them.

It is true that lending is a key part of capitalism and that the global economy is only growing more financialized, which makes bankers' roles crucial to its functioning. But before bankers are ordained into some pantheon of benevolence, they must squarely face the reality experienced by those their institutions have left behind and deliberately harmed, and they continually shy away from doing so. Dimon, as Wall Street's longest-standing CEO and the leader of the country's largest bank, is particularly outspoken. But he is not alone, nor is his tendency to extend his commentary far beyond the limits of his expertise unusual. Another leader who loves to project an Olympian level of moral superiority is BlackRock's founder and CEO, Laurence Fink.

By the time the 2020 presidential election cycle began, Black-Rock's holdings had grown to over $8 trillion in investments and the firm employed approximately 16,000 people around the world. Fink had the ear of world leaders, including not just Donald Trump but France's president, Emmanuel Macron, and one of German chancellor Angela Merkel's biggest rivals, Friedrich Merz, a BlackRock board member. Fink's firm seemed mighty in its influence. Former Black-Rock employees quickly surrounded presidential candidate Joseph R. Biden and, once Biden beat Trump in 2020, swooped in to help the president-elect find the right people to serve in his administration.

The transition from Trump to Biden had clear implications for Wall Street and for large companies in general: They were going to have to get nicer. They'd have to care more about the environment and climate change, be fairer to their employees and to the defenseless masses in general. As Fink framed it in his letter to investors in 2021, it wasn't a change driven solely by the presidential transition of power; it was a broader movement by BlackRock's customers, including pension funds and other large money managers entrusted with the retirement savings of non-elite people like teachers and firefighters, toward "sustainability." Companies were going to have to be more open and direct with the public, including their own shareholders, and they were going to have to more actively try to fix the problems plaguing the world, including economic and racial inequality.

Fink's letter positioned BlackRock as a leader in this movement. The firm would hold the companies in which its clients were shareholders to higher standards on all these fronts. It was as close as any person or entity on Wall Street would get to being—or appearing to be—"progressive."

But back at the home office, things weren't all that progressive looking. Non-white employees had a nickname for the place—WhiteRock—and they were either quitting or speaking out in protest—

or both—in droves. Not that there were droves of non-white employees to begin with. Just 5 percent of BlackRock's workforce in the United States was made up of Black employees, and only 3 percent of its directors—higher-level managers—were Black.

When Essma Bengabsia went public with her story in February 2020, she was not alone—not even, it seemed, an outlier among non-white employees. Just days before she posted an account of her treatment on the internet, a Black woman, Brittanie McGee, had taken BlackRock to Manhattan federal court, claiming that over the course of six years at the firm she had been marginalized, humiliated, and passed over for promotions despite receiving excellent performance reviews before eventually being forced to leave after telling human resources officials that she was experiencing racial discrimination. The most striking details in McGee's lawsuit weren't the specifics of her mistreatment. (They matched the stories of other employees; there was nothing particularly out of the ordinary in them.) Rather, McGee had spent so much time talking to BlackRock's head of employee relations, a woman named Tara Smith Williams, who was also Black, that the two had built up a rapport with each other and were able to speak frankly.

Williams had only recently joined the firm herself after working for eight years at JPMorgan Chase, and that is another likely reason for her frankness. McGee claimed in her lawsuit that Williams admitted to her that BlackRock had massive problems with diversity. The list of managers who had never, ever worked with a Black person, Williams told McGee, was "pages long." There wasn't even much diversity in the human resources department. Overall, she said, BlackRock's efforts had been "pathetic" so far.

After George Floyd's murder in 2020, BlackRock had pledged to increase the number of Black employees at the firm. But McGee told Williams that nothing had changed in her division, and Williams agreed: Nothing had changed. She explained that BlackRock's overall approach to its whiteness was driven by "convenient ignorance." It was fine to publicly praise the virtues of diversity, but nobody was willing to take a close look at their own behavior or the makeup of their teams.

There was more than just this private moment of candor to show how aware BlackRock's top managers were of its problems. In early February of 2021, Essma posted an account of her experiences and departure on the internet. It had an interesting, rather unexpected effect: Manish Mehta, BlackRock's global head of Human Resources, sent a companywide note two days after Essma's account came out. Its title: "Creating a More Inclusive Experience for All of Us."

Mehta was careful to say that BlackRock would stand by its decisions in the specific discrimination cases that had come to light—including, presumably, Essma's, since he never specifically named any. "Even though we have not found evidence of discrimination or harassment in these recent cases," he wrote, "we know that there are instances where individuals have not lived up to our principles."

He listed the ways employees could raise concerns about discrimination and harassment and vowed to "share more details" about BlackRock's diversity goals for the year soon.

Mehta's memo was also peppered with assertions that BlackRock was, at its core, a good and inclusive place already. The memo began with the claim that BlackRock's culture was about "creating an inclusive, equitable environment," and that this culture was "central to our success." The bad behavior everyone was talking about was "not who we are" and "not what BlackRock stands for." (Which was it: that things were great or that they weren't?)

Essma wasn't the only employee who wanted to make sure the public knew that things were *not* going well at BlackRock. Two weeks after Mehta's memo went out—it was almost immediately leaked to the press—Essma published an open letter to Fink on the blogging platform Medium that was coauthored by Mugi Nguyai, another former employee who reported having experienced racist treatment at Blackrock before being fired after reporting it to Human Resources. Essma had said that every word and action by BlackRock officials responding to her complaint, from her direct boss and her colleagues to the human resources representative tasked with investigating her claims, was designed to make her feel like *she* was the problem. Mugi's account was eerily similar.

BlackRock issued another memo: "Working to Enhance Our Culture of Belonging and Inclusivity."

"Some of our people have experienced the firm in a way that is not inclusive. Whether the behaviors that cause this are intended or not, they are not acceptable," Mehta wrote, even as he continued to insist that the specific stories that the public was getting from former employees weren't true. ("We disagree with the portrayal of our firm in today's blog post.")

It was again a mix of acknowledgments that BlackRock would need to do better and assertions that the firm's culture was already inclusive and respectful. It reminded employees that BlackRock had previously vowed to increase the number of Black employees at the firm. It added that, soon, there would be more details about how BlackRock was changing its procedures for investigating employees' discrimination complaints. Rarely is the public storm around a single company so concentrated that it is possible to observe two contradictory things at once: the company's quest to keep its public image clean and its human resources department's private dirty work.

NUMBERS AND NETWORKS

Just because they are mostly out of sight does not mean that conditions like those at BlackRock are rare. The percentages of Black employees working at various top-brand Wall Street firms are right around BlackRock's level, maybe a little more, maybe a little less, but nowhere near the proportion of the Black people making up the total population of the United States. At PIMCO, the well-known, $2.2 trillion bond fund based in Newport Beach, California, there was not a single Black partner or managing director for fifty years, from the firm's founding in 1971 until March 16, 2021, when two employees became the first Black men ever to be promoted to managing directors in the firm's history. The promotions, which PIMCO said were based entirely on merit and had nothing to do with optics or politics, came after a group of women working in the fund's legal department sued, claiming gender and race discrimination, and later became part of a group of twenty-one current and former PIMCO employees who signed a letter to top managers detailing its abuse of female and minority employees.

PIMCO is enormous. There are scores of little Wall Street firms, like boutique investment banks and money managers with a niche focus, that are too small to attract much notice. Inside these firms, in general, protections for Black employees—if there are any Black employees there to begin with—are even weaker. One Black woman who worked for a hedge fund and spoke to me on the condition that I not name her or the hedge fund told me that after she had formally complained that she had been passed over for more than one promotion while watching less qualified white men get the raises and titles they asked for, the hedge fund's leaders asked her if she could explain to her boss and the rest of her team how to be less discriminatory. After reading my stories in the *New York Times*, a white man reached out to me to describe the ways in which his former firm, a small investment bank based in Chicago, had tried to put the two Black employees who worked there on display, to signal that it cared about diversity. Little League moves like these are not categorically different from what goes on at top-name places like BlackRock or PIMCO, but these larger firms always manage to make themselves less vulnerable to reproach. They have bigger budgets for teams of lawyers and public relations employees dedicated to keeping their public images pristine.

Black Wall Street employees have told me that as they move through their careers they become part of an informal yet robust network of advisors, helping each other through difficult periods, coaching younger colleagues, and providing listening ears to all in the network—anyone who is Black—who seek help.

Jacob Walthour, a money manager who began his career at Morgan Stanley in the early 1990s and worked at big-name firms like Lehman Brothers, Moore Capital Management, and Citadel Investment Group before starting his own firm, Blueprint Capital Advisors, said the network's most important rule was that if someone reached out, the overture was never ignored.

"When I went to Lehman I was given five people to get in touch with," Walthour told me. None of the five worked at the same firm. One was at Lazard, another at Bear Stearns, a third at a white-shoe law firm. "They became my advisory board," Walthour said. "I never talked to anyone inside Lehman; I had these other people whose job it was to make sure I didn't make any mistakes."

Walthour said that the network's members made it clear to each other that any discriminatory treatment they might be receiving was something they would just have to get through. Going to Human Resources was out of the question. It wasn't a rule; it was simply the truth. I asked Walthour what the network was for, then, if not to help its members get justice when they were being mistreated by bosses or coworkers. What advice could its members give?

"Unfortunately the answer would be: 'Just let it go.' But you felt better just talking to somebody else about it. They would make you feel better by telling you a story about something that happened to them or something that happened to another peer of yours somewhere else.

It hurt less because other people were being hurt, too, which is sad, but it would work to just kind of talk you off the ledge and remind you of how far you've come and how much worse it could be."

Even Walthour, who, in 2021 when we had this conversation, was in the midst of suing the state of New Jersey and BlackRock, accusing them of stealing one of his asset management models, said he thought things had improved since the 1990s and early 2000s. It was easier to speak up now, he said.

And, one must wonder now, whether surely in *some* cases human resources officials can help victimized employees get relief. It can't be *all* bad.

A particularly grim example of a successful discrimination complaint also came out of Standard Chartered. In 2017, Sobara Simon-Hart, another Dubai-based employee of the bank, formally complained to its HR team that a white woman had been making racist comments to her with such intensity and frequency that she was no longer able to concentrate on her work the way she wanted to. It had begun the day the woman, Lauren, had joined Sobara's team—they were lawyers together working on Standard Chartered's trading floor—when the two had gone out to lunch together as part of a larger group. Lauren had told the group she was especially glad to be working in the area of Dubai where Standard Chartered's office was located, because, unlike other parts of the Emirates, it was full of Europeans. "I'm *so* glad to be around white people again—yay!" she'd exclaimed. Sobara had rolled her eyes and chalked it up to obtuseness, but things had gotten worse from there. Once, Lauren told Sobara she would never understand the feeling of conditioner in her hair because it was too wiry. Another time she made a comment about Sobara's bottom. And their shared boss seemed to favor Lauren over Sobara, which made everything worse.

Sobara's claims were investigated and the bank determined that Lauren had indeed made the lunchtime comment—another person who had attended the lunch remembered hearing it, too—but that there was "no evidence to corroborate" the other incidents, so the claims related to them were "not upheld." Sobara's boss told her that human resources officials had recommended that "no further action" be taken about the situation, emails filed in UK court showed.

Sobara's career at Standard Chartered ended with her complaints. She took medical leave and was treated for depression, and after the bank asked her to return to work and she pointed out that her managers had not changed anything about her situation to alleviate the source of her stress and trauma, like moving her or Lauren to a different team, Standard Chartered fired her.

FIVE

UNSAFE AT ANY LEVEL

Kayode Odeleye and I spoke for the first time in March of 2021, the day after Oprah Winfrey interviewed Meghan, Duchess of Sussex, and Prince Harry about the racist abuse Meghan had experienced at the hands of the British royal family. Meghan had revealed that while she was pregnant with her son, Archie, at least one member of the royal family had expressed fears about what skin color he would have when he was born and had worried that he would be too "dark." Meghan was told that Archie's royal status would be inferior to that of his cousins—and presumably that of a baby born to two white parents—and the family later refused to grant Meghan and Harry a security detail.

The interview with Oprah came up in my conversation with Kayode, not because I asked him about it, but because, while watching it, Kayode had thought of another story of racism in rare air. The coverage of the British royals had reminded him of what had recently happened at Credit Suisse.

Tidjane Thiam, a Black man born in Côte d'Ivoire, became the CEO of the massive Swiss bank in 2015. It was a watershed moment for the banking industry. There had never been a Black CEO at any big bank before. The closest any Black executive had ever come to that kind of power in finance was Ken Chenault, who'd held the top job at American Express, but Amex was not a bank. Neither was TIAA (founded as Teachers Insurance and Annuity Association of America), another large financial company that had already had a Black CEO.

When they hired Thiam, Credit Suisse's board had said his risk management expertise was exactly what they were looking for. At that point, Credit Suisse's image needed some repairs. Its bankers had recently had to admit to authorities that they'd made a business out of illegally helping Americans hide their fortunes from tax collectors. Credit Suisse had also fallen behind its rivals in the wealth management space, and it had had to slash parts of its investment banking division to stay profitable. Against this dismal background, a *Times* reporter described Thiam's appearance at the bank as "uplifting."

But right from the beginning there were signs that Thiam would be subjected to things his predecessors had not had to face. Even the *Times* coverage suggested that this might be the case: The paper's 2015 story introducing Thiam to the wider world began with a tidbit about how he had been advised to bring a change of clothing to one of the annual shareholder meetings at his old job, where he was CEO of the British insurance company Prudential, because shareholders might throw eggs at him in disgust over a recent takeover bid he'd made for a rival insurance business. What CEO, even an unpopular one, had been threatened like that, even as a joke?

By the time he arrived at Credit Suisse, Thiam already knew that the color of his skin could affect his ability to get and keep jobs, even at the highest levels. Earlier in his career, when another British insurer let him know through an intermediary that he was being considered for the top job there, he replied, "Well, I am very happy to interview. But frankly, you need to tell them that you found someone who is black, African, Francophone, and six foot four."

But as my colleague at the *Times* Kate Kelly later discovered, the wariness of a lifetime as a Black man in finance still failed to keep Thiam from being blindsided.

The Credit Suisse job turned out to be a test of how a bank's highest ranks would treat a Black man. No position was freer from bureaucracy and violent corporate machinations than a CEO position. There would be no human resources department to gaslight Thiam if he reported discrimination. The only people governing his employment were Credit Suisse's board of directors itself.

The board turned out to be an unyielding embodiment of the white wall.

Five years after his arrival, Thiam was forced to resign. A deputy of his had admitted to spying on a former high-level Credit Suisse banker suspected of trying to lure other employees away to a rival bank. Thiam took the blame for the incident even though he had no direct involvement in it. The stories of his departure all focused on "Spygate," as it was called, but Kelly, my *Times* colleague, decided to dig deeper. She found something entirely different.

"Whether it's labeled racism, xenophobia or some other form of intolerance, what's clear is that Mr. Thiam never stopped being seen in Switzerland as someone who didn't belong," Kelly wrote in a story in the *Times* in October of 2020. She discovered that Credit Suisse board members liked to party in blackface and that, near the end of Thiam's tenure, they'd hired a Black performer to dress up like a janitor and dance around for a birthday celebration he attended.

That wasn't all. The real conflict in "Spygate," it turned out, traced back to a phenomenon that many Black Americans are familiar with: the nosy, disapproving neighbor.

Thiam had a nosy neighbor in Zurich, where Credit Suisse is headquartered. But this man wasn't just any neighbor. He was a Credit Suisse executive himself, and Thiam had promoted him to run the bank's private wealth management business. Soon after being promoted, the banker had bought the house adjacent to Thiam's, shocking the CEO. To try to protect his privacy from his own subordinate, Thiam and his partner planted a few trees on their property to block their new neighbor's view into their house. The banker began to complain about the new trees. The conflict escalated: In 2019, the neighbor showed up at a holiday party that Thiam (his boss!) was hosting and started badgering Thiam's partner about the couple's landscaping decisions. Eventually, the fight got so heated that the banker quit Credit Suisse. The spying scandal followed; it was this man whom the bank's other leaders worried was poaching Credit Suisse employees.

The conflict between Thiam and his nosy banker neighbor was essentially a power struggle animated by racism. Just two months after Kelly's story appeared, another report described the same phenomenon in even more detail. It had nothing to do with banking, and it took place thousands of miles from Zurich, in suburban New Jersey, but the fact pattern was eerily similar: A Black family was relentlessly harassed by a white neighbor over a series of choices they made about how to arrange and improve their own backyard. At the height of the conflict, the white neighbor appeared on the Black family's property and started yelling at them—she didn't like their new patio—then called the police and falsely claimed that one member of the family had tried to assault her. Allison P. Davis chronicled it in a *New York Magazine* story called "The Karen Next Door." Thiam's absurd experience with his neighbor was similar. And it had cost him his job.

As for the spying incident, as Kelly pointed out, it was not even the worst spying scandal of its era. At the same time, at Barclays in London, CEO James E. Staley, another JPMorgan alumnus and erstwhile Jamie Dimon rival, was caught trying to ferret out the identity of a confidential whistleblower who had alleged that Mr. Staley was personally involved in wrongdoing inside the bank. This effort had the added evil of retaliation, which British law expressly forbids. And unlike Thiam, Staley was actually found to have done something wrong after authorities investigated. He was fined £642,000 by British regulators, and Barclays' board clawed back another £500,000 from his pay package. Yet no one forced Staley out over the matter. He enjoyed the support of the bank's board for another three years, until he resigned on November 1, 2021, over another regulatory investigation, this one into his ties with the convicted sex offender Jeffrey Epstein.

Kayode's heart ached when he thought of Thiam. "It's painful that at his level it could happen," he said.

Kayode had watched Thiam go down at the same time that he was trying to claw his way back to a solid footing at Standard Chartered. Seeing this parallel conflict come to a hopeless ending was incredibly demoralizing. "I saw the writing on the wall at my level: They don't want you there," he said. If Thiam couldn't make it, what could Kayode possibly hope for?

"It brought it home that you're never going to be welcome, no matter how good you are."

IN HER OWN WORDS

In 2021, the scarcity of successful Black leaders in finance became even clearer when one of the most powerful Black women ever to work on Wall Street changed jobs.

Thasunda Brown Duckett was, for a time, a figure akin to JPMorgan's corporate do-gooder mascot. A Black woman who had rocketed through the bank's upper ranks to become CEO of its consumer business, "T," as everyone called her, was beloved. And perfect. Never was she plagued by gaffe or scandal, by regulatory scrutiny or palace intrigue. Her enthusiasm for JPMorgan as an institution was as unwavering as her public image was pristine. Whenever Jamie Dimon and his top lieutenants wanted to swat away suggestions that they were

not welcoming to women or non-white people, T's public presence got
an extra boost. A profile here, a speaking engagement there—nothing
vulgar, but the message was clear: *Look at this powerful Black woman
whom we have promoted and nurtured*, the bank's communications
machine seemed to be saying.

And then she was gone.

In the spring of 2021, T got a better job. Roger W. Ferguson Jr., the
CEO of the big asset management firm TIAA and a Black man, was
retiring, and he recruited T to be his successor. It was the first time in
the history of a Fortune 500 company that one Black CEO would be
followed by another. And entirely apart from its historic nature, it was
a huge move for T. She would be second to none in a storied organization. Not just *almost there*, as she had been as CEO of one of JPMorgan's business lines, but *there*, right at the top. She enthusiastically
took the job, and JPMorgan executives bid her a hearty and friendly
farewell.

She left behind a huge hole. JPMorgan's operating committee, the
governing body of executives at the top of its roster that included its
CEO Dimon as well as other key executives like its chief risk officer,
its chief operating officer, and the heads of various businesses, had no
more Black faces. (T had been promoted to the committee in September of 2020.) With the departure of just one executive, any claim that
the bank was being led by a diverse group of people was greatly
diminished.

T has never said a bad word about JPMorgan. I have watched her
from afar, and I reached out to her while reporting this book not because I observed any visible mistreatment of her by the bank but because I felt a duty to find out whether she would want to contribute to
it, having ascended to a height in her career that so few other Black
women had ever reached. I got just the response I was expecting: a
polite rebuff.

I stumbled upon an interview she did for a conference on women in corporate America. Her interlocutor, Jana Rich, was already a trusted friend of hers, not a stranger like me. The two women spoke over Zoom in an interview that was later posted on YouTube, and Rich, I could plainly see, knew where the boundaries of the conversation needed to be. This was no place for a searing interrogation. It was all positive, vague, full of smiles, awash with goodwill.

It was early May when the interview took place, and T had only been in her new role at TIAA for a couple of weeks. She appeared radiant on-screen, never letting her wide smile fade.

"I am so thrilled to get a chance to have a girl chat," Rich said introducing the conversation. "Welcome to your new job!"

"It's so good to see you," T said. "I'm so excited about this conversation we're going to have."

About halfway through the twenty-minute interview, Rich asked a question that elicited a surprisingly revealing answer from T: "What would you say to women and especially women of color who are facing barriers to their advancement, the types of microaggressions that they have faced in the workplace. Any words of wisdom or inspiration for them?" Rich asked.

Still smiling, T gave this answer:

Oh, yeah. First and foremost, I think we have to know that we are worthy and deserving of everything. And be unapologetic about it. When you are having those microaggressions or some of those slight remarks where they are almost questioning your existence, as if your gender or your complexion was the only reason why you got the job, then they were lazy because they didn't even do the research.

So you don't even need to own that narrative. But I would say it's important to know that you are worthy and deserving, because, quite frankly, the biggest hurdle that we have to overcome many times especially as Black women is the mental gymnastics that we do in our head when we see and feel these microaggressions and just feel like we can't get ahead.

Secondly, know that your voice is necessary and required and do not dim your light. And in order to do that—and that is why I love this conference—the power of the sisterhood. That's where we have to connect. We have to say: "You know what? I might be the only Black woman in a senior role in the company, but there's my white sister or my Asian sister or my LGBTQ sister," that we have to come together and say: "Hey, I need you." And so, I think we have to create that space for that vulnerability, that space for us to really share what's on our minds and in our spirits so that we can navigate these waters collectively and together.

And then lastly, lastly, I would say is: Be unapologetic of the impact and the power that you have to make sure that that next Black girl or that next woman or person of color does not have to have the exact same road that you just traveled. We have to make it a little easier for the next person, and that is why we cannot give up, even when we are dealing with the storms that we all face and will continue to face until we see a lot more representation of the sisterhood at every level of corporate America or just business in general.

They were gentle, they were oblique, they did not mention JPMorgan, but the words offered by T, the powerful role model, told a simple story of struggle.

SIX

THE FRIENDLY GUY NEXT DOOR, EDWARD JONES

Once I got to know Linda Friedman, the lawyer whose firm has handled a large portion of the racial discrimination lawsuits against big financial firms, I started to realize just how plentiful and how varied Black financial industry employees' horrible experiences could be. Friedman got into the habit of alerting me to any interesting or consequential cases she was working on that had reached a certain stage of maturity and were ready for public attention and scrutiny. She was usually up to her eyebrows in Wall Street employees' painful stories, so I came to understand that whenever her name popped up in my email inbox, I was about to absorb a tale or two of real woe. But I was unprepared for both the severity and the volume of the stories her firm had collected about a brokerage firm known to sell itself as the friendly guy next door.

Edward Jones, a St. Louis–based firm, boasts about its 19,000 advisors' abilities to help everyday Americans cut through Wall Street's gobbledygook and find simple, commonsense ways to grow their nest eggs. "Making sense of investing" is how they put it in their marketing materials. The company's advisors are supposed to be the kind of folks who can sit down at a stranger's kitchen table and organize whatever financial mess is before them. They're approachable, lovable, not as slick as the big-timers in New York. And they're everywhere, in storefront offices across the country, in neighborhoods that aren't necessarily the center of anywhere.

The company aggressively recruits people to join its ranks, not just recent college graduates but people in the middle of their careers who have good jobs and defined directions for their lives, families, some money, stability. Edward Jones does not simply recruit new financial advisors with its eyes on some distant goal to expand or dominate the industry; it recruits them because it has to do so, constantly, to survive. It counts on a constant stream of new recruits to keep revenue flowing into the firm, and warns its investors each year that if too many of its advisors leave for other companies without being replaced, its business could suffer.

Sometimes, moving to Edward Jones is a good idea, but it's a bad bet if you're Black.

. . .

Wayne Bland was not new to the wealth management industry. He'd worked at Vanguard, a big mutual fund company, for several years starting in 1998, doing marketing and compliance jobs for the firm. In the course of his time there, Wayne learned a great deal about the rules governing mutual fund management and sales of the funds' shares to unsophisticated investors like the people who often became Edward Jones's customers. He briefly left the industry to open a restaurant with his family in Charlotte, North Carolina, where he lived but returned in 2007 as a financial planner specializing in insurance for LPL Financial, a San Diego–based wealth management company.

Wayne left LPL a few years later to launch his own financial planning consultancy, Bland Retirement Services. But he soon felt like he had a little too much on his plate. He had to do his own marketing work and monitor his own activities to be sure they adhered to financial regulations, as well as set up his own appointments with clients; it all added up to the work of three or four people being done by just one.

"I was spending more time trying to operate the business and 40 percent less working with clients," he said. "Edward Jones offered to handle my back-office stuff." He wanted to keep doing what he was doing no matter which firm he worked for. Edward Jones's recruiters told him that this was not a problem. Once he joined their ranks, he could do as he liked. Even after getting that reassurance he hesitated, since business in general was good, but the Edward Jones recruiting team finally convinced him in 2014.

Wayne set his sights on a wealthy part of the Charlotte area named Ballantyne. He knew the plush surroundings would play well with his managers, appealing to Edward Jones's philosophy of capturing neighborhoods rather than just clients. This one was a series of planned communities, neighborhoods full of repeating patterns of houses all built at the same time, set on curving streets with names that all adhered to a single theme. One community had fine wine as its theme; there was one street called Riesling Court and another called Russian River Place. Carpeted with verdant golf courses and dotted with homes luxurious enough to have their own swimming pools, it looked like a great place to find new customers, especially because the community itself was new. These weren't the people whose money was being managed by the same firm that had protected their parents' and grandparents' fortunes; their riches were of a newer mint. They were, in a word, gettable.

He told his new bosses that Ballantyne would be his territory. But within a few weeks of his joining, Edward Jones's regional director sat him down for a talk: Sure, it was up to Wayne to decide where he'd like to work, but it would really be better—and management would be much happier—if he were to choose a different neighborhood instead. Managers in the area were desperate for someone who could take on Steele Creek, a neighborhood that was a bit more out of the way and less secure than Ballantyne. It was tucked behind the airport, on the edge of a big reservoir. The homes were a little smaller there than in Ballantyne, and a little older. Something, Wayne thought, felt off.

His sense of discomfort rose again when he flew to St. Louis for a big training program the Edward Jones recruiters had gushed to him about. Instructors there told him the key to building up a successful business was knocking on strangers' doors and introducing himself as a financial advisor. He was one of only two Black trainees in a class of around forty-five people. And he quickly began to catch snippets of conversation that made him think that not everyone in the class was being relegated to backwaters like Steele Creek. Other trainees boasted about having their own offices inside some of Edward Jones's many storefront setups and being given lists of clients worth $15 million, $40 million, offering the chance for instant profitability. Wayne did not have an office—he had to work from his kitchen table or his car—and no one had given him any clients. He knew enough to realize that these gifts of business were the real secret sauce of the Edward Jones model, not the door knocking they were telling him to do.

Something's not right here, he said to himself.

"JUST LEAVE IT ON THE PORCH"

The St. Louis training session was unsettling in the extreme. Wayne quickly realized he'd picked up more casual knowledge of wealth management techniques as a Vanguard employee than the instructors at the training facility seemed to have.

"I was waiting for the training to start," he said. "You kept antici-pating they're just warming us up, there's got to be something more to it."

Wayne knew enough to know that the wealth management indus-try was full of pitfalls for unsophisticated advisors. If you sold a cus-tomer a financial product that was too risky or did not make sense for the customer's portfolio, you could get sued by the customer or even fined by a regulator. Advisors had to strike a delicate balance between the act of persuasion essential to the sale of any product and a mind-fulness of a customer's best interests and his or her ability to under-stand the product's risks. Surely the authorities at Edward Jones had something to teach new recruits about the subtleties of the business, right?

But instead of expert knowledge about the world of retail financial products, in Wayne's view, the trainers imparted little more than plat-itudes about how to pleasantly introduce oneself to a stranger answer-ing the door.

"You kept hoping: 'Well, I guess, after break, when we come back, we're going to really get into it.' There was no 'it'; it was always just scratching the surface. They would say: 'Okay, we're going to talk about mutual funds,' but there was no meat."

Wayne already had his doubts about knocking on strangers' doors. He was a Black man living in the South, after all. He held no illusions about what people would see when they looked at him standing on their stoops.

The other Black recruit in Wayne's training program was worried about the same thing. She was from Atlanta. Wayne watched as she raised her hand during one of the door-knocking lessons and said that she worried that the method would make people in her neighborhood uncomfortable.

"The answer was: 'This is how we have done it; it has worked in the past.'"

St. Louis was where Wayne first heard the names Goodknight and Legacy, programs through which some Edward Jones recruits were handed clients or given extra office space by more established investors. He tried to ask instructors what these programs were, but no one seemed to want to explain them. So Wayne found a group of young, white trainees sitting together in a classroom, laughing. He had heard their chatter: A few of them had failed their licensing exams but had been sent on to training anyway and had even been given clients to look after.

Everyone in the group was wearing a suit and tie. Wayne introduced himself and began to learn a little about each member. One was getting into wealth management after having been in the fertilizer business. Another had worked in a fabrication plant. They were from Georgia, Tennessee, the Great Lakes, all in their twenties or thirties, and they knew absolutely nothing about the financial industry.

One particularly chilling event came when Wayne's training class had its "visiting vet" session. An established financial advisor who was assigned to be the class's mentor appeared and began giving a demonstration that immediately seemed suspect to Wayne. Hooking his phone up to a projection system in the room, Wayne remembers the advisor calling one of his clients and, without letting the client know that a classroom full of strangers was listening, proceeding to try to convince him to move his retirement money out of the Vanguard mutual funds in which it was invested and roll it over into an IRA that the advisor would help manage.

"Listen, I talked to my wife about this," the man on the phone said, his voice quavering slightly. "She did a little research on Edward Jones and she thinks I should just slow down, because Vanguard has been really good to me."

There was silence in the room. The advisor hosting the call was clearly flustered. "Well, you can listen to your wife," he told the man on the phone as his face turned red. "But Vanguard is going to charge you a bunch of fees and I'm just trying to save you some."

Wayne did not say anything, but he realized he had just heard the advisor lie to a client. *Your wife is right*, he thought. *You should be glad you're married to her.* Vanguard offered shares in mutual funds that did not carry transaction fees.

After Wayne returned to North Carolina, his discomfort with Edward Jones's practices only grew. Advisors in his region would gather on the first Thursday of every month for a big meeting during which managers would present a new financial product to sell. It was often a single stock, like shares of an oil and gas exploration company. Wayne felt that not every client could handle buying every stock that the advisors were told to sell, but it was also what his bosses expected from him. "Everyone can own this," they told him when he suggested a particular product wasn't suitable. What's more, Wayne couldn't get by with just lip service to his bosses about whether he'd called every client and offered each of them the product. He had to log all his calls into a central system so his bosses could check to make sure he had made them.

Sometimes, just to make it look as though he had made his required sales calls, Wayne would reach out to a customer and shoot the breeze rather than put on the hard sell. He'd log the call for the company records but use that time to ask about the kids or chat about sports. He knew his fellow advisors could not be trusted to exercise the same discretion.

"When you're at a company like Edward Jones with limited training, you can only repeat what they tell you," Wayne said. "You don't really understand."

Alongside his worthless calls to clients he'd already recruited, Wayne was still being forced to walk around Steele Creek and knock on strangers' doors. "Just leave it on the porch!" some people shouted through their closed doors, mistaking Wayne for a deliveryman. Once, after he had knocked on a door and waited several minutes with no answer, Wayne turned to go to the next house and saw a police patrol car roll slowly down the street. His heart climbed into his throat as he met the eyes of the white police officer checking him out, but he managed to smile and nod, and the officer continued past without stopping.

He learned that some of his white counterparts had been given little cards shaped like hotels' DO NOT DISTURB tags to hang on people's doorknobs that said "Sorry I missed you!" They bore the advisors' names and numbers and served as a way to make contact with homeowners who were out all day. Wayne had not been encouraged to order these cards for himself, and he could see why. He did not want them. "If somebody saw or heard me trying to leave that on someone's door, I would probably get shot," he told me. "I live in a different universe. I can't touch anybody's doorknob."

IN THE CULT

Eventually, Wayne found out that Steele Creek was a neighborhood haunted by the ghosts of older, failed Edward Jones trainees. He started to suspect that various aspects of his struggles at work existed not by unfortunate accident but by design. How many times did his supervisors need to hear about the trouble he had as a Black man walking around in a residential neighborhood? He could not possibly be the first person to experience these problems. Hadn't the men and women who'd tried and failed before him left any useful impressions behind—lessons that could be learned and passed on by managers?

"It just didn't make sense to me that you could be this oblivious, but the more I thought about this Goodknight program, the more it became clear that there were two Edward Joneses operating in parallel universes," Wayne said. "At some point it began to seem like it wasn't really real. They can't really expect you to succeed like this. It doesn't take a rocket scientist to see that you just can't make it like this."

And Wayne was not succeeding. He had not been able to attract enough clients through door knocking to sustain a decent salary on top of the expenses Edward Jones was deducting from the commissions he brought in every month. He began dipping into his retirement savings and leaning on his wife for help. He did not understand why Edward Jones was keeping such a large portion of his commissions. In fact, when he first started bringing in commissions, his paychecks—which, during his training process, had provided a steady if modest income—suddenly went to zero.

When the first zero-pay day arrived, on a Friday, Wayne called an Edward Jones administrator to find out what was going on. It was already a dark period in Wayne's life. His father had recently died. He had just gone back to making his depressing sales calls. The one bright spot was to be the paycheck, because Wayne had just signed up two new clients, each of whom had bank account balances with enviable numbers of zeros trailing their starting figures. Now this. The administrator could not explain exactly what had happened to Wayne's paycheck but said that it was definitely not a mistake, as he had suggested. Something in the tone of the conversation made Wayne feel that even asking about it had been a false step by him in the company's eyes. He started to wonder if he had accidentally joined a cult.

His feeling that some ugly truth lurked under the company's shiny surface was reinforced by almost every interaction Wayne had with his field trainer, a man whose territory was just over the state line from Steele Creek, in South Carolina.

From the first time he met his field trainer, Wayne pitied him. The man had grown up in Clover, South Carolina, on the other side of the reservoir from Steele Creek. He kept his office in York, a town just down the road. It was a town where everyone knew everyone else. And it seemed to be the man's whole world. Wayne looked at him and saw that if he left Clover, he would not have any idea where to go. Edward Jones was his life.

The company made sure things stayed that way, too. It hosted events for advisors and their families that included special training sessions just for wives. Wayne called them "indoctrination ceremonies." At one of them, which Wayne's wife attended, she reported afterward that the women were told that Edward Jones had to come first, before family considerations, and the sacrifice would eventually pay off. Another woman turned to Wayne's wife and said, "This isn't right."

After that, Wayne and his wife realized there was no point in her attending future sessions. Wayne's field trainer and his wife attended every one of them together. When Wayne would see them there, he sensed something unnatural in their cheerful attitudes.

"I could see it in his face; I could see it in his wife's face. They would smile, but underneath they knew there was something wrong."

One afternoon the field trainer visited Wayne in Steele Creek and accompanied him on a door-knocking session. It was something that was supposed to happen regularly, but this was the first time Wayne's trainer had ever come out, and Wayne knew he might not get another chance to talk candidly with him. He turned to the man: "You told me all the things you like, but tell me what you don't like about this place," he said. "No company is perfect. What don't you like?"

The field trainer had nothing to say.

"EDWARD JONES IS HIRING ANYBODY THESE DAYS"

As a Black man, Wayne knew he was a member of an extremely small group in finance. His employers made sure he did not forget it. Back at Vanguard, he had frequently been pulled into the firm's diversity work, and he had participated energetically. Having the chance to mentor young employees and think about ways to find new Black recruits had made his work feel even more meaningful. Imperfect, but par for the course.

Not long after he started at Edward Jones, Wayne's bosses made him the regional specialist on diversity and inclusion. But he soon realized that conditions were different from the way they had been at Vanguard. He was suddenly saddled with demands for extra work, and he was expected to be a symbol for the company to highlight and look to for inspiration. And yet he could not find anyone willing to talk to him about what the company might be able to improve about its hiring or training practices in order to help minorities. At Edward Jones, he came to feel that no one actually wanted to hear his views on diversity.

"Every time I brought something up, they would shoot it down," he said. "I realized I was window dressing."

Selection to the company's diversity committee granted Wayne access to internal reports on how Edward Jones treated Black employees—"the scary part," as Wayne put it. He could see that not a single Black advisor was allowed into the Goodknight program. He saw reports with the performances of different groups of advisors—white men, white women, and so on—color coded in green, yellow, and red. The green-coded groups were the people who were doing the best—the white men. Black advisors were in the red group, lit up like a stoplight. They were struggling.

The reports, Wayne said, were made by an analyst in St. Louis who appeared not to realize that he should not be sharing them with the entire committee. Those red flags would come to mind when Wayne got his first taste of just how open some EJ employees could be with their bigoted, racist views.

It was at the summer regional conference, the biggest event of the year for Edward Jones advisors. Each year the conference was held at a fancy resort, and this time it took place at a hotel with a golf course on Hilton Head Island in South Carolina. Advisors were encouraged to bring their families with them. It was a grand place, a complex of sturdy white buildings with a front entrance mimicking a plantation house's flanked by giant live oak trees that gave way to an emerald-green lawn and, beyond it, the golf links, flat but lush, to which advisors and managers rushed in competition. Families splashed in the limestone-clad swimming pool and later dressed for the evening—khakis or smart suits for men and skirts or sometimes cocktail dresses for their wives—to attend soirees in a sparkling, thick-carpeted ballroom. The events were partly paid for by mutual fund companies that wanted Edward Jones to sell more of their products. Company representatives would host smaller breakout dinners for the advisors and their families, a chumminess in which Wayne saw a conflict of interest. Still, it was his duty to attend, and a trip to Hilton Head for his family didn't sound so bad. His wife and three of his five sons, ages eighteen, sixteen, and fourteen, accompanied him.

The first incident occurred at the hotel swimming pool. The Blands had just eased themselves into the water when Wayne sensed that someone was staring at him. He looked up and saw two white women standing five or six feet away from his little group, transfixed. Not swimming, not splashing; they were just staring. Glaring, really.

Wayne moved in the pool so that his body was in between his wife and the two women. He did not want her to see the looks on their faces, so unmistakably full of hate. One of the women, still meeting his eyes, said:

"Man, Edward Jones is hiring anybody these days."

Wayne later found out this stinging remark had come from the wife of one of Edward Jones's senior regional leaders.

Breakfasts at the conference kept up the painfully awkward feel of the week. Wayne had learned long before joining Edward Jones the special rules of behavior that he had to follow as a Black man in finance. He had to be impeccably dressed in the best suit he could find, his shoes shiny and spotless, his hair perfect. His name tag had to be prominently displayed at all times, to confirm to everyone else that he belonged in the room. He took to bringing a newspaper to the 6:30 a.m. buffet each morning, a kind of outward-facing security blanket so people would not feel uncomfortable when they noticed him sitting alone. And he always sat alone. Not because he wanted to but because, in following his preestablished rules of conduct, he inevitably arrived so early that no one else would be seated when he entered the room. As other attendees filed in, rare was the EJ employee willing to take a seat next to him, the conference's "sore thumb." He would watch as the other tables in the lavish hotel ballroom filled to capacity with white advisors chattering away. He would bury his head in the newspaper and try not to think about it. Always, and always toward the end, someone would come up to him and take a seat at his empty table to break the ice, and he would feel a shot of relief mix in with his frustration.

These little slights piled up on Wayne like wet leaves throughout the conference, so that by the time, a couple of nights later, a regional manager named Jim Paolone ran up to his family and shouted about a dance contest, Wayne had been inured to the shock.

The Blands were one of only two Black families at the event, a party with almost four hundred people in attendance. Paolone's eyes were alight as he pointed to Wayne's sons.

"Are these your boys?" he shouted. "How great! We're going to be doing a dance contest and we're going to be doing the 'stanky leg'!"

Wayne smiled politely. His wife had to stop herself from rolling her eyes. His sons just stared.

Only after they got home to Charlotte did Wayne tell his wife about the women in the pool.

"HOW'S THIS FOR DIVERSITY?"

In spite of it all, Wayne started to win a few clients. Big clients. But instead of being rewarded, he received another reminder of where people like him stood at Edward Jones.

There was a team-building session at the Mellow Mushroom, a pizza restaurant in Rock Hill, South Carolina, just across the state line from Charlotte. Wayne had just won a $6 million client, and word was going around about his victory. He sat down with pride at a table alongside some members of the company's leadership team. But instead of compliments for his work, one of the men—all of whom were white—gave him a glance and turned to a colleague.

"He got a six-million-dollar client?" the man said. "How did *he* get a six-million-dollar client? He's not even going to *be* here, anyway!"

Wayne was sitting a mere three feet away, well within earshot.

"You can't pay attention to this person," Wayne's field trainer, who was sitting with him, said. But the field trainer himself told an Edward Jones regional leader about the incident, who called Wayne the next week to talk about it.

"That guy is not on the leadership team anymore," the regional manager said.

Wayne later found out that that was a lie. Not only was that guy still a leader but his office, a prominent one in the Edward Jones network, was in Ballantyne—a locale Wayne had targeted to build his business.

"That's the day I started to check out," Wayne told me. He went home and told his wife what had happened. She was furious.

Not long after, Wayne was invited to give a presentation about diversity to the leadership team. When the meeting let out, Wayne found himself in a hallway behind three men, one of them Paolone, the man who had invited his sons to do the "stanky leg" at the dance competition. Paolone appeared to think the three men were alone. He didn't see Wayne, who was heading in the same direction, trying to get to the men's room.

"How's *this* for diversity?" Paolone whooped, raising one hand above his head and jabbing a raised middle finger in the air. Seconds later, he turned and locked eyes with Wayne, who left, wordlessly shaking his head.

"I HOPE WE CAN COUNT ON YOU"

Toward the end of 2015 it was clear that, no matter how hard he worked, Wayne's career at Edward Jones was doomed.

He started to plan an exit but knew he had to be careful. At the first hint his managers got that he was looking for another job, he'd be fired so quickly he wouldn't have time to contact his clients and let them know.

After the incident with Paolone, Wayne was moved to an EJ office in Lake Wylie, South Carolina, a little south of Steele Creek, sharing space with Jon Kingston, an established Edward Jones financial advisor. Wayne was under the impression that Kingston would be leaving soon, and the practice—and clients—could be his.

Although he now had a storefront where he could work, Wayne did not have an office per se. Kingston had a side business collecting and selling antiques, and he had commandeered the only extra space in the Edward Jones unit to use for storage. Whenever Wayne wanted to meet with clients, he would have to lead them carefully through the narrow space not taken up by a tea cart that looked like a movie theater popcorn machine and a large dining table that occupied almost all of the floor space in the room.

Wayne and Kingston did not exactly hit it off in the new space; they never had a single one-on-one meeting, and when Jon would arrive in the mornings he would pass by Wayne's room without a word. Kingston had no business reason to bemoan Wayne's presence. Under a system by which advisors with their own offices got production credits, Kingston got paid extra for housing another EJ employee.

After a month, Wayne tried to put his foot down about the antiques. He went on Edward Jones's procurement system and ordered the standard office furniture that belonged in all advisors' offices. It arrived, but Kingston refused to move his things, and so Wayne's furniture stayed in the hallway for six weeks. The receptionist handling their calls eventually got so annoyed by the mess that she alerted the head office to Kingston's refusal to accommodate Wayne, and he was forced to move the merchandise.

Shortly thereafter, Kingston was gone. But the office did not go to Wayne, nor did his clients. Another advisor, a white man named Ryan, showed up and took on Kingston's $25 million book. Wayne got a call from another senior financial advisor in the region, Todd Tyrie:

"I hope we can count on you to help him."

It was March of 2016, and Wayne had had enough.

"I really began to accelerate my departure," Wayne said. "I started looking around to see what to do next." As soon as he could, he quit and opened up an independent practice as a registered investment advisor, which meant that he had to convince financial products companies to let him sell what they had to offer. Many refused, saying—or hinting—that they were worried that if they did business with him and Edward Jones found out, the company would cut them off.

ON THE BLACKLIST

Wayne continued to struggle in his search for a new job in the financial industry after leaving Edward Jones. He became one of the lead plaintiffs in two separate lawsuits against the company, which made his future in the industry even more precarious. In one of the lawsuits, Black EJ employees described the company's systematic exploitation and abuse of them and their managers' open displays of racism. The other suit focused on its refusal to acknowledge the dangers of imposing its door-knocking strategy on them and on the exploitative structure of the EJ training program. The employees said EJ's requirement that trainees repay their training costs if they left the company within three years of their start dates as financial advisors was predatory. Wayne knew the risks of sticking his neck out by suing a large financial company, but being prepared for them didn't make the disappointments he faced after going public about his treatment any easier to endure. Some promising interviews at a bank in Raleigh suddenly went cold in 2020, and Wayne suspected that someone at the bank had googled him, found the lawsuit bearing his name, and decided he was too hot to touch. This was not unfounded paranoia; he'd already resigned from the board of a Charlotte-area charity that provided free healthcare to poor residents after overhearing two other board members, both of whom worked for Wells Fargo in Charlotte, discussing the Edward Jones lawsuit that Wayne had participated in. The same law firm that had handled it—Linda Friedman's firm—had also brought a racial discrimination class-action case against Wells, and the executives were noting the connection to each other. Wayne stepped away from the charity, concerned that his presence could jeopardize Wells's status as one of its primary donors.

He carried on selling insurance and making ends meet with bits and pieces of work.

"As far as this industry, I'm done with it," he said. "By the time my sons are a little older or they have children, maybe it will be different."

• • •

Felicia Slaton-Young didn't need what Edward Jones was offering. It was 2013. She had a job at a bank in Chicago that helped get minority businesses up and running. She liked the work, a hybrid of for-profit and community-building activities, and she was good at it. She was paid well enough to rent a small house for herself, where she lived alone, and to buy a Honda CR-V, a little black SUV she loved the way some people love their Mustangs and Corvettes. That car represented her stability and her freedom to choose, to assess what was best for her and to determine that the best was within reach. All was well for Felicia.

But a friend of hers, a white woman (Felicia is Black), kept calling her. They had worked together years earlier at another bank, Wachovia, which was bought by Wells Fargo during the 2008 financial crisis.

Felicia wanted me to know that whatever Wachovia's reputation for bad mortgage lending had been—the bank had nearly collapsed under the weight of the bad loans it had made to tens of thousands of borrowers during the housing boom in the early to mid-2000s—its workplace culture, at least in the office where she was located, was outstanding. Her coworkers were friendly, caring, and supportive. The warm and fuzzy memories she had of working with her friend added to the credibility of this friend's raves about Edward Jones.

"The culture is amazing," the friend told Felicia on the phone. She said it was similar to Wachovia's. "I think you would love it; I think you would thrive. Would you be interested in just speaking to a recruiter?"

It was hard for her to think about abandoning the work she was doing. But she was curious, and she admitted to herself that she did feel a sense of uncertainty about where her career would go next. Perhaps this opportunity was the answer.

"I was just kind of open to whatever the universe had available," Felicia told me, thinking back to that worry-free time. "I said I would be open to listening if someone calls. It would be on my terms: 'I'm not really thirsty for anything right now.' A recruiter called. We played a lot of phone tag. I wasn't giving it my full energy. We were able to connect after a few months, talk about what the opportunity was."

The Edward Jones representative told Felicia that she could, for practical purposes, be her own boss. She would have her own branch of a financial advisory business anywhere she fancied in the United States.

"He explained to me the opportunity to build a practice the way I wanted in a community of my choice, the support of marketing and all-around development that I would receive," she said. And on top of that, she recalled, another enticement: "Within five years I would be making six figures."

The recruiter outlined what the beginnings of the job would look like. There was a training period, after which Felicia would have to go out and find business prospects on her own. He was vague on just how that part was done, but she remembers him saying, "Make it your own. Find your clients, build your book the way that you want, because this is your practice."

CRASH COURSE

It took months of consideration, but Felicia eventually struck a deal to enter Edward Jones's training program for financial advisors. It was only after she had signed all the paperwork that she really understood what the move entailed. She would have to stay home and do nothing but cram for exams that would give her the professional licenses she needed to sell stocks, bonds, and other investment products to clients. Without those licenses, she would not be able to do her job, so failure— even delay—was not an option. Unlike other firms, where trainees learned the lessons they needed for their exams over the course of many months while they were introduced to the business by working in an office full of experienced professionals, she would have just one ten-week sprint in which to complete her studies.

Company representatives mailed her preparation materials, sure. A laptop with some do-it-yourself lessons and exams on it. A thick binder full of study materials, pages of information that Felicia needed to memorize if she was going to pass her exams. The number of a hotline she could call if she had questions she could not find answers to on her own. It was fuzzy how she was supposed to accomplish this all at once.

"Between studying and reading and practice exams, it's a lot of time commitment, definitely more than fifty hours a week," she said. Classic cramming. Felicia did the work, in the end averaging almost sixty hours of work a week, and passed her exams. The slog had been painful, but she felt good about herself for getting through it. Now it was time for hands-on training to begin.

Her new employers told her this was not something she could simply read about in a book. This was the time for in-person training, when she would learn the company's "secrets to success." She would soon have the power to build her own wealth as she helped her customers build theirs, but only after she had studied in great detail the patented wisdom of Edward Jones's leaders, the unique ideas they had honed over decades for building up clients. There was a delicacy to their descriptions, and perhaps that made up for their lack of specificity, because Felicia felt she was being told just enough to be kept hungry for more. Eager to know the company's secrets. Eager for the keys to success.

She would soon be told to walk around in a neighborhood of her choosing and knock on every stranger's door.

The so-called secret turned out to be that simple. Edward Jones's leaders told her that the key to becoming a successful financial advisor was for her, a Black woman, to pound the pavement, approach front door after front door, raise her hand and knock, and almost immediately put on the hard sell. Ask whoever answered whether their finances were in order and whether they had any money saved up.

A ROW OF DOORS

This wisdom was imparted to Felicia and the other trainees in periodic big-group meetings that lasted for several days at a cavernous training facility in Arizona where, in a warehouse full of mock-ups of front doors, kitchens, and living rooms, everyone had to practice the company's technique. The doors were set up on a stage with heavy black curtains on either side, facing a vast space for an audience to view a trainer's demonstrations of proper door-knocking techniques. Volunteers from the audience were occasionally selected to act out various scenes with their instructors, and then everyone was sent up to test out their new knowledge on the play sets of strangers' homes. It was part community theater, part boot camp, part magic show.

The task of breaking the ice was not left up to chance. The company gave Felicia and her fellow trainees scripts to memorize. They began with:

"HELLO MY NAME IS_____
 "I AM OPENING UP AN OFFICE WITH EDWARD JONES IN-VESTMENTS.
 "I JUST WANTED TO STOP BY, INTRODUCE MYSELF AND LEAVE YOU SOME INFORMATION . . ."

Felicia had to memorize these lines. They were supposed to get her quickly to a point at which the conversation could get personal: "ARE YOU FAMILIAR WITH EDWARD JONES?" was the first question. Directly underneath it was a note: "(Answer doesn't matter. Just say the next statement immediately.)"

The hard sell began seconds later:

"I CAN HELP YOU GET A BETTER INTEREST RATE ON YOUR SAV-INGS AND (Start smiling!!) I CAN HELP YOU SAVE ON TAXES!!
 "YOU'RE NOT OPPOSED TO ANY OF THOSE, ARE YOU?"

That was the cue for the first question about what this stranger standing in the open doorway might have in savings, whether their money was already being managed by a broker or a bank and what they were earning in interest. The trainees were advised to ask which individual stocks their targets might be interested in buying ("I wonder if you have ever heard of a stock called Procter & Gamble" is one version Felicia remembers), to leave behind business cards, get as much personal data as possible, and return for more in-person visits before trying to call any of the targets on the phone.

The sessions were grueling, beginning at 7:00 a.m. and lasting until 7:00 p.m. Instructors assigned trainees to various roles in mock scenarios to get them to practice their sales pitches, assigning some to be the homeowners who answered the fake doors and engaged in fake dialogue with other trainees who were trying out sales techniques. All the trainees' practice sales calls were filmed and played back for them later so they could learn from their mistakes and improve their form. During one session, Felicia raised her hand and made an observation: None of the practice setups were apartments. They were all stand-alone houses. What should she do if she wanted to knock on the door of an apartment? No one had an answer.

Felicia's trainers explained that the value of this exercise was getting some good contact information for people in the area where she wanted to build her practice. Even if she couldn't immediately do any deals, the basic data would be helpful. They gave her a quota to meet: twenty-five names and numbers a day. She had to upload the names and numbers she had gathered into a central system that her bosses could access to make sure she was doing her work.

"If you have not completed your list, then you should not be ending your day," her bosses told her.

"YOU PEOPLE"

Felicia's first day of door knocking was a blisteringly cold morning in December of 2013, right at the beginning of a weather pattern that even veterans of Chicago winters had a hard time handling, a cruel shock of arctic air forced southward by the destabilization of global wind patterns known as the polar vortex. Lows fell below zero. There were three days that month on which the temperature never got above 18 degrees Fahrenheit.

Hyde Park was where she tried to build her practice. It was a mix of comfortable single-family homes and high-rises full of well-to-do urbanites. Around 60 percent of the faculty of the University of Chicago lived there, and the university's imposing campus, often criticized as a fortresslike enclave that too easily kept its neighbors away, was located there as well. The high-rises in the area were guarded by doormen and entry codes. The few private houses that existed were large and imposing. And the people who were home during the weekdays were not, on the whole, friendly.

"What I would get is: 'Why are you on my porch?' 'Why are you in my community?' 'What are you doing here?'" Felicia said. "It's not that African Americans are not in Hyde Park, but those are not the doors that you would knock on." Black people, to many white people living in the area, represented the undesirables with whom the university had periodic clashes.

She made a checklist for herself, a series of conditions she had to maintain in order to get through her door-knocking rounds each day. First of all, no matter how cold it was, she would look unmistakably like a business professional ("as much as you can under layers of coats"). She made sure her hair and makeup were perfect, even when the wind howled and the cold made her eyes water. Then, after knocking on a door or ringing the bell, she always made sure to step back from the doorway so that her entire body was visible to anyone looking out at her from inside the house: "It's a mental preparedness that if you chat with any other African American in any other sales program, whatever that is, it's what we do. We know we have to look a certain way to be seen as someone that's legitimate, to be seen as a salesperson who is on that porch in that space at that door for a reason that is not crime related."

Edward Jones's training officers did not cover any of this. Black trainees were told that it would take them longer to establish client rosters, but they were not told why. Even as the company acknowledged that there was an observable pattern of struggle for Black trainees, its insistence on door-to-door sales was unwavering. White trainees seemed to log successful door-knocking sessions left and right; Black trainees toiled for much longer before scoring any wins.

"What would normally take a white man or woman seven tries to convert a prospect they just met to a client, it would take an African American twice as long to get to that step," Felicia said. "The recruitment process didn't mention just how difficult this is going to be because of the color of my skin."

Strangers would yell at Felicia throughout the course of her day:

"Get the fuck off my porch!"

"Why the hell are you here?"

"You people are always coming onto our porches looking to take things!"

You people.

The response was demoralizing. There were days Felicia ended up in the driver's seat of her car, frozen in fear and shame, trying to steady her breath and reset her brain in preparation for the next pitch. Sometimes she would call a friend and chat just to feel she was not completely alone. Sometimes she and a colleague in the trainee program who was also out knocking on doors would give each other pep talks. Sometimes, when the colleague asked her what she was going to do next, she admitted that she could do nothing but go home for the day. Defeated.

Felicia devised her door-knocking strategies based on what, in her imagination, would be least offensive to the people she was visiting. She would go out as early as possible so as not to interrupt people after they had become too engrossed in whatever their main tasks were that day. She would rush to finish up before it got too dark in the evenings, especially because she still had studying to do for Edward Jones's program at night. She also had thank-you notes to write. Everyone she spoke with got a thank-you note. It was part of the formula.

Edward Jones had assigned her a mentor, a guide to whom she was supposed to turn if she had a problem with door knocking. Hers was a white man who ran an Edward Jones office in a Chicago suburb lined with single-family homes. It was her responsibility to drive out to the suburbs to see him every week or so.

During one of these conversations, Felicia described her difficulties in Hyde Park. The high-rises didn't lend themselves to the strategy, she explained. And some of the free-standing homes were gated, so it was impossible to get up to their front doors. Felicia wanted to expand the geographic reach of her solicitations. She wanted to use other channels to introduce herself to new people, collect their information, and try to convert them from prospects to clients.

His response did not instill confidence in her future at the firm.

"You people are always looking for the easy way out," he said.

You people.

"I just kind of looked at him like 'This is not the easy way out,'" Felicia said. "I said: 'You have no idea how this community works. This is not Orland Park, where it's tree-lined single-family homes. This is a neighborhood of high-rises. If I want to get two hundred, three hundred people to know I exist, I have to figure out how to get into the high-rises.'"

And even without her mentor's blessing, she did. Felicia started reaching out to the organizations running the buildings. She wrangled invitations to speak to groups of residents at condo and co-op board meetings and other community gatherings. She volunteered on the weekends handing out water and granola bars at charity runs and slipping her business card into locals' hands as well. But rather than reward her resourcefulness, Edward Jones's managers insisted that she continue to focus on door knocking.

They also pooh-poohed her when she tried to talk to them about her mentor's "you people" comment.

The first person she went to for help with her mentor was a white woman, a full-fledged financial advisor who worked in the nearby suburb of Evergreen Park.

"I don't think he really meant anything by that," the woman said. "I don't think you should take it personally."

But Felicia knew exactly what the term "you people" signified. It was racist, demeaning, a way to lump all Black people together and saddle them with smears.

"I didn't need anybody to validate it. I was there; it was just him and me alone in a room," she said.

The regional manager overseeing the Chicago area, another white man, reacted in near-identical fashion when told of the offense. He advised Felicia not to take it personally and said that the mentor, who had been with Edward Jones for years and years, had probably not meant anything by the "you people" remark. Felicia told him that she did not feel comfortable working with the same mentor anymore.

Felicia was soon informed that she had been moved into a new group of financial advisors that was based in a different part of Chicago. She would be assigned a new mentor, and although her primary territory would still be Hyde Park, she would now have an office to go to on the south side of the city, on State Street. It was an exciting opportunity, they told her, that had opened up suddenly when a financial advisor there resigned from the company to take a job somewhere else. She would be able to pick up some of the clients that the departing advisor had left behind. The woman handling administrative work in the State Street office told Felicia that the lease on the space had just been picked up for another five years. Fate had taken a happy turn.

THE OFFICE

On her first day, Felicia was handed a list of clients and told to call them and introduce herself. These clients would be hers, if any of them still cared to do business with the firm. She began sending out introductory letters: "Hi, I'm Felicia," each letter said, and went on to explain that she, Felicia, had stepped in for the old advisor and would now be in charge of the office.

On her second day, a manager called and told Felicia that the office would be closing down and that her calls to clients should be to inform them of the change. She had to sign her name to another batch of letters conveying a message far less sunny than what had gone out the previous afternoon. The new letters warned clients that the office would be closed within two weeks. From EJ's perspective it was a long-planned office move, but from Felicia's it was a complete surprise. No one had explained why she had to start working at an office that was closing down.

"It is like whiplash in a flash," Felicia said, reliving the day in her memory. "I'm feeling foolish."

Over the next few days, she and an office assistant embarked on a mad dash to stay on top of the practical parts of the shutdown, and they had to do it blind.

"No one tells you how to do that: Who orders the boxes? Who prepares the moving people? I was, like, 'Okay, they must have this all worked out.'"

They did not. A week before she had to leave the space, Felicia called Edward Jones's home office and begged for directions. She got little practical advice, but there was one piece of good news: She was being moved again, this time to an office that was just about to open up in Hyde Park. There would a seasoned advisor there with whom she would share an administrative assistant. The arrangement was part of an exciting new pilot program. Felicia and her compatriot would be pioneers. But, in fact, she never learned the program's name or got a clear explanation for what it was supposed to entail.

Once she joined the Hyde Park office, Felicia had to start paying into the common pools of money that went toward the office cleaning crew, the window cleaner, printer paper, staplers, pens and pencils, and other overhead costs. She owed this money even though she was barely making any of her own. The clients she managed to attract weren't ultra-rich, just comfortable, which limited the fees she could earn by buying and selling financial products for their portfolios. Meanwhile, her new mentor, who did not work in the same office, barely spoke to her. Over the course of nearly three years, Felicia can only recall meeting with her twice to discuss her career.

She asked other people for help, and tried to soak up as much practical wisdom as she could during the massive meetings she and her trainee class still attended from time to time in St. Louis. There, she did meet people for whom the Edward Jones promise was being fulfilled. These trainees were hitting the sales and earnings targets everyone had been given when they first joined the company, modest as they were.

Take-home pay for the first year was supposed to be around $50,000. For the second year the goal was $75,000. By the third year, a six-figure number ought to be within reach. By year five, the door knocking would be just a sliver of an advisor's routine.

None of that was happening for Felicia, and the more successful trainees she met, the clearer the reason became. These happy folks had all been initiates of either the Goodknight or Legacy corporate program designed to develop trainees into productive EJ assets, handing over lucrative existing clients from established or departing advisors. One woman, Felicia remembers, had taken on clients whose business was worth a total of $50 million, gifted to her by several different advisors. When Felicia asked the regional manager how she could get herself into a position to be given clients by older advisors, he said that there were no clients left to spare. The client list Felicia had been handed upon her arrival at the State Street office amounted to almost $13 million in assets, but there was no departing advisor guiding Felicia's takeover of them. They were the leftovers of an office that had failed. The trainees who were benefiting from Edward Jones's legitimate windfalls had one thing in common, Felicia noticed: They were white.

Another reality was becoming clear: Edward Jones was actually sucking money away from Felicia. It was a penalty she never expected when she signed up for the company's training. Once she joined, after she had signed all the paperwork and could not reverse her decision, she found out that if she quit before three years had passed, the company would try to recoup $75,000 from her: the cost of training her, they said. But Felicia wasn't going anywhere, and those dollars were being drained away still, going toward overhead expenses for her shared office. It seemed like the company was trying to recoup its training costs even though she was still working there. And no one was willing to talk to her about the fact that she was saddled with such steep operating expenses even as she struggled to get her new business going and start generating her own revenue. At the beginning of her second year, she was making less money than she had when she started the training program. But when she asked her superiors for guidance about how to improve her performance, they told her to keep doing what she was doing. They simply offered to extend her training period by a few months to give her extra time to get up to speed.

"All you get is: 'You're doing great,'" she said.

Felicia started to worry about her personal finances. She was plagued by the feeling, as she met with clients, that she should not be telling them what to do with their money when she could not hang on to her own. She loathed the office, where everyday expenses were draining her bank account. After months of working there, she uncovered a secret: Her office was infamous for its limitations. The community from which it drew business could barely support a single advisor. As Wayne Bland had in Steele Creek, Felicia was becoming just another in a string of failures.

NEARING STARVATION

As the weeks and months wore on, Felicia started to burn through her savings to pay her bills. When they ran out, she dipped into her retirement account. Then one day she realized there was nothing left in reserve.

"I had to make some hard decisions: Do I keep my car, on which I had a car note, or my home?" she said. "I'm not making enough money to do both."

At first, Felicia thought she would choose the Honda.

I don't need to stay in the house. I have a gym membership and I can shower there every day, and I can stay in my car, she thought. *I need the car to get around to all these places to meet with people.*

But Felicia's friends wouldn't let her do it. She took the CR-V back to the dealership, marring her credit score in the process. She was earning just $1,300 a month, sending some of that money to help her mother with expenses like medicine and gas and electricity bills, and still paying for a major share of the office expenses. Now she could no longer afford to actually go to her office every day. She tried to choose the days on which she took public transportation wisely, to economize, and to figure out how to keep her clients from realizing what was happening to her.

"It was the first time in my entire life that I had to make $50 in groceries last a whole month. I learned that it's doable; that meant no eating out, being real clear about what my meal plan was, and every now and then I had friends that would kick in $50 for this or pick up a few groceries."

Even so, Felicia sometimes ran out of food. She resorted to making herself popcorn for dinner. "It was cheap and quick to eat and filling," she said.

She couldn't always make rent, either, and felt lucky that her landlord was kind enough to let her pay what she could, when she could, without charging any late fees.

She counted the days until the three-year period was up and she could quit Edward Jones without being pursued for penalty money she could not pay. The total value of the assets she was managing for clients had dwindled to $11 million. As soon as the time was up, she was gone.

By early 2021, things had gotten better for her. She had founded a community group that helped small businesses get loans and grants. She loved her work.

She still did not have a car.

• • •

Wayne's and Felicia's experiences at Edward Jones were not unique. In early 2019, the company disclosed that it routinely lost half of the trainees it recruited into its program because those trainees had "difficulties developing or expanding their businesses." The 50 percent failure rate was not something the company advertised in its recruiting drives or even warned new recruits about after they signed up.

Other Black Edward Jones employees suffered dramatic losses, too. They lost homes, spouses, stability, sanity. In 2018 a group of them sued the company in federal court in the Northern District of Illinois, claiming it was systemically mistreating them, keeping opportunities away from them based on racial stereotypes. A judge granted the case class-action certification, so the group's complaint eventually represented eight hundred people. The lawsuit said that Edward Jones's managers routinely steered Black trainees to knock on doors in low-income neighborhoods where the likelihood of finding someone with enough savings to warrant a financial advisor's attention was low. It also claimed that Edward Jones kept business development opportunities—like the bestowal of established clients—away from Black trainees and that it routinely forced the costs associated with maintaining offices onto only Black trainees, who ended up supporting white colleagues even while they were being shut out of the same opportunities.

Edward Jones denied the allegations and spent three years fighting the claimants before reaching a $34 million settlement with them in 2021, ending the case before it reached the point at which the company would have to share documents that could have revealed whether and to what extent its treatment of Black employees was a series of conscious choices. The firm also moved to settle a separate suit over its attempts to claw back money from trainees who had departed before serving their mandatory three years.

When I asked Edward Jones about the stories Wayne and Felicia had shared with me, Catherine Stengel, a spokeswoman, said that some of their specific claims had never been brought up. She said Edward Jones had a robust protocol for handling employees' discrimination complaints.

"Despite these processes and more than three years of litigation, the accusations that you allege were never asserted," she wrote in an email to me in which she said the firm "strongly denies" Wayne's claims about how Paolone and Kingston behaved in particular. "We agreed to settle this litigation because doing so allows our firm to move forward."

Documents tell a different story. Wayne made a point of reporting the hostile encounters on doorsteps, the moments when he felt unsafe trying to do his job, the slights from superiors and coworkers. He included descriptions of Kingston's treatment of him, Paolone's flip-off of "diversity," and the other regional manager's happy-hour dismissal of his big client win in a complaint he filed with the Equal Opportunity Commission in 2016, which Edward Jones's lawyers later filed as an exhibit attached to one of their motions in the class-action case against the firm. Felicia said that while she may not have reported everything to her superiors, she discussed her struggles in great detail with other Black advisors at EJ, making it nearly impossible to believe that managers did not know what was going on.

Yet neither Wayne nor Felicia could be accused of having a negative attitude. Throughout their tenures at EJ, they poured every ounce of their energies into succeeding in the environment in which they had been placed. In Wayne's case, that included enthusiastically embracing the idea of door knocking when it was raised by EJ's leaders.

"We are dedicated to achieving increased diverse representation among our financial advisors," Stengel said in an email to me. "Any allegation of inequitable treatment that is raised to the firm is taken seriously and investigated, and appropriate action is taken if wrongdoing is identified."

Stengel said that Edward Jones changed its process for giving up-and-coming advisors existing clients under its Goodknight program. In 2018, a week before Black advisors sued the firm, Edward Jones announced to its employees that retiring financial advisors who chose to give their clients to female or non-white advisors would earn "increased compensation."

The avalanche of chilling stories from Black EJ employees was not enough to freeze the firm or its leaders out of the industry—not even close. EJ itself is still embraced as legitimate and basically good by its competitors. There has been no "EJ tax" for having succeeded at and left Edward Jones, even if that success came at the destruction of others.

PART THREE

SEVEN

HOW INSURANCE WORKS
IF YOU'RE BLACK
(IT DOESN'T)

$\mathbf{I}$n 1994, Birny Birnbaum found himself in possession of an enviable amount of power. Insurance executives had nicknamed him the "Dark Prince."

The wiry, soft-spoken Massachusetts Institute of Technology graduate had, for a year already, held the position of chief economist and associate commissioner at the Texas Department of Insurance, the body charged with overseeing every aspect of the insurance industry in the second-most-populous state. This meant a great deal, because, unlike banks, whose most influential regulators were clustered in Washington in various federal agencies, insurers answered to state authorities and no one else.

It was a sweet setup, one the industry had carefully orchestrated over decades. Insurance lobbyists earning top dollars had argued that insurance products were so highly tailored to different people in different parts of the country that there was *no way* blanket regulatory policies could govern their behavior. Whenever members of Congress tried to interfere with this arrangement, the lobbyists would warn that any changes to the structure of the industry's oversight were liable to cause unspeakable chaos in the U.S. economy. In the early 1990s, especially, everyone seemed to share a keen interest in not rocking the boat, since, in the previous decade, 105 property/casualty insurers had failed outright, while hundreds more had teetered on the brink of catastrophe.

Far from being a burden to insurers, having fifty regulators meant the industry could reduce the chances that any one of them would notice broad patterns of misbehavior or muster any impactful resistance against their chosen courses of action. On top of that, many regulators did not particularly care whether the industry was being fair to its customers. Since no single state had the kind of money, organization, or legal heft that the feds had, insurers enjoyed freedom from scrutiny, effectively giving them permission to treat their customers however they wished as long as things didn't get too ugly in public.

The political scientist Kenneth J. Meier had recently described the state of regulatory oversight of insurers in scathing terms. "The commissions range in size from a few dozen employees to several hundred employees; resources range from totally inadequate to sufficiently ample to compete with other state agencies for qualified personnel. A large number of state insurance commissions quite frankly lack the regulatory resources to be an effective regulator of the insurance industry even with help from the National Association of Insurance Commissioners' staff," he wrote.

By contrast, insurance companies had hundreds of billions of dollars in assets and employed a combined total of nearly 2 million people.

But Birnbaum—whose given name was David, although no one called him that—promised to show how much influence a small and scrappy oversight bureau could still have among the industry's Goliaths. When he'd arrived at the department, Texas had been in Democratic hands. Governor Ann Richards had chosen an insurance commissioner with a history of outspokenness on behalf of insurance customers: J. Robert Hunter, who had spent years in the federal government. Hunter's presence had created a naturally welcoming environment for Birnbaum, whose passion was helping consumers. Richards lost her reelection bid to George W. Bush, a turn of events that should have spelled the end of Birnbaum's tenure at the department.

Except it didn't. Bush's new commissioner, Elton Bomer, had taken a liking to Birnbaum after spending two weeks listening to his descriptions of the work he'd been doing, a daily debriefing ritual Birnbaum had initiated in preparation for what he thought would be his eventual departure.

"You can stay on if you'd like," Bomer said. And Birnbaum did. With Bomer's blessing, he continued with his work and assumed a publicly visible position in the department, asking questions during commission hearings at which he appeared alongside Bomer and the department's general counsel. That was how he'd gotten the "Dark Prince" nickname.

At the heart of Birnbaum's work was a quest for transparency. He wanted the department to enact a new rule to force insurers to share basic information with the state about how much they were charging customers for their auto insurance policies and, once a policyholder made a claim, how much money was actually paid out.

This was not an unheard-of request to make of a financial services company. The insurers were already reporting their homeowner policy sales and claims data to the department on a confidential basis—confidential not because the insurers were revealing their secret formulas for writing policies but because the data contained detailed personal information about the policyholders, including their addresses. In addition to the precedent set by this reporting regime on the state level, there was a well-established precedent on the federal level not only for such reporting to occur but for some of it even to be made public.

For a few years already, banks had been required to send similar sales data to the federal government under a law called the Home Mortgage Disclosure Act, first passed in 1975, which Congress updated in 1989 to add new reporting requirements on race, gender, and income. Of course, that information wasn't about insurance policies, but it provided the equivalent amount of data about the home loans banks were making. Getting them to share details about whom they were lending to and at what rates was one way Congress thought it could ensure that Americans buying homes were getting equal treatment. The reporting requirement was in itself a way to keep banks in line. If the banks knew there was a possibility that someone at a regulatory agency or a consumer advocacy group could sit down and compare the interest rates they were charging various customers, they would be less likely to exploit certain kinds of customers, including racial minorities.

Birnbaum thought this trick might work with insurers, too. He had long suspected that companies were charging Black customers more for policies on their cars, and also that they were giving Black policyholders trying to make claims a harder time than white policyholders. But without the data to prove this, his office could not take any action.

The reporting requirements Birnbaum laid out were modeled after those that Congress had imposed on the banks in the Home Mortgage Disclosure Act. The bank data the act solicited was called HMDA data. Essentially, Birnbaum wanted HMDA data from insurers. Companies providing auto insurance in Texas had to report their sales and claims data to Birnbaum's office on a quarterly basis. The information would include the zip codes of all the companies' customers. An aggregated quarterly report would have to be made public.

It was a big step for a state regulator to take, and a rare one. Texas was the first state to start requiring this kind of reporting on auto insurance, and the first to try to make it public. California soon followed suit and was one of only a handful of other states to do so. For a couple of years, while the rule was winding its way through an approval process, Birnbaum felt that he was moving toward a larger goal with a fair amount of momentum behind him.

But by 1996 the momentum had dissipated. The data was being collected, but leadership, including Bomer, was now focused on other things. Tort reform was the biggest political issue in the insurance world, and it wasn't something Birnbaum wanted to deal with. He didn't want to watch as insurers won more protections against customers trying to sue them in court. He didn't want to see them shore up their protections against involvement in whacky disputes between two private parties. At the end of the year, he resigned.

Thanks to the new reporting and disclosure rules, Birnbaum had the tools to do the kind of work that was most meaningful to him on his own—or so he thought.

Birnbaum began to build a picture of how the industry was treating different groups of customers in Texas over time. He overlaid demographic data onto the zip codes in which the insurers had taken various actions and started to create reports on the industry's activities. What he found was that the biggest insurers in Texas did a lot more business in white neighborhoods than they did in Black neighborhoods. The share of their total business was heavily skewed toward white customers.

In April of 1997, Birnbaum, by then the executive director of a consumer group in Austin, the Center for Economic Justice, published a report on redlining in the auto insurance industry, claiming that companies across the board were still treating Black customers worse than white customers and avoiding business in certain neighborhoods where minority communities were concentrated, just as if the Jim Crow era were still in full swing. A month later he published another report showing that two companies, Nationwide and State Farm, were behaving even worse than their peers.

His work quickly attracted attention, and it began to get results. Bomer, still the state's insurance commissioner, announced he had opened an investigation.

The insurers went ballistic.

By October of that year, they had sued Birnbaum in Texas state court and won a freeze on his access to new data and the use of any data he already had. They argued that the information about their sales and claims payouts by zip code—even in aggregate—was top secret, that it was proprietary trade information, which would put it on the same sensitivity level as the recipe for Coca-Cola.

That was what they said in court, anyway. A *Wall Street Journal* investigation published three years later, in August of 2000, revealed that the data had been available the whole time through a trade group's database to any insurance company that wanted it, and that competitors rarely bothered to ask the group about each other's sales and payouts.

The battle between Birnbaum and the insurers lasted for almost four years and spanned two states. They sued him in state court in Texas and California; he countersued in federal court and appealed a federal ruling that affirmed the state judges' decisions to force him not to use his own data. It was a long, complicated, costly fight, through which Birnbaum sustained himself in part by doing consulting work and serving as an expert witness in insurance cases—he would only participate in cases he believed in, he said—after the Center for Economic Justice could no longer afford to pay him.

The insurers won. Not only did they prevent more data on sales and claims payouts from becoming public; they actually succeeded in convincing a few state legislatures to pass new laws outlawing the collection of the data at all. Texas still collects some, but its insurance department no longer has a chief economist, which means that it's highly unlikely that anyone ever looks at what the companies send in. Robust data collection has fallen off in California and Illinois as well. Today, virtually everyone who could use data to study in detail whether insurers are treating their customers equally is barred by law or circumstance from doing so.

Insurers can keep their data secret—so what? Why does it matter? Because insurance companies collect vast amounts of wealth from consumers in order—they say—to help those consumers preserve the rest of theirs. But if they don't give the money back when the time comes, or if they force their customers to pay too high a price for their services, the wealth preservation function is lost. By keeping data on their policy pricing and payouts secret, insurers make it impossible to find out whether they are indeed performing the service they advertise to all Americans.

The concept is simple: Anyone who buys a car or a house has sunk a major chunk of cash into the purchase and is more often than not diverting even more of their income stream to the purchase through payments on the principal of and interest on a loan. Insurance is a way to make sure that if something bad happens to that very valuable and expensive purchase, all the money that went into it will not be lost. Total your car? Your insurance will give you some cash to go get a new one. Tree falls on your house? Insurance will help pay to repair the damage, not only so you can still live in the house, but also to preserve its value so that you can someday sell the house for at least as much but hopefully even more than you bought it for. It's a component of the velocity of money. Over generations, it can help turn a poor family into a rich one.

Take Lisa Thompson, a Black woman. She grew up poor in Toledo,

Ohio, and fell in love with a volatile character, a man who drank until he passed out and often disappeared from her life for days and weeks at a time. But he loved her, and she loved him, and together they had four children.

Then one freezing January night in 2000 Thompson's partner was drinking at his local bar. He got so drunk that the bartender took his car keys away from him, but with a surprising burst of dexterity he snatched them back and fled the bar. He got into his car, gunned the engine, and slammed the vehicle into a telephone pole. He died instantly. Thompson got $10,000 from his life insurance policy. She was twenty-eight years old.

She used the money as a down payment for a small two-story house in Toledo. Her sister helped her out with the mechanics of the purchase, and she and her family spent the next twenty years there. For Thompson, as for the vast majority of Americans, her house was the most important purchase she would ever make, and she loved it. But she was still a single mom with four kids raging around and was often out of work. The house fell into disrepair. It needed major improvements that Thompson couldn't afford. So, in 2019, she turned to a local program that offered homeowners grants to help fix their blighted properties.

The program had one requirement: Thompson needed to have homeowner's insurance. That turned out not to be too difficult. A big brand-name insurer, Allstate, agreed to write her a policy, and Thompson signed up and began paying the required premium. Things seemed to be going well, except for one last problem: Thompson was told that she had to fix a hole in her roof immediately or she couldn't keep her insurance and would not be able to access the city program.

Thompson hired a group of roofers willing to work on her extremely limited budget. To keep costs down, they told her she would have to buy her own supplies and have them ready for the men who showed up to work. Thompson obliged and over Memorial Day week-end that year, she drove to another part of town to stay with her daughter and the roofers got to work. They had a small portion of the job done when their boss approached Thompson and asked for more money. He told Thompson he was afraid she would not be able to pay him or his men. She insisted she could pay and that they should finish the job. But that night thieves came and stripped away what the roof-ers had applied to Thompson's roof. They loaded the other materials she had purchased into a truck. They climbed through the hole they'd opened in the roof and ripped out her water heater. They took some copper pipes. Thompson's house was stripped bare. Putting it back together would cost thousands of dollars.

For nearly a decade already, Allstate had been personifying the things that could go wrong in a homeowner's life in TV commercials featuring a character called "Mayhem," played by the white actor Dean Winters. Sometimes Mayhem was a dog rampaging in an empty home, scratching the walls and floors and smashing expensive décor. Some-times he was a thief. In 2019, Mayhem was a car thief who video chat-ted with a man in another part of town at a sporting event to inform him that he was about to steal his car. This was an ad that frequently ran during prime-time TV hours in the same season when the thieves invaded Thompson's home, and it was eerily similar to her experience in that, before the thieves struck, Thompson got a text message from a member of the roofing crew warning her that she might be robbed if she didn't give the roofers more money. Allstate's message in the commercial was that its policyholders would be protected against this sort of thing.

"If you've got cut-rate car insurance, paying for this can feel like getting robbed—twice," Mayhem said near the end of the spot, before a final cut to a soothing conclusion.

"You're in good hands with Allstate," Dennis Haysbert, a Black actor with a deep voice, said at the end of Allstate's commercial, as if to counteract the anxiety Mayhem may have caused viewers. But Thompson found that, contrary to what Haysbert's reassuring voice had told her on TV, Allstate was not going to make anything better.

When Thompson filed a claim, an Allstate adjuster suggested that she had orchestrated the theft herself. The company opened an investigation into the matter, which dragged on for months as rain fell through the holes in Thompson's roof and insects and mice moved into its uninhabitable interior. Neighbors took Thompson to court over her blighted home, filing nuisance reports designed to force her to improve the looks of her house or pay fines to the city.

In December of 2019, more than six months after the theft and long after Thompson had filed her insurance claim, Allstate forced her to go to a lawyer's office in Toledo and sit for a four-hour deposition. The company said it wanted her to speak about her life while under oath. Nothing less than that would do. Thompson had to tell the story of her partner's death again, of her history in her own house, of her past at work, her health, her children—everything. The session ended without any new conclusions by Allstate but plenty of pain and annoyance for Thompson.

Six more months went by. In June of 2020, Allstate sent Thompson a letter saying it needed more time to investigate her claim. The company said its investigation could last as long as another six months. In the meantime, Thompson kept having to go to court for the nuisance claim. On two occasions, when her lawyer, a fair-housing advocate in Toledo who was helping her deal with the trouble she was in because of her house, explained her situation to a judge, other people—Black folks—in the courtroom who heard Thompson's story approached her to say that they were experiencing similar problems with their insurance companies. Thompson had no way of gauging just how common her experience was, but she knew she was not alone.

I found out about Thompson's story late in 2020, and in the course of reporting a story about racial bias in the insurance industry for the *New York Times*, I asked Allstate for a comment on the case. A spokesman for the company told me that Thompson's claim had been denied because Allstate determined that she hadn't been living in the house when the theft occurred. I went back to Thompson and asked her: Did you know Allstate had denied your claim? She said she did not. I went back to Allstate and told them that Thompson thought they were still investigating her case. I had even seen a copy of the letter Allstate had sent her in June asking for more time to complete the investigation.

Allstate's spokesman refused to share any more details with me, but a company representative contacted Thompson and told her that her claim had been denied—all the way back in June—and that the denial letter had been sent to the blighted, empty house. It had later been deemed undeliverable by the U.S. Postal Service and returned to the company. The representative apologized on behalf of the company.

At the end of one of my conversations with Thompson about her ordeal, she asked me to remember one thing: Allstate, which was now saying it could not possibly pay her insurance claim, had had absolutely no problem taking her money each time her insurance bill came due.

• • •

Thompson's situation is extreme, and it might at first seem unrelated to her race. After all, she is poor. It is common knowledge that insurance companies routinely look for reasons to deny claims, and that poor customers' cases are the easiest to dispose of because those customers are the least likely to fight a denial. In fact, when insurers do have to pay out claims, they refer to those payouts as "losses," and where else is one to cut one's losses than among the people least able to fight back against unjust treatment?

But insurance industry experts—including lawyers who help customers fight their denials, as well as public adjusters, who help claimants get more money from insurers after an accident—say that non-white claimants have a much harder time with the claims process in general than white claimants do. One public adjuster I talked to, Jeff Major, who travels around the country helping people with their claims after major disasters like floods and fires, described the treatment of minorities by insurers as an unspoken but widely practiced convention in the industry that can be boiled down to three things: Deny, delay, and disbelieve. Adjusters are supposed to decide whether to pay customers' claims based on how they feel about the customer, whether they think the customer is trustworthy. This fuzzy, unscientific convention leaves plenty of room for adjusters' individual biases to come into play. And just as in widely accepted and blatantly racist American convention, Black neighborhoods are called "sketchy" and Black teenage boys are called "men" and "Section 8" is shorthand for a place where poor Black people live, Black insurance claimants are somehow suspicious.

While Allstate's treatment of Thompson might seem uniquely bad, the reality is that Allstate is no worse than any other big-name insurer. In the course of my research, I found stories like Thompson's connected with other companies. I also found others that were not like Thompson's at all, because although the people at their centers were also Black, they were not poor.

Where insurance is concerned, if you're Black, it doesn't necessarily help to be rich. One insurance lawyer I talked to recalled a Black family living in a wealthy San Francisco suburb who were deposed by their insurance company because, after a fire destroyed their house, the adjuster handling their case simply refused to believe that their sheets and towels had come from the luxury department store Neiman Marcus.

I spoke with a woman in Dallas, Althia Hawthorne, who lived in a predominantly Black neighborhood south of the dividing line between Black and white communities in the sprawling metropolis, Interstate 30. Hawthorne lived a comfortable life thanks to a long career as a postal worker. She owned her home and had lived there for twenty-four years when, in the spring of 2017, a hailstorm ravaged her neighborhood. In its aftermath, neighbors surrounding her started to find damage to their roofs and to hire contractors to fix it. Hawthorne could not climb up to her own roof to check it. She was seventy-two and suffered from multiple sclerosis. But a neighbor's roofer agreed to check for her, and he found what Hawthorne had feared: The golf ball–sized hail had punched holes all over the roof. The roof needed to be replaced, at a cost of around $15,000.

Hawthorne called her insurer, State Farm, and filed a claim. But the company sent an adjuster to check to see whether the damage was real, and he determined that the roof needed to be patched only in certain places.

From the moment the adjuster, a white man, walked into her house, Hawthorne felt something was wrong. He seemed to be talking down to her, she said. He acted like he was doing her a big favor by visiting. He clambered up onto her roof and took a look. It wasn't so bad, he said. He did the math: Hawthorne's deductible was $1,200. Patching the roof wouldn't cost much more than that. State Farm sent Hawthorne a check for $200 and called it a day.

Hawthorne did not accept the adjuster's determination. She asked a contractor she'd found on her own for a second opinion. It came back the same as the first contractor who had looked: The roof needed to be replaced, and the cost would be well over $10,000. State Farm would not budge. Hawthorne hired a lawyer who was used to fighting such decisions. For four years, while she was waiting for the case to be decided, her roof remained in its state of disrepair. In November of

2021, the two sides reached a confidential settlement. The terms are secret, but Hawthorne got her roof fixed.

The treatment of Black claimants is so blatantly bad because insurers have so much room within the process to decide whom to believe and whom to suspect. Individual adjusters are supposed to use their intuition when examining claims, and they are free to add whatever material they want to their case files as they investigate.

In one instance, Provident Life and Accident Insurance Company, a disability insurance provider, added an article from a website called Militant Islam Monitor to the file of a Muslim psychiatrist with an eye disease who was making a disability claim. The company, which eventually stopped paying the disability claim, later said in court it had not relied on the article in its investigation but offered no explanation for why its adjuster had included the article in the case file.

The most striking example I encountered of the hardships wealthy Black insurance claimants have had to face was in California, where Deonne Burgess, a Black woman with a high-powered job as the global payroll director of the packaged food producer the Wonderful Company, suddenly found herself fighting with her homeowner's insurance provider, State Farm, for every doorknob and light fixture she needed to replace after a broken pipe flooded her house.

Burgess was not poor, uneducated, or intimidated. She was proud of her success. She'd bought a newly built house in Inglewood, a majority-Black city in the Los Angeles area that was experiencing a bit of a renaissance. She drove a BMW. She had nice clothes and nice furniture. When State Farm refused to replace what she lost, she was furious.

Burgess's adjuster did not reject her claims wholesale; he nickeled-and-dimed her on little things: a carpet that stretched throughout her upstairs and was partly ruined; a door that had gotten so warped and swollen from water damage that it no longer closed. State Farm did not want to replace the whole carpet even though replacing only the damaged portion would make the floor look mismatched and patchy. (California law requires insurers to pay for replacements that preserve a home's continuity.) The adjuster argued that the swollen door was unrelated to the water damage.

Burgess called State Farm out on its mistreatment, first to the adjuster, to whom she argued that if she were white and living in Malibu she would never have to haggle over the details over which they were disagreeing. Then she shared her story with me. State Farm said her assertions were without merit, but after my story ran, late in 2020, I began to hear from other people around the country about how the company was behaving, and the evidence started to pile up that State Farm's treatment of Burgess as a Black woman was no accident.

There is no way to quantify the amount of money insurance companies drain from Americans each year by collecting premiums on policies and then refusing to pay claims on them. State Farm is a private company and therefore discloses comparatively few details of its yearly and quarterly financial activity. But each of the single-page summaries it releases of its annual reports contains a few telling lines showing how the company's claims payouts and any expenses it incurs related to them form a simple zero-sum balance with the amounts it collects each year in premiums plus what it earns on investments. Its earnings are quite simply premiums and investment income minus payouts and their related expenses. The fewer claims State Farm pays, the more money the company earns. What's more, its institution-wide focus on denying claims has been publicly documented, most notably in a federal court case brought by two sisters who claimed that, while working as contractors for State Farm, they observed a broad effort by the company, with orders coming directly from its Illinois headquarters, to fraudulently avoid paying claims brought by victims of Hurricane Katrina.

(Black people were disproportionally hurt by the storm. A Congressional Research Service report found that 44 percent of all Katrina victims were Black and 73 percent of Black people living in Orleans Parish in Louisiana, where the storm hit hardest, were displaced by flooding or other damage, compared with 63 percent of non-Black people in the same area.)

A jury found in favor of the sisters and ordered State Farm to pay $750,000 in damages and almost $3 million in legal expenses for the case. The judgment was upheld by the Supreme Court in December 2016.

One particularly strong accusation of overt racism at State Farm appeared in a lawsuit filed in federal court in Chicago in 2019. A Black man, Darryl Williams, accused State Farm of failing to pay for damage it ought to have covered on an apartment building he owned.

Williams, world-weary and in his mid-fifties, was proud of the real estate business he had built. His company, the Connectors Realty Group, owned a small portfolio of buildings that he rented out to people and businesses on Chicago's South Side. It had taken him nearly thirty years to build up his properties to the point where he felt he could make a business out of them. During those decades he'd worked as a social services counselor, a security guard, and a police officer. He was used to juggling multiple jobs at a time in order to earn enough to save and invest.

The jewel of the portfolio was a three-story building on the corner of Seventy-Ninth Street and Lowe Avenue, where there were six apartments and two commercial spaces. It was there that an accident occurred that, thanks to State Farm, would prove fatal to Williams's entire real estate business.

Someone had left a bathroom window open during an arctic blast; the pipes froze and burst, causing flooding in the building and forcing other tenants into hotels. Williams was juggling bills for the repairs and his tenants' temporary arrangements, and he was in a tight spot. Williams claimed that the adjuster assigned to his case had told him right off the bat that she thought it was his fault that she could not get in touch with the tenant who left the window open to verify the story.

"We have a lot of fraud in your area," Williams said the adjuster told him. When he asked her what she meant by that, she said: "South Side of Chicago and you-all's neighborhoods."

Williams immediately reported the conversation to State Farm.

He never had to deal with the woman again, although State Farm denied that she had made the comments. After that, various representatives assured him that they would "take care" of the situation, and he believed them. He needed desperately for his insurance company to reimburse him. In order to keep his tenants safe and fulfill his obligations to them, Williams had started using his own savings to pay their hotel bills when the Connectors Realty Group ran out of cash. He was rapidly going broke. And without State Farm's help, he could not fix the building and let his tenants move back in and start paying rent again.

On top of these other bills, Williams was beginning to receive bills from the city of Chicago. The broken building was in violation of a score of local codes, and as its condition worsened, the code violations piled on. Williams had to go to court, and the city threatened to simply take the building away from him.

State Farm agreed to pay for less than 15 percent of what it would cost to fix the damage.

Williams had to sell the building in a fire sale to a group of investors in New York who quickly flipped it, extracting value from it that he himself could not access because of the bills he owed. He had to give everything he made in the sale to Chicago to pay the violation fines. Meanwhile, the building itself remained empty, boarded up. Some sort of clerical failure resulted in the tax bills for the building still going to Williams, another headache he'd have to deal with before the nightmare of his losses could end.

Williams's lawyer, Ken Anspach, hired a statistician and used Illinois's sunshine laws to get data on insurers' claims payment history from the state's insurance regulator, the Illinois Department of Insurance.

Back in Birny Birnbaum's days as a regulator, Illinois was one of the most aggressive collectors of insurance industry data of all the states. By the time Anspach went looking for data, it collected information only on customers' insurance claims, delineating which claims had been paid and which had not, at the end of every calendar year. The data wasn't specific to any one insurer; it was aggregated to show simple totals of paid and not-paid claims, but it did identify each claim by zip code. The department kept the data hidden from public view unless someone specifically requested it.

Anspach's data researcher analyzed the payouts and found that, over a period of six years, insurers consistently paid more claims in white neighborhoods in Chicago than in Black neighborhoods. State Farm had long been the biggest provider of homeowner's insurance in the state of Illinois, and its coverage spanned both Black and white areas in Chicago, so Anspach felt that it was reasonable to extrapolate from the statistician's findings. It appeared that State Farm had business everywhere, but the claimants in white neighborhoods seemed to actually be reaping the benefits of having their homes insured, while the claimants in Black neighborhoods were not.

Anspach decided that Williams's experience was not his alone; it was common among State Farm's Black customers. When he filed Williams's suit, he argued that it should be certified as a class action so any other Black policyholders who had gone through similar experiences could join. State Farm tried and failed to convince a judge not to let the class claim go forward, but Anspach was asked to provide more evidence to justify class certification.

State Farm's spokesman Roszell Gadson told me Williams's claims, as well as Althia Hawthorne's and Deonne Burgess's descriptions of the company's treatment of them, were "baseless." (I asked him about Hawthorne's claim before State Farm reached a confidential settlement with her.)

"These allegations do not align with our values and are without merit," he wrote to me in an email. "State Farm is committed to a diverse and inclusive environment, where all customers are treated with fairness, respect and dignity. We are committed to paying what we owe, promptly, courteously, and efficiently."

MEANINGFUL ACTION

While Williams's case made its way through court, another effort was also underway to explore how widespread discrimination in the insurance industry really was. This was led by consumer advocates like Birny Birnbaum, who wanted the federal government to step in and mandate some kind of disclosure by insurance companies that would let researchers compare their treatment of different customers.

In the fall of 2020, Birnbaum and another consumer advocate, Douglas Heller, proposed that a federal advisory committee inside the United States Treasury Department start looking at the inadvertent effects the industry's policies might be having on minorities. Even if insurers weren't consciously trying to cheat their Black customers, it might be possible that the way they operated was producing an uneven outcome.

This form of unequal treatment is conceptualized as behavior that has a "disparate impact" on a minority group. "Disparate impact" is the passive sibling to "disparate treatment," the kind of discrimination that is unquestionably outlawed by the Civil Rights Act, the Fair Housing Act, and the Equal Credit Opportunity Act, among other federal laws. Behaviors that have a disparate impact on minority groups are also supposed to be no-nos, but the space is grayer. Federal courts have disagreed over whether "disparate impact" as a concept applies to certain industries, including insurance, and the agencies, like the Department of Housing and Urban Development, that are tasked with actually enforcing the law governing disparate impacts have, under different presidential administrations, changed the rules implementing the law, so that it is sometimes easier and sometimes much harder to meet the standards for proving a disparate impact claim in court.

The committee considering whether to study disparate impact or proxy discrimination was called the Federal Advisory Committee on Insurance. It had nineteen members, some of whom were the leaders of insurance companies like Amerisure, Aon, and Liberty Mutual. There were also state insurance regulators, academics, and consumer advocates like Birnbaum serving on it.

Birnbaum and Heller submitted a one-page proposal for a study that would look at the unintended consequences of home and auto insurers' sales practices. In making it, they used another term, "proxy discrimination," interchangeably with "disparate impact." Was there proxy discrimination occurring, especially in the way insurers were choosing to use digital advertising to find new customers and the way they were using artificial intelligence to decide how much to charge those customers? They wanted a mandate to investigate, and their proposal left plenty of room for the other committee members to give their input and help set the parameters of the study. The one requirement would be that insurers would have to turn over the data necessary to make the study meaningful on a national level. But even though the CEOs on the committee professed a redoubled dedication to racial justice—George Floyd had been murdered just four months earlier—they thought this sort of study was wrong.

The proposal met its end on September 29, 2020, when the committee met (virtually, of course; the coronavirus pandemic was raging) and voted on the proposal.

"This truly is a critical issue for our country and our industry right now," said Gregory Crabb, the CEO of Amerisure, a property and casualty insurer that issued policies across the country. Crabb said that he supported the idea of fixing racial inequalities but that the Federal Advisory Committee on Insurance proposal would cause "confusion." State regulators could look at the issue instead, and they had already said they would. This federal study would just be duplicative. Crabb voted against it.

"I do appreciate and agree with co-chair Birny's and the rest of the committee's desire to take meaningful action on the topic of race and social justice. However, the proposed study is not that meaningful action," Crabb said at the meeting.

It was a textbook example of the habitual way in which corporate leaders pour cold water on initiatives that threaten their interests. "Race and social justice" could have been swapped out of Crabb's statement in a Mad Libs–style game and replaced with many other issues like "climate change" or "drug pricing" or "criminal justice reform," and the result would be the same. As a financial reporter, I had already seen the sort of faux concern in Crabb's comments countless times.

As I watched a recording of the hearing, I was reminded of the financial brokerage industry's response to a rule, briefly implemented by the Department of Labor at the end of President Barack Obama's second term, requiring financial advisors to act in their clients' best interests. There were all kinds of objections to it from lobbyists for big financial brokers, including one that sounded just like Crabb's: Yes, we need to fix the problem of bad actors in the advisory industry taking advantage of their clients, but not with this rule. It simply wouldn't be effective, so it shouldn't be tried.

Think about the alternative: If industry leaders really cared about fixing racism in their business, how could they begrudge the experts who might root it out the opportunity to try? What would a study idea like the one Birnbaum and Heller proposed really cost? The expense of having to send over data that each company already had at its fingertips, thanks to the sophisticated analytics tools the industry and other financial firms routinely use to maximize their profits—what could that cost be? How many individuals, out of tens of thousands of employees, would have to spend time putting the data together? What would the impact be on the company's productivity? Nothing. It would not even be measurable within these companies' multibillion-dollar budgets. So where did the energy come from to oppose this gnat of a proposal, if not from the fear of being exposed?

Just like that, after one four-hour meeting, Birnbaum's latest attempt to get the insurance industry to cough up specific data on its behaviors—data that could be used to improve Black Americans' financial health—was dead.

· · ·

Plentiful evidence of the insurance industry's racism has been around for years in the court papers and testimonials of customers, former employees, and experts. In the 1990s, fair housing advocates sued Nationwide, State Farm, Prudential, Travelers, Liberty Mutual, and Allstate for discriminating against Black customers and won settlements in each case.

More recently, housing advocates won a round of cases that forced insurers to end a practice in which they were refusing to write policies for apartment buildings and other residential properties that had renters receiving Section 8 public housing assistance.

But despite the fact that insurers had to pay millions of dollars in damages as part of the settlements, and despite the implicit idea baked into the settlements that, although they never had to admit to wrongdoing, the companies would try to improve their cultures in the future, there is no evidence that the major insurers have made meaningful changes. Consumer protection experts say they are still charging Black customers higher rates, and anecdotal evidence suggests that they still try to deny Black policyholders' claims more frequently, too. There is no way to know how big the problem really is, thanks to the lack of available data that researchers could use to track sales and claims patterns.

All the available evidence—that which has been gathered within the industry's data sharing system while it was active, as well as that which has been scraped from the surfaces of real life outside it—points to one thing: Insurers are not helping Black Americans preserve wealth the way they help white Americans. Through neglect and active abuse, they are taking it away. By trying to keep their products away from Black customers—by taking Black Americans' premiums and keeping them instead of paying out their claims and by withdrawing coverage from buildings were Black tenants live—they are not just maintaining the status quo of inequality; they are exacerbating the problem. Their behavior is letting the other forces of chaos in America deplete the carefully won gains Black Americans have achieved. They are actively contributing to the racial wealth gap and doing everything they can to prevent regulators and lawmakers from noticing. Without a major overhaul in the regulation of these companies and their accountability to the public, this trend will no doubt continue.

EIGHT

THE PROBLEM WITH
THE MACHINES

One Monday morning in May of 2021, the Twitter account representing an insurance app called Lemonade started churning out a string of statements that quickly made it a target of scorn and ridicule on social media. Lemonade was billing itself as an alternative to the traditional insurance industry, offering policies to renters, homeowners, pet owners, and those desiring term life insurance, and relying on artificial intelligence as its secret weapon. The tweet thread the company published that day showed how this could be a very powerful weapon indeed.

"We collect about 100x more data than traditional insurance carriers," the thread boasted. It went on to describe how, when Lemonade customers filed claims, the app required them to record videos detailing each claim, which the company then analyzed "for signs of fraud."

This, Lemonade said, had really helped improve business.

"This ultimately helps us lower our loss ratios (aka, how much we pay out in claims vs. how much we take in), and our overall operating costs."

This made the internet's eyeballs pop out of its head.

Prominent researchers had been sounding the alarm for years already about the discriminatory results of AI's attempts at facial recognition. Algorithms used for both commercial and law enforcement operations were found to consistently misidentify non-white people. Consumer advocates pounced on the recent avalanche of studies showing that AI programs discriminated against Black people in particular, and added that Lemonade's approach was, overall, "super creepy."

Lemonade deleted the thread following the backlash and apologized. "We do not use, and we're not trying to build AI that uses physical or personal features to deny claims (phrenology/physiognomy)" . . . "We never let AI auto-decline claims" . . . "Our systems don't evaluate claims based on background, gender, appearance, skin tone, disability, or any physical characteristic (nor do we evaluate any of these by proxy)," the company said in a new Twitter thread. In a blog post published the same day, it explained that any customer videos its algorithm flagged as potentially fraudulent were sent to human investigators for review. (As we learned in chapter 7, human insurance adjusters often display a great deal of bias in their treatment of claimants and in their decisions on which claims to pay.)

There was a less-remarked-upon aspect of Lemonade's thread, however, that was equally as important as its description of a problematic approach to AI: The insurance start-up had, seemingly accidentally, explained its use of machine learning and the benefits of AI to its business with breathtaking transparency. If only we, the consumers of financial services, could be this lucky every day.

Artificial intelligence is created by training a computer to analyze a large array of data and identify meaningful patterns. Financial firms use it to make choices about whom to advertise to, whom to hire, and whom to lend money to. There is an aura of cleanliness around AI—the term, anyway—that big companies cling to, as though machines, in all their gleaming perfection, create an entirely new, sterile space where purity and correctness replace human baseness. Banks and other financial institutions have begun to tout AI in an abstract fashion. But their descriptions are often so abstract that they make little sense. What they reveal is that AI is the black box inside financial firms into which a great deal of data is fed. Most of the time, the public is left guessing about what happens after that.

In September of 2019, for instance, Michael Corbat, Citigroup's CEO at the time, recorded a very short video titled *Mike Corbat on the Future of AI* for the business software company Salesforce. The web page where it was displayed exhorted visitors to "learn how AI empowers employees and creates new possibilities."

Corbat's speech was part of a video collage of clips of corporate leaders talking about how AI related to their companies. He said:

When you think of the application of technology today, what I love about it is, it's got the ability, in so many positive ways, to change things. How many times have we all been frustrated when you end up going to a call center, and having to enter a fourteen digit code and remind them of your mother's maiden name and the first pet you ever had? Today, AI allows us to actually know who you are without having to do any of those things. When I think of AI and the collection and storage and use of that information, we've got to be mindful of the responsibility that we take in terms of our customers. And making sure that we're safeguarding that information and using that information in a way that benefits them in their lives.

Corbat seemed to be suggesting that AI would let customers get past security barriers designed to protect them from fraud with less of a hassle than before. At first it seemed like he might be referring to voice verification or even facial recognition programs that helped users log into mobile banking apps faster or helped them get past identity checks when calling customer service. By the fall of 2019, when the video of Corbat was posted, many American banks had already begun using these tools.

But the second half of his statement suggested that there might be a problem with "Big Data," as one might call the vast amounts of information gathered by the digital surveillance that is now standard at companies across the financial industry and far beyond it. There were slight hints of an answer: If Citi could use computer programs to holistically track its customers' activities, it could teach those programs to recognize breaks in a customer's normal activity patterns that could indicate fraud. This, too, was a type of technology that banks had already embraced enthusiastically by mid-2019. Many of them were using software to track their customers' online behavior, including what kinds of computers they were using and even the physical quirks of their online browsing: how they held their smartphones, for instance, or how they clicked on various web links, a category of data collectively called biometrics. If a customer's biometric patterns deviated from the normal baseline created from hours and hours of surveillance of that customer, perhaps that was because it was not actually the customer who had logged into the online bank account portal. An alert would be sent to the bank's fraud department: time to restrict the account and check to make sure the customer was aware of the activity.

Detecting potential fraud or suspicious activity among customers is something banks are constantly trying to do well, something they have had to pay attention to throughout the history of their existence. Their duties go beyond keeping customers' funds safe. In the United States, financial institutions have a ton of responsibility, conferred upon them by anti–money laundering laws, to know who their customers are and report any potential illegal activity they see to authorities. All the largest banks have many layers of fraud detection programs that consist of a combination of computer analytics and human investigators. Often the computer programs flag potential fraud instances to humans, who have to follow up on the leads provided and make a determination about what really happened.

Viewers of the video could only make educated guesses about what Corbat was describing, because he did not explicitly describe any program or goal. I later found out that he was not even thinking of a specific program being run by Citi but rather referring in general to the ability to use voice recognition to identify customers. In any case, relying on computers to do work formerly assigned to human beings is trickier than it might first appear.

A CUSTOMER SERVICE BOT AND ITS CREATOR

For several years already, some banks and online lenders have been using automated customer service functions to help their customers get help with specific problems. One of the biggest traditional banks relying on AI for customer service functions is Capital One, the tenth-largest United States bank, which has lately tried to cast itself as a subprime alternative to some of the other behemoths—the Spirit Airlines of the banks, perhaps—a place willing to offer credit cards to people with lower credit scores and checking accounts to small-dollar depositors. Part of keeping its own costs low has involved automating some customer service functions and encouraging customers to do most of their banking business online rather than at Capital One branches.

The customer service AI function Capital One implemented was the first of its kind. Its developer, Dr. Tanushree Luke, patented its design. It was named Eno, giving it a vaguely human spirit that was supposed to make real humans feel more comfortable interacting with it.

Eno was designed to engage customers in digital chats and use the information the customers provided to route them to specific services. If someone had a question about a credit card bill, for instance, the chat program could analyze that person's account information, speech, and customer profile and decide exactly what to do next. Did the customer need to be sent to an internal collections team, or to a sales team that could handle some sort of service upgrade?

It might have seemed simple to create a program like this, but it was not. Similar to the voice automation that many companies adopted years earlier, the Eno chat function had to be able to understand a wide array of words and phrases that different customers chose to use in their chats. Then it had to process that information and create its own responses to the customers' questions. The responses had to feel to the customers as though they were more than just crudely matched pairings of answers and questions that would make the customer feel trapped in a digital world of "frequently asked questions." They had to feel like real responses. They had to make the whole interaction seem smooth, effective, and pleasant. The program had to send people to the right places, and it had to keep from accidentally failing to do business with various kinds of customers lest the bank run afoul of equal credit and antidiscrimination laws.

And in deciding how to answer customers' questions, the algorithm did not just look at a small sample of customer histories or credit scores. It used data that connected customers' preferred devices—smartphones versus laptops—the models of these devices, the kinds of cars the customers drove, even the colors of those cars. An ocean of data went into predicting what kinds of financial decisions each customer was most likely to make and how Capital One could maximize its own revenue based on them.

Dr. Luke and her team succeeded in this complex task, even patenting their creation. It was, in a very significant sense, the first of its kind in banking. Other banks rushed to develop competing versions of it.

Capital One had taken a bold step in hiring Dr. Luke and getting her to design its product. Her background was in government work. She'd had jobs at the Department of Homeland Security and the Defense Department, where she was a technical lead on a project developed under the Defense Advanced Research Projects Agency, the laboratory for ultrapowerful new military technologies. She was, in short, no slouch, and she was proud of her work at Capital One.

In public appearances, Dr. Luke, who had a PhD in theoretical and mathematical physics from George Mason University, seemed, above all else, fearless. She was confident in her own brainpower, but it was more than that. She wasn't afraid to talk about things that others around her didn't seem to want to talk about.

Maybe it was because she was a woman in the vastly male world of computing and programming. Maybe it was because she was a Brown woman. Whatever it was, she displayed a motivation to care about whether something she was doing was right or just or fair in a way that many other people working in her industry simply did not. She had long been outspoken about the dangers of hidden bias in algorithms and had emphasized that proper testing, as well as diversity among the people actually writing new programs for machine learning, were essential.

At Capital One, she realized that the banking industry wasn't just far behind other industries when it came to developing their own AI tools; AI was the banking industry's veritable Wild West. Regulators did not know how to police it. Banks did not know whom to hire to create it or monitor it. Some of the people working on writing new code for banks had taught themselves the coding process by reading about it on the internet, which meant that they understood far better how to get a computer program to follow steps A, B, and C than to go back through a completed program and design a test that would reliably show whether the program was working, including whether it was doing exactly what it was supposed to do and nothing more or less.

Wherever she went, Dr. Luke warned her listeners, whether they were coworkers, students, or peers in the tech industry, that, on a whole, not enough was being done to make sure that AI was used by companies for ethical purposes only, and with plenty of safeguards to prevent bad unintended consequences.

That was her reputation when, in November of 2019, another big bank, the Minneapolis-based U.S. Bank, announced with great fanfare that it had lured Dr. Luke away from Capital One to be its new head of AI.

THE UNACKNOWLEDGED HISTORY OF DATA

In 2019, AI was not only being developed by banks to help reduce their employee headcount and streamline their customer service operations; it was also widely touted as being the solution to the problem of discrimination in the financial industry. Computers were, after all, pure, cold engines of logic.

This public image of AI persisted despite the fact that data scientists had been pointing out for years that using AI to make lending decisions could actually end up being more harmful to minorities than traditional methods were. The Harvard- and MIT-trained mathematician Cathy O'Neil laid out how AI could perpetuate inequality in her seminal 2016 book, *Weapons of Math Destruction: How Big Data Increases Inequality and Threatens Democracy.* In a chapter devoted specifically to the financial industry, O'Neil pointed out that, even when they work, computer programs that help banks advertise and even lend to customers can end up causing existing unfairness to become more entrenched. For example, she noted that a credit card issuer that uses AI to decide which customers should be offered which credit cards in online ads may end up trying to sell cards with higher rates and less favorable lending terms to people living in neighborhoods where data analysis shows people more frequently default on loans. So potential credit card borrowers in those neighborhoods, even if they are responsible individuals, won't even get to see an ad about a card with better features because a computer has decided it is not right for them. The specific example she picked to show this happening was Capital One, Dr. Luke's old employer.

O'Neil had begun raising an alarm about AI's use in financial services years before that. In 2013, on her personal blog *Mathbabe*, she examined the online lender LendingClub's methods for evaluating potential borrowers. LendingClub gave less weight to traditional credit scores and more to an analysis of the ocean of data that could be gleaned about applicants from the internet, including the identities of their friends (courtesy of Facebook) and their web browsing history. But because the company was relying on AI, O'Neil said, no one who had been denied a loan from the company would ever know for sure the details behind his or her rejection.

"People denied loans from LendingClub by a secret algorithm don't know why," she explained. "Maybe it's because I made friends with the wrong person on Facebook? Maybe I should just go ahead and stop being friends with anyone who might put my electronic credit score at risk?"

LendingClub and other similar companies say that customers are actually treated more fairly by their programs than by big banks. And some research has borne this out. In 2018, economists compared some of LendingClub's decisions to those of big banks on similar unsecured loans and found that LendingClub's use of so-called alternative data—information scraped from the internet—allowed the company to make more affordable loans to customers who would have only been given subprime terms from traditional banks. But these positive outcomes do not come from a process any less shrouded in secrecy than the negative ones. O'Neil's point was that without a clearer picture of how each algorithm works, including the accuracy of the specific datasets that are fed into it and the stability of its performance over time, customers are at the mercy of a collection of inaccessible forces against which they are utterly powerless.

Despite these concerns, reliance on AI in banking and finance has continued to grow, driven in part by traditional banks' worries that if they did not start incorporating AI into their operations, they would be left behind by financial technology start-ups (colloquially known as "fintechs"). By the time Dr. Luke started her new job, AI was already acting as a fulcrum in the financial industry, the point at which the balance of power tipped to fintechs. Not only did letting computers make lending decisions let the companies do more with less; the programs they were running were supposed to make better decisions about whom to lend to. And they were supposed to make those decisions more quickly than human bankers could.

In theory, this might have been—and may someday be—true. As we have seen from the mystery shopper surveys, the "Please Use Caution . . ." emails, Frank Venniro's "Section 8" comment, and the scores of examples of Black bank customers meeting failure or even terror when trying to do basic banking business, there seems to be a benefit to taking human interactions out of the lending decision process.

But before that ideal outcome is possible, another major problem with this good idea must be solved. The data being fed into these decision-making programs was gathered by humans, organized by humans, and *created* by humans living in a world populated by humans, not machines—a world that, in 2019, when Dr. Luke moved to U.S. Bank, some Americans were acknowledging with greater and greater clarity was full of anti-Black forces, while others still had their heads in the sand. Replacing human bankers with computers was not going to be enough. Not on its own. This is especially true when banks seek to rely on algorithms to make decisions about whom to lend to and at what rates. The information contained in a borrower's basic profile has been skewed by injustice. Credit scores are based on payment histories that Black Americans in some cases have not had the chance to build up, as well as on court judgment histories that reflect the unequal treatment of Black Americans by the U.S. justice system. They remain the centerpieces in any lending decision, whether it is made by humans or machines, and they are the sum total of decades of discrimination.

Frederick Wherry, a Princeton sociology professor, put it this way in an interview with *Forbes*: "The data used in current credit scoring models are not neutral; it's a mirror of inequalities from the past. By using this data we're amplifying those inequalities today. It has striking effects on people's life chances."

The personal profiles of Black bank customers have never been the same as those of white customers, because at each point in American history, at each turn this country has taken, a new force has put negative pressure on its Black citizens. These forces have been documented in myriad ways. Data scientists ought to be taking them into account when they create programs that remove the human heart from the machinations of everyday business. Yet there is no indication that any of this history is being incorporated into AI algorithms.

In her book *Race for Profit: How Banks and the Real Estate Industry Undermined Black Homeownership*, Keeanga-Yamahtta Taylor, a Princeton professor, described in great detail the mid-twentieth-century policies that banks, real estate agents, and the federal government used in tandem to keep Black families away from white neighborhoods, to corral them in crumbling cities in housing that was so dilapidated as to be nearly worthless, and to use those squalid conditions to impugn them and further justify de facto segregation long after it was supposedly outlawed by the Supreme Court and the Civil Rights Act. "The cheating of Black communities and homeowners continues to skew economic outcomes and shape racist housing policies," she wrote.

Things didn't improve much in the four decades after the period Taylor studied in depth, either. A 1974 law, the Equal Credit Opportunity Act, made it officially illegal to deny loans to people based on race and other protected categories, but banks and other lenders simply switched tactics, turning their focus to a practice that Taylor calls "predatory inclusion." When forced to deal with Black customers, banks pressed them into loans with higher interest rates and absurd terms. Even before the 2008 financial crisis blew banks' predatory practices wide open, research by economists at the Federal Reserve and the Wharton School, the University of Pennsylvania's business school, found that subprime loan terms were more likely to be imposed on Black borrowers than on white borrowers.

In the years leading up to the 2008 crisis, banks not only failed to offer Black borrowers reasonable mortgage terms; they actually marketed bad loans to Black communities. The most famous case of this practice was perpetrated by Wells Fargo, which sent mortgage salesmen to Black churches in and around Baltimore to get church leaders to convince their congregants to refinance their existing loans to new ones with higher interest rates. Justice Department officials found the bank had overcharged home loan fees for 30,000 minority borrowers and had deliberately steered 4,000 people into mortgages with predatory terms.

The attempts to recoup the value that the big banks extracted from them have not extended as far as any effort to help them erase the blemishes the banks' predations left on their records, even though this extraction of value has not gone completely unnoticed.

In federal court cases filed in 2013 and 2014, the city of Miami accused the four largest United States banks—JPMorgan Chase, Bank of America, Citigroup, and Wells Fargo—of doing things similar to what Wells Fargo had done in Black and Hispanic neighborhoods in Miami. The effects of the banks' predatory lending practices were so bad, the city argued in its lawsuits, that they had damaged local public finances. A rash of foreclosures had destroyed property values in various parts of the city and had materially reduced its tax base.

(The banks countersued and won a Supreme Court ruling that significantly raised the bar for Miami to keep its original lawsuits going. In 2020, the city dropped the suits, but not before copycat claims had been filed in other parts of the country, in Los Angeles, Oakland, Sacramento, and Philadelphia. Wells Fargo settled a suit in which Philadelphia had made similar accusations for $10 million in 2019.)

Credit scores aren't the only measurements that can help banks automate their lending decisions. Their own lending histories could factor into their models, creating a bad-data double whammy. That's because, even as Black borrowers continue to be treated differently when seeking mortgages, one of the powerful mechanisms built into federal bank regulations to identify these differences is being hobbled by the banks.

The Home Mortgage Disclosure Act was designed to shame banks into treating their customers equally by forcing them to disclose a plethora of details about each home loan they make, including the race and zip code of the borrower receiving it. HMDA data is indeed a powerful tool; it is publicly available, and regulators and economic justice groups use it to track banks' behavior in poor and non-white neighborhoods.

Banks, meanwhile, have long complained that HMDA imposes an undue burden on them and on their customers. The tedious forms bankers and customers have to fill out when completing loan paperwork are longer and more complex thanks to HMDA requirements, they say. When Donald Trump became president and put his own appointees in charge of various bank regulators, banks were told by these regulatory agencies that they would not be penalized for failing to turn in data for some recent years.

But the holes in HMDA data are bigger and older than any conditions created by the Trump administration. An economist for the federal regulator overseeing the country's biggest banks, the Office of the Comptroller of the Currency, observed that, in 2000, almost a quarter of all new home loans lacked race indicators on their HMDA data, while race was missing in almost half of all refinancings. What was more, there seemed to be a trend in which, over time, banks were reporting less and less race data for their mortgage loans. In 1993, only 11 percent of new mortgages were missing race data, while 12 percent of refinancings lacked it.

The OCC economist, Jason Dietrich, concluded in a paper published in 2002 that banks' failures to report the races of the customers to whom they were issuing mortgages was making it harder for their regulators to assess whether they were following fair lending laws. But that was just the most immediate consequence. The missing data has the potential to skew any analysis an algorithm may try to make of lending patterns for various parts of the country. If redlining went undetected and unpunished back then, the record left by banks' activities from that period looks normal and good. If it is normal and good, it can be part of a benchmark. And if it is part of a benchmark, then it can make present-day redlining invisible, while banks' automated lending decisions appear normal and good.

All these past hurts ripple and blur the financial profiles of millions of Americans, bleeding into their credit scores, their borrowing history, and their property values. So-called neutral data is actually a hollow chamber in which these wrongs echo. Add to that the fact that racism itself still factors directly into the dynamics of the housing market. Even now, individual Black homeowners, no matter how wealthy they are, have found that appraisers value their properties at lower potential sale prices than those at which the comparable homes of white people are valued.

There is no way for the public to determine whether this history— or the current uneven reality it has helped produce—is factored into algorithms that make credit decisions. It is a problem that O'Neil says has created one of the hottest discussion topics in the world of AI but that has not been publicly addressed so far. Banks are incredibly tight-lipped about the specifics of their back-office operations, from who does what in their information technology departments to what specific programs they may be seeking to introduce into their vast digital architectures. They do not issue reports about these operations, nor do they often encourage the people running them to speak publicly.

The only thing we know for sure is what does not exist: There is no special requirement for programmers working at financial firms to learn about this legacy or pay attention to it. Regulatory requirements for AI programs say that the programs can't overtly incorporate observations about protected classes, like minority groups, gender differences, or religious affiliations in their functioning. Programs must also be tested to make sure that they don't unintentionally discriminate against protected classes. But the regulations do not call for any particular historical reckoning with the data they use.

What's more, AI is getting complicated. That means that it's harder to test whether a computer program's "thinking" is biased, because the program is almost incomprehensibly sophisticated. A group of researchers from Tulane University and the University of Maryland put it this way in an article on bias in financial algorithms, published in 2019 in the *Fordham Law Review*: "Much of contemporary AI is either opaque or so complex that an effort to explain its 'reasoning' would be about as useful as a map of all the synapses and other chemical reactions in the brain that occur when, say, a manager decides whether to grant or deny an employee's request for a vacation day."

HER BRIEF TENURE

Dr. Tanushree Luke had an idea for how the safeguards on AI could be strengthened and its potential to accidentally discriminate against minorities reduced: For a start, she was in favor of hiring people who understood these histories to write programs. She also thought it was important to make sure that programming teams included people who came from a wide range of backgrounds, so that they did not all think alike. The teams could not be staffed exclusively by white men who all shared the same ideas about how technology could solve the world's problems.

These were very simple ideas, but in espousing them, Dr. Luke was revealing herself to be part of a small vanguard of tech developers who were publicly, pointedly, rejecting the Silicon Valley status quo. Specifically, they sought to separate their work from the concept of post-racialism, the idea that special programs to help non-white people—and Black people especially—succeed in the United States were no longer necessary because the economic and societal problems created by racism had been fixed and that, furthermore, it was no longer acceptable to *see* or *talk about* race, that everyone needed to move on. This view had a firm hold over the community of start-up founders and software developers whose inventions were being released into the global commercial sphere faster than anyone could keep up with how they worked and what their true purposes were, let alone track their long-term impacts on the people using them.

When Dr. Luke joined U.S. Bank in 2019, there had already been some public discussion about the toxic embrace of post-racialism in

Silicon Valley, but it was happening mainly in the pages of academic journals or on the margins of tech media coverage rather than at the center of popular public discussion. What *was* happening in public was the opposite. Two years earlier, a Google engineer named James Damore had written a memo, first circulated internally at the company and then leaked to the internet, called "Google's Ideological Echo Chamber," in which he argued that the company's efforts to hire more non-white people and more women amounted to discrimination against white men. Google fired Damore after the memo became public and caused an uproar, but Damore simply doubled down on his position. Along with another former (white male) Google employee, he sued the company for discriminating against white men with unpopular political views. Plenty of people were outraged by his manifesto, but they were mostly outsiders looking in. Damore's fellow Silicon Valley insiders did not seem as repulsed by his ideas.

Damore's case was not put to rest until mid-2020, when the two sides reached a confidential agreement. It was still alive when Dr. Luke set up her office with a window inside U.S. Bank's great gray granite-and-glass headquarters in downtown Minneapolis.

At the bank, Dr. Luke found herself in charge of a newly created department overseen by some deeply traditional banking executives. One of her bosses, Derek White, had been lured away from an important job at Spain's second-largest bank, Banco Bilbao Vizcaya Argentaria. He had been BBVA's "global head of client solutions," a fancy way of saying that he was in charge of the entire suite of digital touchpoints the bank was trying to use to engage customers scattered across a vast landscape of locations, including the United States, Spain, parts of Europe, and South America. Under White, the bank was trying to transform itself from an old-fashioned paper-pushing business to an ultramodern operation that would combine traditional things like loans and account services with new ways to make money from borrowers and account holders, most of whom depended on computers and the internet. White had spent three years at BBVA and had just recently arrived at U.S. Bank himself when Dr. Luke started her new job. White was the freshest hire above her level. The other people Dr. Luke would have to work with were U.S. Bank veterans who knew little about the tech industry and who told White and Dr. Luke that they would have to build an AI department from scratch.

Dr. Luke may have started out with grand plans, but not long after she arrived she realized that U.S. Bank was not a welcoming environment for her. It wasn't just that one or two colleagues weren't nice; the hostility came from every direction. Other employees refused to accept her authority, contradicting her in meetings, ignoring her directives, and generally opposing her in any way they could. Data scientists she had hired, whom she trusted, were cut out of discussions held by other, longer-tenured programmers at the bank who were members of a different group called the "Innovation Team." When one of Dr. Luke's top deputies disputed the methods and the quality of data that another programmer had used to come up with a particular AI function, the programmer initially refused to share the spreadsheet containing the raw information that was being fed into the function. Innovation Team members also pooh-pooed Dr. Luke's deputy's concerns about how the program worked, claiming it would become more accurate over time, "once implemented."

And the more Dr. Luke and her trusted team members tried to push back against the bad behavior they observed, the more resistance they met. The bank's chief innovation officer, Dominic Venturo, who was Dr. Luke's direct boss, appeared, in the eyes of observers, uninterested in having her shake things up. Dr. Luke's team members viewed Venturo as being dismissive in meetings, talking over her, questioning her presence for some gatherings, and even shouting her down.

In the meantime Dr. Luke was finding things that seemed to her to be big violations of bank policy and possibly even the law. About six months after her arrival, she filed a complaint with U.S. Bank's ethics hotline based on her belief that a team of employees who were supposed to be entertaining proposals for software from outside vendors were actually using the pitch meetings with these vendors to steal their ideas and try to copy them internally. There was no question that the same team that reviewed outside proposals was also responsible for coming up with their own product ideas, but until she raised a concern about it, no one had seemed to care about the conflict of interest their twin duties posed. When she asked a few employees to examine the pitches the team had received and compare them to that team's own proposals, things started to get spooky. Two of the employees she assigned to do the review said that they were concerned that their activities were being monitored by human resources officials at the bank.

She also thought she had found problems with one of the few AI programs the bank had up and running. It wasn't customer facing, but its problems did not bode well for future creations by the bank's programmers. The algorithm, which was supposed to sort corporate trust deeds, appeared to be doing the right thing only half the time—sometimes less than half the time—and the rest of the operations it performed produced the wrong outcome, she thought. She filed another formal complaint.

Eventually, the deputy she had hired to be her top programmer left for another job in the tech industry. Dr. Luke tried to enlist White, who was two levels above her, to help her make things right with the faulty AI program, but then he left suddenly, too, in September of 2020, taking a job at Google with a title far beneath the one he had at U.S. Bank. Once he was gone, things got even worse.

Despite the strife she was experiencing at work, Dr. Luke was still the public face of U.S. Bank's new AI push. In early October, the bank's official Twitter account bragged about a public presentation Dr. Luke had just given in which she had explained her views on the necessary steps for making an AI algorithm "ethical."

In the presentation, Dr. Luke had emphasized the need for sustained attention and concern by developers and managers. Checking to see whether a program was working properly and ethically could not be treated like a one-off task, she warned. The presentation consisted of a detailed description of how laborious a task keeping AI ethical really was. It was ironic, given that Dr. Luke seemed to feel that none of the things she was talking about were things she was allowed to implement at U.S. Bank.

The process she described to viewers involved applying separate checks and tests to every step in the process of developing a new algorithm, beginning with a check on whether the data that the program would use was complete, bias-free, and of high enough quality to be useful. Once the dataset was verified, Dr. Luke said, programmers had to be challenged to explain how data went into the model they were building and how it came out. If they couldn't answer those questions, their model might do things they did not expect it to do. After those tests were complete and the model was built, it had to be tested again, especially to see if it could be scaled up to function at the volume of computing at which programmers eventually wanted to rely on it. Did this work? Next came the monitoring, which, Dr. Luke said, should continue for the entire time the program was in use. Did it "drift" away from its original purpose? Did new problems crop up after its program was repeated enough times? This stage required endless vigilance, because algorithms learned from their past experiences, Dr. Luke explained. They formed habits, similar to the kinds of habits people formed. They had to be kept on track.

"Diverse talent is vital to our digital strategy at U.S. Bank," a bank official wrote in a Twitter post to the bank's main account that month that featured Dr. Luke's smiling face. "That's why it's a priority for us to elevate and support women in digital and tech, through events like our AI hackathon. Read more from our head of AI, Dr. Tanu Luke."

In reality, things were falling apart inside U.S. Bank's AI department. But as little support as Dr. Luke had in U.S. Bank's highest ranks, she was beloved by her direct reports. The bank's tech team had found her presence refreshing. She didn't think like a banker; she thought like an inventor. More importantly, she treated the grunts in the IT department with warmth and respect.

During Dr. Luke's final months at U.S. Bank, conditions in the wider world of tech development were rapidly changing. In early December, a high-profile whistleblower rocked the programming world by speaking out about race and gender discrimination in tech. Google's technical cohead of ethical AI, Timnit Gebru, abruptly resigned from the company and tweeted that she had been forced out. The *MIT Technology Review* called her Google's "star ethics researcher."

At the heart of Gebru's dispute with Google was a draft paper she had coauthored that the company did not want her to publish. It criticized methods that Google and other tech giants were using to design and train programs that could understand language and respond to it. Among Gebru's criticisms was one that touched on something Dr. Luke had long feared: that racial and gender bias could seep into the programs by virtue of the data they were using to "learn" about language. If a language-processing program used too much data—conversations scraped indiscriminately from the internet, for instance—it would inevitably get used to the foul content that permeated sites like Reddit and other social media platforms. Hateful language abounded there, and feeding it into the language programs would make the programs "think" it was all normal and okay. The larger the dataset used in these training programs, the harder it would be to audit it for that kind of bad input, Gebru and her coauthors argued.

Over the following days, more news about Gebru's time at Google trickled into public view. Gebru revealed that the team she led, which was supposed to act like a watchdog for the work that Google and other big companies were doing in AI, was isolated and their suggestions were ignored. She had been outspoken, she said, about the lack of diversity in Google's own ranks, and that had not won her any supporters in the company. In an email to employees explaining the company's side of the story, its head of AI said as much, criticizing Gebru for an email she had written to a group of employees in which she warned them that it was basically not worth pushing for more diversity until the company's own leaders acknowledged their responsibility for the current state of affairs.

Dr. Luke's sympathizers inside U.S. Bank watched what was happening to Gebru and feared that they were living through a similar destructive act by U.S. Bank's management, one that targeted Dr. Luke. Some of them tried to formulate ethics complaints of their own, hoping to highlight sexism, harassment, and bullying. But the widespread practice the bank had in place of deleting employees' emails after just six months, including the emails of high-level employees, presented a major barrier to making any claims. Anything they might have tried to say about what they saw happening to Dr. Luke would be hard to back up.

In early December, Dr. Luke gave a talk to a group of employees about how her team was going to try to use AI to eliminate bias in U.S. Bank's hiring practices. She never got the chance to execute that plan. Just a few days later, she was gone. The bank said nothing publicly. It sent out a notice to employees on the day she left, and only afterward did Dr. Luke send out her own farewell message. No one had a chance to say goodbye.

By the summer of 2021, the bank was running 150 different AI programs, according to David Palombi, a U.S. Bank spokesman, and they were being used for things like detecting fraud and figuring out which products to market to which customers. Palombi said that the bank subjected its programs to independent reviews and audits to make sure they were working correctly and had a "senior-level" team focused on ethical AI, as well as a group of people devoted to "model risk management."

"We can deploy AI subject-matter experts to validate all models in development and production," he said, "whether we've created the model internally or not."

The officials who looked into Dr. Luke's ethics complaints declared to the bank's leaders that they had found no problems in the areas that Dr. Luke had formally raised concerns about: the faulty algorithm and the copycat software developers.

Palombi said that a unit inside U.S. Bank's legal department oversaw ethics investigations and that, since the unit's members were outside of any business lines, they were "essentially an unbiased third party reviewing ethics complaints."

U.S. Bank considered the whole episode closed.

REGULATORS TRY TO CATCH UP

Dr. Luke's story shows how hard it can be for data scientists who are vocal about their ethics concerns to keep their footing at big banks, where long-entrenched cultures are hard to shake up. It is one of the few windows into what life is like in the back-office environment of a big bank, where the programs that affect the lives of millions of customers are created and tested. Problems like the ones Dr. Luke faced at U.S. Bank can easily get in the way of efforts to test and retest specific algorithms for bias, as well as any broader push to make a company's tech workforce more aware of the many ways bias can enter into their work. Even when things go smoothly, that is a monumental task. There is no particular formula that can be applied to a collection of data to produce a binary finding of either "biased" or "not biased." A cottage industry of tech start-ups offering products that let companies test their finished models for biased outcomes is growing.

Cathy O'Neil is part of it. She now runs a consultancy designed specifically to help companies identify and eliminate bias in their programs and make them more ethical. No big bank had ever hired her, she told me in June of 2021.

When AI bias is caught, it is usually thanks to researchers who study particular kinds of programs and discover that they do not work the way they should, or because maligned people come together in a group and hire experts to investigate what is happening to them. They then have to rely on lawyers to help them sue the offender for discrimination, a task that companies have for years been trying to make more difficult. In 2013, for example, the Department of Housing and Urban Development created a rule requiring any business using AI to decide whom to lend to for home loans and whom to advertise to for housing projects to test the algorithm first to see if it unintentionally discriminated against any minorities. That was not all. The rule also required these businesses to probe their own capabilities and see if there was a *better* way to make these decisions—and to prove that they had undertaken this exploration should any regulator ask to see their work.

Banks and other financial firms hated this rule. They banded together and—relying on their lobbyists at trade groups like the American Bankers Association and the Housing Policy Council to serve as the public face of their effort—lobbied Trump administration officials at HUD to scrap it. The Trump officials at HUD offered them one better than what they had asked for: They devised a new rule that made winning a case against a company for accidental discrimination nearly impossible. It was such a reversal from the 2013 rule that—after George Floyd's murder in 2020 and the ensuing displays of new awareness in corporate America that racism was alive and well in the United States—the biggest banks realized that supporting the new HUD rule would not be a good look for them. Representatives from JPMorgan, Wells Fargo, Bank of America, and Citigroup each wrote to HUD—and publicized their letters—asking officials not to go through with the rule change. HUD officials did not listen to the banks. So, for a brief time between August of 2020 and the early days of the Biden administration, legal protections against accidental discrimination by lending and housing algorithms basically did not exist.

The revised rule was suspended after Trump left office, and the Biden administration later tried to revive the stricter 2013 version. As the financial services industry's power grows or ebbs, so does the ability of victims of the kinds of discrimination most likely to occur when AI is used—the passive, hard-to-detect, impersonal kind—wane and wax. Anyone suffering from discrimination remains at the mercy of this political cycle.

As of mid-2021, the Consumer Financial Protection Bureau, the agency created by the 2010 Dodd-Frank financial regulations, which were supposed to be a response to the 2008 financial crisis and were designed to strengthen protections against predatory behavior by financial firms, had not brought a single public case against a financial firm for discrimination involving AI. The agency has not even publicly disclosed how many people it employs to monitor financial companies' use of AI, but its leaders have admitted that they need to beef up their capabilities.

In general, regulators say that the way the financial industry uses AI is not fundamentally different from many of its earlier practices. Banks and other lenders have been using automated lending decision programs for years already, and they have been using computer programs to figure out people's credit scores for even longer.

This view seems to disregard the fact that AI has taken these more traditional practices and bent them at a right angle. New data is being woven into decision-making programs, and banks and other financial firms are also relying more now on programs that predict the future. These programs scour vast oceans of data and look for patterns, so that a program might end up concluding that the number of times a bank customer orders takeout from a food delivery app on a Samsung smartphone can help project the likelihood of that customer opening a new credit card within the next twelve months.

Regulators say they're hip to this kind of thing and its many ramifications, but as of mid-2021, the Office of the Comptroller of the Currency, the agency that is in charge of policing the largest American banks, did not employ a single computer programmer on its staff. The economists that have tested banks' models for decades are now inspecting their newly designed algorithms.

There is evidence to suggest that regulators might not yet know how much they don't know about financial companies' reliance on AI. Two months after Joe Biden took over as president from Donald Trump, five financial regulatory agencies—the Consumer Financial Protection Bureau, the Office of the Comptroller of the Currency, the FDIC, the Fed, and the National Credit Union Administration—sent out a broad request to the financial industry, including banks and other lenders under their purview, asking for information on how they used AI in their day-to-day business. The agencies said they wanted to hear not just from the banks themselves but from all interested parties, including consumer groups, trade organizations, and any other members of the public who had something to say on the subject. The goal of the request, the agencies said, was to help them "better understand the use of AI, including machine learning, by financial institutions; appropriate governance, risk management, and controls over AI; [and] challenges in developing, adopting, and managing AI." There was a distinct "blank slate" quality to the request, as though the regulators were hoping an avalanche of information would help them decide what to do next.

A TEST CASE

In 2019, Goldman Sachs and Apple launched a new credit card together. The Apple Card promised to "help customers lead a healthier financial life" by combining traditional card functions with a personal finance app designed to give customers more insight into their own behaviors, thus potentially lowering their interest rates. But less than a week after the card's debut, two Twitter users with large followings—both white men from Silicon Valley—began complaining that the card appeared to be discriminating against their wives.

"The @AppleCard is such a fucking sexist program. My wife and I filed joint tax returns, live in a community-property state and have been married for a long time. Yet Apple's black-box algorithm thinks I deserve 20x the credit limit she does," David Heinemeier Hansson, a software developer, posted in November of that year. His criticism was soon echoed by Steve Wozniak, the cocreator of the Apple Computer along with Steve Jobs, who said in another tweet that the "same thing" had happened to him and his wife. "Hard to get a human for a correction though. It's big tech in 2019."

Heinemeier Hansson and Wozniak were attacking Apple, but the credit algorithm the card relied on was actually designed and managed by Goldman. The controversy sparked by their tweets led to the first and only public example of a regulator addressing questions about fairness in a bank's credit algorithm. In this case it was New York's state regulator, the New York State Department of Financial Services.

The DFS's investigation took almost a year and a half. Regulators interviewed people at both companies—Goldman and Apple—and studied loan decision data provided by Goldman, including 400,000 Apple Card applications submitted by New Yorkers, which they analyzed to see if Goldman's decisions about whom to grant a card and how high individuals' credit limits should be violated any laws against intentional or unintentional discrimination. They concluded that there did not seem to be any intentional or unintentional discrimination. They also reviewed the work Goldman was doing to evaluate whether it was adhering to fair lending laws and were satisfied that the bank was checking its own operations for unfair decisions.

In their report on the matter in 2021, officials said that much of the criticism the Apple Card faced in its first days could have been avoided if Goldman and Apple had just taken the card's rollout a little more slowly. The companies should have explained their policies better instead of sticking to an opaque decision-making process that spat out credit decisions quickly but did not offer any insight into how they were reached. With regulators looking over their shoulders, Goldman executives made some changes to the program, the biggest of which was to introduce a way for people who had been declined an Apple Card or offered a card with a very low credit limit instructions for how to improve their applications and build up their credit scores.

The DFS's final report offered no details on the structure of the specific program Goldman was using to make its Apple Card decisions, and the bank has never shared that information publicly, either. In Cathy O'Neil's view, banks should have to spell out their programs' designs for the public. The standard question, O'Neil says, is: "What is your evidence that what you're doing is fair?" In her view, banks should answer that question as an industry standard. The problem, she told me, is that in most cases "they don't have an answer."

NINE

ON THE DIVERSITY CIRCUIT

The dimly lit ballroom in the Detroit hotel was vibrating with nervous laughter. Everyone was watching a short, white-haired white woman in a white sweatshirt and jeans who stood facing the seated audience, holding a microphone.

"Will every person in the room who considers themselves a member of the white race please stand?" she asked. Commanded, really. Gingerly, a smattering of people rose from their seats.

"Get up!" she yelled, pointing at a pale, skinny man sitting in the second row.

The man stood up and looked around. His shoulders curled forward as though they could lead the way for the rest of his body to fold over and disappear. On either side of him, rows and rows of audience members remained in their seats.

"Now," the woman with the microphone said, "will everyone who considers himself or herself to be a member of the Black race, please stand?"

Most of the rest of the audience rose.

"Now the Brown race," she said. "Now the Yellow race. Now the Red race."

Eventually, everyone in the room was standing, wondering what was going to happen next. The leader of this little show, the woman with the microphone, was Jane Elliott, an eighty-six-year-old former elementary school teacher from Iowa who had attracted national attention when, following the assassination of Dr. Martin Luther King Jr. in 1968, she had designed a lesson for her third-grade class by separating the students according to the color of their eyes and convincing them that one eye color indicated mental superiority over the other.

The results of this designation were astounding: After being told they were inferior, the students marked for discrimination did worse on tests in reading and math, while the group of kids who were told they were superior immediately started accomplishing things in their schoolwork that they had been unable to do before the separation. They also quickly got used to lording over members of the "inferior" group, acting like a miniature Stanley Milgram army.

Elliott's experiment had been repeated many times, filmed for TV, described in newspapers. She began traveling all over the country, giving lectures about discrimination and the evil and arbitrary separation of Black people from white people. She endured death threats and harassment. She eventually stopped teaching schoolchildren and began producing materials and lectures for companies and local governments seeking to combat racism in their own ranks. By September of 2019, when I saw her, she was fearless, rather famous, but totally unknown to most of Wall Street.

I heard her speak while attending the annual meeting of the Association of African American Financial Advisors, or "Quad-A," as its members called it. I had been talking to Ricardo Peters for months, but I had not grasped the enormity of what there was to observe about racism in banking. I did not even know what I didn't know, but I suspected I might learn from the experience of attending this conference. I flew to Detroit and checked into the upscale hotel where the conference was taking place, across the street from the complex of dark, gleaming midcentury cylindrical towers that make up General Motors' imposing headquarters.

The conference, overall, was a mix of discussions about diversity in the financial industry and presentations by successful financial advisors on business development and specific investment strategies. I soon found myself in a room full of financial advisors, watching a presentation by representatives from JPMorgan Chase. There were four people squeezed onto a small stage, looking out at an audience of a few hundred. Three of the presenters, Jacqueline Campbell, Jason Tinsley, and September Hargrove, were Black. One, Laura Stone, was white.

As is often the case with glossy corporate presentations, JPMorgan's focus was on JPMorgan and how great a company it was. It began with a video describing the bank's activities in Detroit, which had, over the past several years, become a major public relations pitch point. Jamie Dimon had made sure his face was next to every new announcement about JPMorgan's donations to local community development groups or to its own grant program for small businesses. While the dollar amounts were minuscule compared to what JPMorgan was earning each year, the program was one of the most successful attempts any bank made during that period to erase the memory of the damage Wall Street investment banks had caused by underwriting a reckless municipal borrowing spree in the early 2000s that ended up forcing the city into bankruptcy in 2013 and leading it to implement large-scale shutoffs of its water system in 2014. The bankruptcy decimated the city's infrastructure so badly that some Detroiters risked death waiting for ambulances that never came because of barely functioning emergency services.

In 2014, JPMorgan began directing money in the form of donations and for-profit capital allocations to existing community development efforts in the city: By September 2019, the bank had committed $155 million over five years, or 0.03 percent of its profits over the same period (though potentially less than it had earned underwriting the city's water and sewer authority's bond issuances over the previous decade). The bank also began publicizing each contribution with a media blitz that made it seem like JPMorgan bankers had galloped into a completely deserted hellscape and brought it back to life.

The five-minute video, set to upbeat guitar music, drew hearty applause from the audience when it was over. Next on the stage, Hargrove, a vice president whose title included "Detroit Program Officer," was saying things like "The passion Detroiters have for Detroit, it gives you goose bumps."

Earlier that day I met a man who had worked at JPMorgan in Texas for a number of years until his manager told him he wasn't "a good fit" and had made moves to fire him. He quit before the company had the chance to strike its final blow and opened his own independent advisory business in which, he said, he had been successful. He was Black, of course. I looked around the room for him as the video ended. What could he be thinking, watching the speakers?

The next presenter was Jacqueline Campbell. At the speaker's podium, she moved with the energy of a dancer or a preacher, lifting her arms, tilting her head back, drawing out some of her words into long, suspense-filled utterances charged with electricity. Sitting there, not knowing anything about her, I thought: *Wow, now there's an employee who has really drunk the Kool-Aid.*

Jaqueline was telling a story. She was talking about how she was *called* to do the job she was currently doing for JPMorgan, serving in a role called "head of diverse advisor experience," which seemed to make her the point person on diversity in the bank's retail financial advisory business, the part of JPMorgan that put wealth managers in Chase branches around the country.

Jacqueline's story focused far less on what she did in her job on a day-to-day basis and more on the moment she pitched herself for the role. She had such a conviction, she said, that she scheduled a meeting with business leaders, including the head of the wealth management business, Eric Tepper. Since she lived in Chicago and the business heads were in New York, they figured she was proposing a simple phone call and blocked out half an hour on their schedules. But Jacqueline wanted to see their faces. She rose before dawn on the day of the meeting and caught the first flight to New York, surprising everyone when she announced herself at the entrance to JPMorgan's towering Midtown Manhattan headquarters. Riding on the strength of her conviction that she needed this new job, and with encouragement from her mother, whom she'd called from the airport, Jacqueline convinced the big bosses that she should become the wealth management division's diversity officer. She concluded her story with a quote from Marianne Williamson, the new-age spiritualist who was running for the 2020 Democratic presidential nomination.

"We are all meant to shine, just like children do," Jacqueline said.

A year and a half after I saw her presentation, I learned the full story of Jacqueline's mission and the meaning of her decision to tell it to the Quad-A audience. But at the time I had no idea how much more lay behind her speech.

The discussion onstage next took a turn in the direction of the bank's diversity ranking. Laura Stone was saying: "If we hired every single diverse advisor in the industry, we wouldn't move the needle."

This was a talking point that she often used, I found out later, based on an industry-wide statistic showing that only 4 percent of all financial advisors were Black, a much lower proportion compared to the general population. By then, the panelists were discussing the dreaded "Pipeline Problem," a concept deeply rooted in the collective consciousness of corporate America, spanning industries and geographies, seasons, job titles, and time itself, in which companies can't hire more people who aren't white men because . . . well . . . qualified people who fit that description just don't exist. If they did, of course, the decision-makers would hire them. A cartoonish version of the same lament would land Wells Fargo's CEO Charles Scharf in hot water in the summer of 2020, when Scharf told employees in a companywide memo that there was "a very limited pool of Black talent to recruit from" and that, "while that might sound like an excuse," it was simply the unfortunate reality.

The JPMorgan presenters were essentially saying the same thing, but no one in the audience seemed to mind. Someone suggested that in the financial advisory business the Pipeline Problem was a vicious cycle in which the absence of non-white financial advisors was perpetuated by the absence of non-white financial advisors.

"You can't be what you can't see," Stone said, nodding.

Tinsley said a minute later: "Money is green and everyone in this room is capable of having not just Black clients but diverse clients."

The audience was receiving these tidbits of wisdom and encouragement with soft murmurs when the JPMorgan representatives opened up the floor for questions. A woman stood up and made a long statement about the way big companies publicize their process for recruiting more Black employees. It was a preamble to a question, and only a close listener would really have heard the question itself when it came, but it did come. It was this: There are dozens and dozens of historically Black colleges and universities in the United States, but most big companies, including JPMorgan, seem to know only three of them: Howard University, Morehouse College, and Spelman College. Wouldn't it be better if JPMorgan were to go to some of the other HBCUs to recruit as well? Wouldn't the bank, perhaps, find a bigger pool of qualified applicants if it looked at a wider swath of institutions?

"That is so interesting," Stone said, closing her eyes a little bit while leaning back and nodding at this observation.

"It's complicated. It reminds me of this story that I heard recently about the final exam in a class at Harvard—I think it was Harvard—and this professor, on the final exam, made the last question: 'What is the name of the janitor who cleans this room?' And his point was that if you don't know the answer, then you can't make it out there, because you don't have it in here."

When I asked JPMorgan's representatives later why Stone had told the story, they said that she had told it before and was in fact in the habit of relying on it, but usually when talking with students or recent college graduates. She likely had not understood the question, they said. The story itself was first told by the CEO of Charles Schwab, Walt Bettinger, in an interview in 2016 in which he was asked what memorable lessons he had learned in college. A business strategy professor had shocked him with the question on a final exam during his senior year, he explained, and he had been unable to answer it. The name of the woman who cleaned his classroom was Dottie, he later learned. "I've tried to know every Dottie I've worked with ever since," he added.

The incongruity of the response stood out to me as a listener, because it seemed to show the tick . . . tick . . . tick of the silent calculations in Stone's head. Someone had stood up during a talk about diversity and brought up something about colleges, and somehow Stone's mind had gone instantly to the neglected janitor.

(I learned later that JPMorgan can actually list seventeen HBCUs from which it occasionally recruits students. The institutions are divided up into two tiers; eleven, including Morehouse, Spelman, and Howard, but also others, like Florida Agricultural and Mechanical University, Morgan State, and North Carolina Agricultural and Technical State University, are on a list labeled "preferred," because they are closer to the bank's business hubs and better known to its leaders. Six others, where the bank is less active but says it is trying to strengthen its relationships, are called "priority.")

The questioner sat down and the discussion moved on, and the audience never learned of these categories. Just before the session ended, Stone said that JPMorgan's retention rate for non-white bankers was low and that that was obviously a problem. And she said that the bank wasn't recruiting enough minorities for development programs in its retail banking and advisory businesses. Tinsley told a brief story about a successful recruiting mission he had just been on to Morehouse.

What did this session add up to? The most important things, in my view, went unspoken. JPMorgan had recently agreed to settle a giant lawsuit brought by Black financial advisors who said the bank was systematically mistreating them, but that was not discussed. The only safe topics in a presentation on diversity were broad statements, oft-repeated statistics, rehearsed stories. And yet the audience had come away fairly encouraged, feeling that a great deal of information had been conveyed and interest expressed.

I found the man from Texas in the hallway during the next break. When we'd met at a dinner the evening before, he'd shared his story with me but had also expressed his fear of being identified. JPMorgan was a big, powerful institution that could blackball people from the advisory industry with great ease, he explained. I agreed never to mention his name. When I caught up with him and asked what he thought about the bank's presentation, he smiled and shook his head. "God bless them," he said. "I hope they were being sincere."

THE HIDDEN ACTION IN CLAIMS ABOUT DIVERSITY

In *The Reorder of Things: The University and Its Pedagogies of Minority Difference*, the Yale professor Roderick A. Ferguson chronicled the path American universities took to bring civil rights movements on their campuses under control in the 1960s and 1970s. Students were protesting against the mistreatment and exclusion of minorities from campus life, from academic study areas, and from the many disciplines in which their places in the world and their contributions to history, culture, science, and art might be studied, and the administrators in charge realized that these protests posed a threat to their control over the institutions. They couldn't ignore the protests but they also felt they could not acquiesce to what the students were demanding, precisely because the students wanted them to give up control. Instead, as Ferguson wrote, the academy let the members of these movements "stretch" its conventions "so that previously excluded subjects might enjoy membership." But, he added, minorities' new inclusion came at a price: Acknowledging their existence and letting them participate would mean they would have to "fall under new and revised laws."

Ferguson postulated that governments and corporations, unquestionably dominated by white men, imitated this model in response to similar challenges to their authority by minorities demanding equal rights. "State, capital, and the academy began to affirm minority difference in ways that seemed to resemble the social movements but actually stripped those movements of their goals of redistribution," he wrote.

This is a good concept to keep in mind while examining the financial industry's approach to diversity. At the heart of the struggle for Black Americans to gain equal footing in this country is the question of who has control and who has money. Nowhere is this formula embodied in a simpler form than in the financial industry, where money is the subject and the object, the occupation and the goal.

Here's a recent example that demonstrates how large institutions view the concept of diversity as dangerous: In 2019, when Democrats

assumed control of the United States House of Representatives, a historic change took place on the committee tasked with overseeing the
financial industry. For the first time a Black woman would be in
charge. Maxine Waters of California, who had been in Congress since
the early 1990s, was taking over. Bankers and their lobbyists couldn't
stand her. One lobbyist, Richard Hunt, described her in 2012 as having been "very hostile to banks over the last several years," neglecting
to mention that the last several years had included a massive financial
collapse brought about by the biggest banks, which had ushered in the
worst global recession since the 1930s.

One of the first things Waters did as the chairwoman of the House
Financial Services Committee was to rearrange its subcommittees.
She combined two long-standing subcommittees and created a new
one: the Subcommittee on Diversity and Inclusion. This move turned
out to be highly controversial within the financial industry. Bank lobbyists asked Waters's aides on Capitol Hill: Why was this necessary?
What would it accomplish? And why was the financial services committee the only one of the many congressional committees to set
about creating such a subcommittee? Why would banks have to endure more scrutiny than any other industry? It did not seem fair to
them. They did not want to be in that spotlight.

When the subcommittee met for its first hearing, the industry's
fears were realized: Waters gave an opening statement highlighting
the industry's poor track record on hiring and retaining non-white
employees. She pointed out that a Government Accountability Office
study had found that the financial industry actually had proportion-
ally fewer Black employees in senior roles in 2015 than in 2007.

The complaints about Waters's new committee led to more than
just idle chatter. When Democrats took over the Senate in 2021, the
committee in that chamber overseeing banks briefly explored its own
diversity subcommittee. Staff members working for the Senate Bank-

ing Committee's chairman, Ohio senator Sherrod Brown, started to plan for a diversity subcommittee. But they soon scrapped the plans. Republicans on the committee were not going to agree to it. It was a fight that would be too costly to wage, the staffers decided. They dropped the idea. A subcommittee looking squarely at minority representation in financial services clearly posed a threat—to someone.

"While we would have liked to have created a new subcommittee like my colleagues in House, the committee rules in a 50/50 Senate made it impossible," Brown wrote to me in a statement when I asked what had happened to the subcommittee. He added that even without a separate subcommittee he would continue to push banks "on issues like diversity, racial equity, climate change, and their commitment to workers."

Waters's committee seemed tame in comparison to some other recent attempts by officials overseeing the financial system to address racial inequality. But opposing any focus on racial equity in the financial industry has remained a mainstream political position, as evidenced by a statement blasted out by Pennsylvania senator Pat Toomey, the ranking Republican on the Senate Banking Committee. In the spring of 2021, Toomey had little to lose and almost no reason left to showboat: He had already announced he would retire at the end of his term. Yet one of his biggest concerns was that the Federal Reserve, along with other regulators and Congress itself, might be overstepping the boundaries of their mandates by using some of their resources to explore racial economic inequality. At hearings convened by Democrats who held the majority and got to choose the direction of the committee's work, he repeatedly argued that there was no need to spend the committee's time focusing on racism and its economic impacts. He also began pressuring Fed officials to stop focusing on racial equity, warning in letters to three regional Fed banks that a collaboration among them called "Racism in the Economy"—which had produced a series of public panels highlighting current academic research into economic inequality in various parts of the financial system like housing and banking—amounted to dangerous overreach.

"This subject matter is fraught with ideological assumptions and interpretations," he wrote in a letter to Minneapolis Fed president Neel Kashkari. "It is not the proper role of the Federal Reserve to be engaging in political advocacy."

Toomey demanded that each regional bank that participated in the "Racism in the Economy" series turn over all planning documents related to the series and asked that each institution brief him on the origins of their "sudden and alarming preoccupation with the political advocacy" he believed he had identified in the conference series. Several days later, his press office shared out an editorial in the conservative newspaper the *Washington Examiner* applauding his efforts to rein in the Fed titled "We Don't Need a Woke Fed." And when the Fed official in charge of supervising banks appeared before the committee for a hearing that month, Toomey repeated his complaints in a statement at the beginning of the hearing, also emailed to journalists in a press release.

By contrast, what is not at all seen as dangerous is the conventional and mostly empty speech about diversity issued by corporate leaders. Legal scholars have shown how the "symbolic gestures" companies make to show courts that they have "policies and procedures" in place to prevent discrimination, including their assertions about having "zero tolerance" for racism, serve to protect them from costly legal battles and big payouts; making anodyne statements about diversity is another component to companies' efforts to protect the status quo, which helps keep the people who have long been in charge of them from losing control. This component consists of the many forms of acting out an embrace of "diversity" through a collection of philanthropic, marketing, and public relations gestures.

Companies have to create visual representations of "diversity"—including printed material, digital images, and TV advertisements that convey an abstract "after" (the present, supposed achievement of equal status for minorities) while carefully avoiding any reference to the "before" (a time in which racism and redlining were the stated order of things)—often by trying to depict non-white people interacting with their employees and benefiting from their services. They also have to make gestures representing inclusivity in their own operations, from promoting affinity groups to publicizing any efforts they make to hire non-white employees. And they must demonstrate "concern" for minorities by making philanthropic contributions to causes that supposedly benefit minorities.

This is all typical of the financial industry, with various firms' practice of this basic set of behaviors varying only in intensity of expression. It might actually be harmful instead of good.

"When our appointments and promotions are taken up as signs of organizational commitment to equality and diversity, we are in trouble," Sara Ahmed writes in her book *On Being Included: Racism and Diversity in Institutional Life*. "Any success is read as a sign of an overcoming of institutional whiteness. 'Look, you're here!'" That's bad, Ahmed writes, because it actually makes pointing out the enduring whiteness harder. "Our talk about whiteness is read as a sign of ingratitude, of failing to be grateful for the hospitality we have received by virtue of our arrival."

The anodyne talk of diversity can be used as a shield against discussions of specific and unflattering problems. This also helps keep the topics of racism and representation on the margins of corporate life. Companies and their managers think the subject of "diversity" is the purview of people who count as "diverse"—which is a nonsensical euphemism that white people in the white-collar world use for minorities. This is clear to anyone who goes to a conference like the 2019 Quad-A conference, where most attendees were Black. There are very few white people who think this has anything to do with them. I had observed this separation a few months earlier in 2019 in even starker fashion when I participated in the Securities Industry and Financial Markets Association's diversity conference, which was held in New York.

SIFMA, as it is commonly known, is a large and powerful financial trade group that lobbies Congress and federal and state regulators on behalf of financial brokers, including retail wealth management firms and Wall Street investment banks—really, any institution large or small that trades in the financial markets or manages money. There are more than five hundred member firms in the organization. Together, its members are responsible for three-quarters of all trading revenue U.S.-based firms generate, and the money managers belonging to the organization oversee $45 trillion in assets. SIFMA is powerful and ruthless, and attending one of its annual conferences is like going to a giant uptight party for bankers that lasts several days. Each conference involves the complete takeover of a big luxury hotel somewhere like New York or Washington. There are swanky cocktail parties at night. By day the place swarms with charcoal and navy and leather and starch. It is an ocean of white faces.

SIFMA's diversity conference, by contrast, was held at its New York offices, which are located far downtown on Broadway, near Wall Street, in a building with an antiquated gilt lobby and plodding elevators. It's not the place for a grand production, and as I looked around the single room that housed the entire conference—bare, white, windowless, lit with fluorescence, decorated with only a whiteboard on one wall—I estimated the audience size at 135 people. Almost everyone in the room was either female or non-white or both. The conference was not an annual event. SIFMA only holds a "diversity and inclusion" event every other year. When I asked a spokeswoman why, she said that, basically, that was the pace at which developments in the

D & I space were occurring. There was no need to talk about the subject more frequently.

Quad-A's annual conference, too, appeared to be seen in 2019 as a backwater or a niche event, judging from the way banks participated in it. A standard part of every one of the biggest banks' marketing operations involves serving as a "sponsor" of important events. Sponsor banks' names are repeated over and over again in the printed material that goes along with whatever it is they're helping to pay for, whether it's a sports event, a conference, or a show put on by a cultural organization. Quad-A's leaders called for sponsors of its annual conference to participate at different levels. The largest sponsorship a bank could buy was called a "platinum" sponsorship, followed by other levels in descending order: "gold," "silver," "bronze." The most any bank forked over to have its name associated with Quad-A the year I attended the conference was for a "silver" sponsorship. Each bank had decided it was not worth their while to go any higher.

Banks never talk about their own whiteness. They stick strictly to assertions about their "achievements" in diversity, being careful not to get too close to any straightforward references to racism. This delicate operation was on full display at the Quad-A conference. For example, JPMorgan handed out flyers there, 8½-by-11-inch pieces of paper printed with a photograph of two Black people in business attire talking to each other in a blurred-out setting approximating a large corporate office. Accompanying the photo was this text:

DIVERSITY AT CHASE

Diversity at Chase is essential to ensure our businesses can continue to grow and provide value for our customers, employees, and shareholders. We are proud to recognize the importance of diversity and inclusion and support these initiatives in our hiring practices year-round.

As Chase Wealth Management continues along a Diversity &
Inclusion journey, we are building on work we've done to be certain
that we are creating diversity of thought, experience, ideas and
background.

Through our efforts, we foster a great team and a respectful,
inclusive culture. The people of Chase are genuine, approachable
and sincere in the desire to help customers achieve their financial
goals.

At the bottom of the flyer was a web address for JPMorgan's career web page—not a page specifically focused on hiring non-white people but its careers home page—subtly suggesting the achievement of an equal playing field in the hiring process.

This assertion of goodness was more aspirational than it first appeared. Someone had printed thousands of these flyers for the conference less than a year after JPMorgan settled the class-action lawsuit brought by its Black wealth managers in which its practices were described as anything but inclusive and fair. But a discussion of "diversity" was no place for talking about the bank's past mistakes or its efforts to repair its own wrongs. Those were two separate streams of its corporate consciousness entirely.

In her book, Sara Ahmed describes statements like the one on Chase's flyer as "speech acts," which, rather than simply describing a separate, observable state of being, create a new force, imposing a belief through repetition and dissemination, willing it into reality. If Chase's marketing department puts out enough material saying things like *We foster a great team and a respectful, inclusive culture*, it can override any perception of an opposing reality.

The gathering of Black professionals at Quad-A's annual conference became a stage for the white-dominated financial institutions to act out their "diversity" efforts. But the representatives of the large institutions who appeared at the conference also had to thread their way through some tricky, self-imposed prohibitions. They were not actually there to talk about racism or even acknowledge it. Their interactions had to be strictly positive. They had to eschew any acknowledgment that their organizations had any particular problems with "diversity."

WHEN "DIVERSITY" MEETS "DISCRIMINATION"

Sometimes, a truer, more raw discussion of diversity bubbles up and mixes with the glossier version. This happened at Morgan Stanley when its former global head of diversity, a Black woman named Marilyn Booker, sued for discrimination.

Marilyn had been fired from the firm in December of 2019 after working there for twenty-six years, the first sixteen of which were as diversity chief. She had had to take Morgan Stanley's side while other Black employees complained that they were being discriminated against in blatant ways. They were called racial slurs by white peers, prohibited from participating in meetings, kept away from lucrative client opportunities, and sent to work in poor parts of the country, then blamed for their subsequent failures as though the firm had played no part in them. The same complaints came up over and over again. Marilyn had had to work with the bank to swat them away and project a positive image. Black financial advisors reached a class-action settlement with the firm in 2007, and Marilyn had to interact with a monitor appointed by the judge overseeing the settlement. "No offense to outside monitors," she told me when we spoke, "I'm not convinced that they're that effective. They make a few recommendations and then they leave." This outside monitor was supposed to make sure the bank was hiring more Black employees and treating them decently. Former Morgan Stanley employees I interviewed over the course of three years beginning in 2019 said that things had marginally im-

proved while the monitor was in place but deteriorated again afterward. Marilyn had watched it all happen and had felt powerless.

She eventually moved out of the diversity position to become the
head of a group that was supposed to focus on attracting new Black
clients, a group that Morgan Stanley's white male leaders had chris-
tened "Urban Markets." That did not last long. Marilyn finally went
to her bosses and demanded the leeway and resources to really fix
Morgan Stanley's discrimination problem. It would require big changes
to the way its wealth management business operated, she said, including a fair and transparent system for distributing existing clients
among newly trained financial advisors and keeping tabs on whether
more senior advisors were giving credit to those who really deserved
it when new deals were done. The managers gave her lip service about
wanting to solve the problem, too, and told her to go ahead and start
working on a plan, but they refused to meet with her once she had
prepared a formal presentation for them. Soon after that, she was fired.
She filed her lawsuit in June of 2020 as corporate America chirped
about the importance of racial equality.

In her lawsuit, filed in Brooklyn federal court in 2020, Marilyn
published an internal memo written by another Black woman, Nadia
Jones, who had been tasked with improving diversity and who had
written a scathing assessment of Morgan Stanley's failings in that area
as her last act before leaving the firm herself in 2016:

*You cannot begin to imagine how it feels for a woman of color to be
constantly reminded that neither your credentials, nor your title,
nor your professional accolades, nor your expertise gleaned both
from your professional and social experiences as a woman of color,
are enough to counteract the pervasive and systemic biases that
run throughout this organization.*

Never in my 8 years of doing this work nor in my 38 years of being a Black woman have so many white people, men in particular, told me how to do my job and where best to focus my efforts to help diverse advisors—without consulting, mind you, a single diverse advisor in making that determination.

The dismissal and/or punting of concerns that I have raised—whether that be around the process of strategic leads or syndicate, or whether diversity is a quantifiable premium in this industry (as it has suited managers to be compensated on diversity, but not the diverse advisors themselves)—illustrate this firm's lack of commitment to creating sustainable change. In fact, the very notion of equity for diverse advisors and managers is oftentimes met with arrogant disapproval.

Because this firm is not about deliberately taking a chance on a person of color (as you all have increasingly done for white women, though nowhere near the proportional rate you have done so for white men) by providing them with a safety net should they stumble, but more importantly by ensuring that you have provided them with the resources to succeed. Because D&I work in its purest form is more than the numbers—it's more than the scorecard. It's about what will truly help diverse advisors, not about moving the ever-present, yet mythical, needle.

The net number of diverse advisors has barely changed in nearly a decade and that's because while we are focusing a lot of time on recruiting a diverse workforce, we have done little to nurture those very advisors who are already here.

This was a pretty spectacular blowup, not only because it demonstrated that Booker's condemnation of Morgan Stanley's diversity efforts was not an isolated view, but also because it directly juxtaposed the firm's public gestures with its private, ugly reality. *This* is the kind of conversation that does not happen during the heavily controlled communications banks and other financial firms choose to engage in about the experiences of non-white people in their midst. All my reporting indicates that Morgan Stanley is not materially worse in its treatment of Black financial advisors than any other wealth management firm.

"My story is the same story as many Black people on Wall Street who have lived the same thing," Marilyn told me when I spoke with her in the summer of 2020. "The difference is they aren't speaking up."

• • •

Jane Elliott's presentation took place on the second day of the Quad-A conference. Attendees had already drunk their fill of investment strategy presentations and discussions with representatives of big banks, including not only JPMorgan but also Wells Fargo. Most of the presentations thus far had focused on various aspects of career development: how to find new clients ("Don't think small; don't just stick to Black clients"), how to hire new advisors for a team, how to devise creative money management strategies and explain them to clients. One breakout session I attended was led by the two founders of a wealth management firm called Momentum Advisors, and there were moments when their presentation looked like it was going to break into a frank discussion about discrimination at the big wealth management firms. One of the founders, in describing to the audience the steps that were necessary to start an independent advisory firm and successfully grow it, said as an aside: "If you have not had enough bad experiences at the big firms, you may not be here yet."

Elliott's talk was like a left turn, like a cathartic break in the sobriety of the whole event. "There is only one race on the face of the earth," she shouted at the audience as we stood facing her, after rising from our seats in groups according to our self-affirmed "color."

"You need to get that into your heads and get it now!" She began referring to white people as "colorless people" and said that colorless people "rearrange the environment to fit our needs." Without hesitation, she called upon a few members of the audience, picked on them, even yelled at them. "Give up on the idea of whiteness!" she shouted. "It isn't real!"

I was sitting near the back of the room and, after watching her ridicule a couple of people near the front for various individualistic stances they had taken in response to her directions, I began to worry that she would single me out for something. I tried to obey her every command as soon as she gave it, so as not to attract attention by being slow or seeming unruly. Her talk went on for over an hour, and when it was over and someone turned the lights in the room all the way up again, everyone exhaled and looked around. It was as if we had all just rolled back into the boarding platform of a roller coaster at the end of a ride, our hair blown in all directions, our throats hoarse from screaming, our bodies drained. It was not anyone's idea of a typical conference session.

I turned around and saw a man I had not met but whom I recognized as one of the earlier speakers. He had been sitting in the row behind me during Elliott's talk. His face was full of bewilderment.

He was a Black man, born in East Africa, who worked at a large asset management firm in Boston. His presentation had been about money management strategies. It had been crisp, slightly boring, with a PowerPoint presentation sprinkled with gentle jokes and bland, sunny cultural references.

Our eyes met. "Are you okay?" he asked me.

"I'm fine!" I said. "How are you?"

"I can't believe that talk!" he said. "I was so uncomfortable! I was so worried for everyone she was yelling at individually."

We made our way out of the ballroom and found a table in the break area where we could chat. He told me about his background and what American discussions about diversity and racism looked like to him. He had not been living in the United States for very long. He had moved to Boston from London. Shortly after arriving, his group had been made to sit through a presentation on racial bias. It included a video that repeated a scene in which two people are walking toward each other on a street. At the point of meeting, different things happen in each repetition. In one scenario, one of them is a white woman and the other is a Black man, and the woman crosses the street to get away from the man. My interlocutor explained to me that this made no sense to him and that someone else from the team had had to explain to him that it was supposed to represent the assumptions the woman was making about the man. He had found the whole exercise rather worthless, he said. He did not see racism as a problem in his job at all. As for Elliott's presentation, it would never fly at a Wall Street firm, he thought. It was far too aggressive, far too liberal.

I had the chance to ask Elliott after her talk whether she had ever given one of her presentations to a bank or to any other Wall Street firm. "Never," she said.

THE REAL STORY

In 2021, I learned the real story of Jacqueline Campbell's time as diversity officer for JPMorgan's retail financial advisors: She had been an advisor herself inside JPMorgan's retail business for years and had eventually become a manager, overseeing a team with $2 billion in assets. In September of 2018, Jacqueline watched as the class-action lawsuit by Black financial advisors at JPMorgan was filed and settled. It was the same lawsuit that Ricardo Peters barely noticed while he was in the depths of his hellish final weeks at JPMorgan Chase in Arizona. Having worked at JPMorgan already for many years, Jacqueline felt that she had enough experience to try to fix the problems described in the lawsuit. *That*, she explained to me, was the genesis of her airplane trip to New York, the one she had described as an almost religious experience, a call to action by a higher power, on the stage at the Quad-A conference. She had not said anything at the conference about the lawsuit, nor did she ever speak publicly—or even privately with me—about what she had seen at the bank, whether she had witnessed the sequestration of Black wealth managers in poor neighborhoods or the denial by the bank of any opportunities for them to inherit clients or benefit from a helping hand. Any potential ugliness had been edited out of her presentation to the Quad-A audience, so that all that was left was the good in the story, which had to be put very vaguely lest it touch on the bad.

As it turned out, Jacqueline kept that diversity job for only a year. None of us knew it as we watched her in September of 2019, but she was within weeks of leaving JPMorgan entirely. She quit in November.

PART FOUR

TEN

ON WHITEWASHING

During the most isolating period of the coronavirus pandemic in 2020, I found myself, more than once, cheerfully driving two and a half hours to meet a friend somewhere in the outdoors, halfway between her house and mine. On one occasion we went for a hike; another time it was a walk around a bird sanctuary. Each time, in the car, I listened over and over again to a new record by the jazz musician Leron Thomas, who had taken on an artistic persona named Pan Amsterdam. The music is a collage of Thomas's thoughts, rapped or spoken in conversation and mixed in with his trumpet playing, samples of many other beats and melodies, and the voices of other musicians like Jason Williamson from the British band Sleaford Mods and Iggy Pop. Even though it's a stew of different voices and sounds, the record, *HA Chu*, is infused with intimacy. It's like being inside Thomas's head as he reflects on the music industry, consumer culture, and his own body. Each time I listened during my long drives, I felt as if I were a miniature person swimming in Thomas's thoughts, seeing the world through his eyes as he floated around New York. Thomas is Black.

One track on *HA Chu*, "Al's Courtyard," portrays a scene in which Thomas waits in line to get into a private party at a club and is treated with disdain by the hostess at the door, who complains that she can't find his name on the guest list, then flippantly waves him away by saying, "He's one of Alfred's."

I started to wonder whether I could manage to talk to Thomas. He had a following but was not, I discovered, an untouchable star. He was on Twitter, where I spend way too much of my time. So I followed him, and he followed me back. And I kept hearing new things in his album, like a snippet of an interview in which Thomas says that the structure of the jazz world is the key to understanding American society. "Always study what's going on in jazz," he says on a track that appears to be a recording of him speaking with an interviewer in a noisy restaurant. "For some reason that style of music is the cornerstone of our psyche."

I began to think about that advice as I mapped out this book in my head. The world of banking and finance is, in a way, set far apart from other parts of the public consciousness. People involved in the financial industry seem to rely on the fact that most people outside it regard it as beyond their understanding. It's an attitude that cuts across the political spectrum, one that can be adopted by Democrats and Republicans alike. Don't interfere with the technocrats.

The truth is, we are all a part of the financial system, whether we like it or not. Banks like to say that their business is the whole world. They're the engines that keep it all running. In a sense, they're right. To some extent, we all have knowledge of the banking system—even those of us who pay no attention to the world of high finance.

I suspected that Thomas, even though he had no special connection to banking, might have some important insights on how to root out racism just by virtue of having presented himself to the public, through his art, as a Black man sharing his views about how the world worked.

I sent him a message on Twitter explaining that I was writing a book about racism in the financial system and asked whether he had some time to talk about the parallels between my research and his world. He said yes.

My conversation with Thomas, in December of 2020, was about the music business and not banking. But we were talking about a power dynamic that the two industries shared. What Thomas described basically boiled down to the fact that a very small group of men—older white men—controlled the vast and theoretically diverse world of jazz in the United States.

Thomas described the ways the inequalities in jazz became visible from the very start of a musician's life. Black children, generally poorer and stuck in schools with less funding, could not as easily afford musical instruments.

"You would think that, since Black music has influenced America and the world for a century now, going into another century, you would think that they would do a better job making sure that instruments get to Black schools," he said, and I thought about how the many Black wealth management professionals I had interviewed over the course of two years had told me that some aspects of money management came easier to people who had grown up around wealth. It wasn't that their skills in deciding which investments to make were better; it was that having had parents with rich friends, they could more easily leverage their family connections to find new clients and project an air of legitimacy. So the inequality began early, in both cases. And it continued in college, where the few Black students who could afford instruments and music lessons were suddenly under the control of white college administrators and, for the most part, white music department heads.

Thomas, who grew up in the suburbs of Houston, described what it was like to move to New York and see white jazz club owners control so completely which musicians got to play and what music they performed. He said Black musicians were appealing hires because they fit tourists' expectations better than white musicians, but club owners wanted them to play from only a narrow selection of standards and styles. Rebelling against those expectations was nearly impossible, as was agitating for better pay or more control over the material produced during a performance: "You risk being blacklisted for speaking out to club owners and other musicians because everybody's on a treadmill. Everybody is too busy hustling. We don't have time to get together to organize because we'd be broke."

Here was another parallel: The power imbalances in the world where Thomas was trying to get ahead created their own vicious cycle. The people without power were kept isolated and apart. Starting out in the disadvantaged position meant being kept in that position by virtue of being powerless. Speak out and risk losing everything. The same is true for people trying to advance their careers in banking and finance. Because the industry is still dominated by white men, minorities and women learn that if they manage to get ahead, the best thing to do is to count their blessings, keep their heads down, and try not to make trouble.

Thomas also described an encounter with racism and gaslighting in his work life that was similar to the descriptions Black bank employees gave of what it was like when they experienced discrimination in the office and tried to speak out, only to be told that their employer saw no evidence of discrimination.

"The worst type of racism is the one that's not aware of it, because then it's way more systematic and covert," Thomas said. "All you can do is look at the end result. One club owner I encountered systematically used Black jazz musicians to get the audience into the club. But he started to get mad because they didn't want to play the Cole Porter stuff; they wanted to play the new stuff they were working on. Once the club started to sustain itself, you started seeing more Black jazz musicians being pushed out and white jazz musicians coming in. You talk to the guy and he'll tell you he's not racist—in his head he's not—but the end result is more racism."

So how would Thomas fix things in the jazz world?

"With musicians—the best thing I can talk about—there needs to be more integration in the bands; I think that would be nice. I really get into a problem when I see an all-white jazz ensemble: I'm, like, 'You mean to tell me you couldn't find no brothers?' We can do better. But just things like that—I think if people just started trying to be more aware of how it looks."

Thomas also said he thought there should be far more acknowledgment of how jazz and Black musical traditions influenced other kinds of music, including indie rock. In our conversation, he traced a line from current trends in experimental jazz back to the height of the grunge rock movement in Seattle in the 1990s and then explained how much it all originated from a sound pioneered by Miles Davis.

"The history of jazz itself is integration, and you see the racism and the know-your-place vibes. The club owner has a vision about what he thought jazz was. A lot of times in Black music, we don't like to address this truth, but white people usually get into the music after the fact. It's had its day and it's past its sexual prime. Black people by nature are naturally innovative to survive. They're always 'counterculturing' the current culture and the racism."

This, too, has parallels to banking. Failing to hire people who look and think differently—and in some cases who think differently because the way they look has led them to have vastly different experiences than those of the majority—leads to a failure to innovate. If everyone thinks the same way, how is anyone supposed to conceive of new ideas and test out which ones work?

These were the thoughts Thomas left me with, along with some suggestions of other people to talk to. They were also in the music business, but hearing from them led me to a major breakthrough in my understanding of how big our ideas need to get if we're going to really address the problem of racism in banking.

On Thomas's recommendation, I reached out to Open Mike Eagle, a Los Angeles–based musician and comedian whose songs are often about contemporary consumer culture and who has devoted a great deal of his work to exploring, as he puts it, "perceptions of Blackness." His subjects include anxiety, depression, buying furniture, the stuff of a recognizable middle-class life. He has even made passing references to banks in his lyrics. He's the kind of writer one could easily imagine might slip an airy, perfectly rhymed reference to Chase Freedom Rewards points into a work of scathing social commentary that also touches on military drones, "post-racial" attitudes, and electoral politics. In 2020, for example, he released a song about how he wanted to blame the dissolution of his marriage on a popular Netflix show, *Black Mirror*. "If it's a love story pick something different . . . ," he warns potential viewers. "If I was petty I would try it as a court case / The goddamn episode raised the divorce rate."

I could see why Leron Thomas thought I should talk to him. Mike integrated commentary about pop culture into descriptions of his own experiences as a Black man in America. He also reflected on the history of the Black American experience in a podcast he created called *What Had Happened Was*, in which he has interviewed some of the most influential hip-hop musicians about their lives and work. But I was still not prepared for the powerful influence his observations would have on me, starting from his description of how he saw—quite literally—racist speech permeating America.

"I spent a lot of my career booking my own tours," he told me when we spoke in early 2021. "Driving through the country, criss-crossing it so many times, being in so many areas where diversity doesn't exist and seeing how I'm reacted to in those places personally, seeing how the act of rapping is reacted to in some of these places, it has given me a stark sense of the racial temperature in the country. I toured a lot through the Obama years, and as much as everybody on the coasts and in the big cities really thought that we had somehow solved racism by electing Barack Obama, one thing I'll always remember from that time is the graffiti in the bathroom gas stations across the country. There were vile things written about Obama in disconnected gas stations all over. This was not the work of a few bad eggs. There were sentiments boiling over. I guess you could connect it to the beginning of the Tea Party rhetoric that was forming in this country. There were people who believed that it was not okay for a Black man to be president. The bathrooms were a great place to get this message out and find people who connected with them."

Mike said he felt personally threatened a couple of times while touring—including when a man in a truck in Redding, California, had called him the N-word and yelled at him to "go home." But he had a theory about what kept racism alive: In his mind it was linked to the unacknowledged trauma that permeates American history. From the Revolutionary War through the Civil War, the Great Depression, various financial panics, and the collapse of the manufacturing sector, all kinds of really awful things have happened to portions of the American population, and there seems to be no common acknowledgment, no mobilization toward a source of comfort or healing from these traumatic events.

"There's a lot of trying to square our reality as individuals with what is told to us as the American dream. And if your reality doesn't meet that standard, there's nobody to go to. There's nobody to say why not," Mike said.

What the country needs, in Mike's mind, is a giant group therapy session. Or maybe not one session with everyone together but some sort of widely distributed therapy, some kind of authoritative ear to listen to the individual and societal pain Americans carry around, and a soothing voice to wisely help them sort it all out. And with that, Mike told me, there must also be an end to the gaslighting that is part of American companies' advertising repertoires.

"We are sold an idea of what it means to be an American or what the possibilities of that are," Mike explained. "Corporate America isn't really interested in our mental health; corporate America is interested in all of our dollars and what corporate America does is they make us feel very special. They make our freedom of choice seem very important. They make personal happiness seem very important. But that's not the truth of our lives. People talk about whether there's such a thing as ethical capitalism, and I think if there were such a thing it would involve them taking a look at that cognitive dissonance."

On TV, Mike said, everything is bountiful and everyone is happy. Houses are big and clean, families are unblemished by tragedy. For Black Americans, who live in fear of trigger-happy police officers and who struggle to deal with the many pitfalls that racism creates in their everyday lives, this is an especially massive departure from reality.

"There's no commercial that will leave you feeling like you might be murdered by an arm of the government," Mike explained. "That's our reality. In 2020, one day I remember very clearly, there was a Tuesday that the music industry decided was Black Tuesday and that they were going to stop operations for a day of reflection in response to the killing of George Floyd, and to the #BlackLivesMatter movement and racial injustice, and I remember that deeply offended me that the music business was coming out in that way. I understood the intent of it, but if we're talking about some sort of ethical capitalism, then the best thing the music industry could do is reflect on itself, reflect on the images it amplifies and distributes to America about the importance of Black life, and see if it reflects that message. I think it needs to reflect on its history of taking everything from Black musicians and leaving nothing. In every possible case it has sought to take the creativity, to not acknowledge the people who have made stuff, to own what it wants to own and to leave musicians penniless and broken with nothing to offer their families in terms of wealth. Only the most successful musicians have been in a position to own their own work and create wealth for their families off of it. It is comical to me that they would want to stop operations for a day and not look at themselves and their behavior."

This, again, held a parallel in banking. In June of 2020, a week after George Floyd's murder, Jamie Dimon walked into a Chase branch in Mount Kisco, New York, and had himself photographed taking a knee just like Black NFL players trying to protest police brutality by kneeling during the national anthem. This was banking's Black Tuesday moment, as Mike had formulated it. And, like the music industry, the banking industry has a centuries-long history of exploiting Black people, not only through predatory lending, redlining, and other forms of racist exclusion and inclusion but also by financing slavery.

By talking to Leron Thomas and Open Mike Eagle, I followed a well-trodden path of ideas put forward by some of the most prominent commentators on racial justice of our time, including my own colleagues at the *New York Times Magazine*'s 1619 Project, most notably Nikole Hannah-Jones. But the specific formulations of these ideas were new to me, and I realized I had not been paying enough attention even to some of the general concepts at hand. Yes, police violence against Black Americans is an abomination amounting to modern-day lynching. So is the mass incarceration of Black Americans. But I had managed to read about the individual horror stories out of which these concepts are built without having a real appreciation of the way everything of value had been snatched from the hands of Black people whose ancestors were originally brought to this land as captives. I also did not understand the magnitude of the gaslighting that has accompanied that endless extractive operation.

Those concepts were new to me, because I had failed to pay attention to what is perhaps the most important element in the broader conversation among Black intellectuals and activists that had been going on for years already about what racial justice in the United States would have to include. I'm not suggesting that this was negligence for which I should be rewarded or that anyone reading this book should emulate. But I thought it was important to note because it shows how many different roads can lead to the same destination, and how easily accessible some of the ideas that often seem cosseted in academia or bound up in the competing op-eds that many Americans tend to ignore really are. There is no advanced degree requirement for thinking about these things, discussing them, and incorporating them into the mix of ideas and principles by which one can live. There is no subscription requirement. There is no fancy vocabulary to memorize.

I started out from a place of ignorance, so I think it is quite significant that, with help from two artists, I found my way to the hottest, most consequential topic in the current discussion of racial justice: reparations.

ELEVEN

REPARATIONS AND THE BIG BANKS

Leron Thomas wanted music promoters to act with more awareness of the influence Black music had on many forms of American pop music, i.e., to stop taking all those good ideas for free. Open Mike Eagle wanted American companies to stop pretending the world was so shiny and perfect and to acknowledge their roles in making it a less equal place. What did this add up to? Both artists wanted the powerful people who got rich off the labor of Black Americans to finally acknowledge all this exploitation and to make amends. To do something real. To stop glossing over the ugly past. As Ta-Nehisi Coates wrote in 2014 in "The Case for Reparations," his seminal essay in the *Atlantic*, "America was built on the preferential treatment of white people—395 years of it. Vaguely endorsing a cuddly, feel-good diversity does very little to redress this."

The idea of finally giving Black Americans some kind of compensation for their ancestors' enslavement over almost 250 years, and for the white establishment having murdered them and stolen their money for another century and a half after that, has been a topic of public conversation that has regularly expanded and contracted within the country's modern discourse, going almost nowhere, but never going away, reliably serving to rile up racists while being seen among many prim liberals as a radical idea that could never actually work.

In its earliest form, it centered on demands for pension payments by the 600,000 members of the National Ex-Slave Mutual Relief, Bounty and Pension Association, a group comprising people who had all been enslaved before Emancipation. These people had given their labor to white capitalists and gotten nothing in return. They thought the federal government should compensate them. Instead of agreeing, federal authorities accused the group's leaders of fraudulently collecting money from its members and giving them false hopes for pension payouts. The group disbanded after its leaders were jailed. One judge who sentenced a slave pension activist to jail for fraud declared: "This scheme of getting money for the slaves is like pouring money into a rat hole and you know it."

The discussion did not end there, but its place in the consciousness of those in power has wavered. It is broadening again, and there is a new momentum behind it, fueled by the stark displays of ongoing injustices against Black Americans, including the murder of George Floyd in 2020 and the April 2021 shooting of Daunte Wright, a twenty-year-old who was killed by police in Minnesota who had pulled him over for having an air freshener hanging from his rearview mirror. In the summer of 2020, the *New York Times Magazine* writer Nikole Hannah-Jones argued for reparations, citing the 2019 Yale study on Americans' misperceptions of the racial wealth gap, and in April of 2021 *Saturday Night Live* featured two of its Black cast members playing a pair of news anchors who, alongside two white anchors, were trying to discuss the day's bad news—another killing of a Black American by police—and who saw reparations as a perfectly reasonable step in addressing the tragedy.

And the way Leron and Mike described the importance to them

of the white establishment coming clean about the past and trying to make up for it, something like reparations has to work, and it's not radical. It's the starting point of a journey toward true equality for Black Americans. Its two main aspects are legitimacy and money.

"To celebrate freedom and democracy while forgetting America's origins in a slavery economy is patriotism à la carte," Coates wrote, touching on the need for truth and transparency from the country as a whole and from its powerful leaders. Those leaders, he said, needed to back up this new legitimate recognition of the past with material commitments.

"Perhaps no statistic better illustrates the enduring legacy of our country's shameful history of treating black people as sub-citizens, sub-Americans, and sub-humans than the wealth gap. Reparations would seek to close this chasm. But as surely as the creation of the wealth gap required the cooperation of every aspect of the society, bridging it will require the same," he wrote.

I did not turn to Coates's essay immediately after my conversation with Mike, because my first step was to process his thoughts about gaslighting through a more personal lens. What I did right after we spoke was think about Germany.

I was raised in a Reform Jewish family, descended from immigrants who mostly came to the United States from eastern Europe at the beginning of the twentieth century. My ancestors came to the East Coast in order to escape the pogroms that regularly swept through the towns in Poland, Russia, and Ukraine where they were struggling to live their lives. I heard some stories of their flight first-hand, from a distant cousin of mine who lived to be one hundred whose brothers and sisters had died in a Polish forest while trying to escape murderous mobs on what turned out to be the beginning of the long journey westward with their parents to New York. My family mostly got out of Europe years before World War II, before the Holocaust. And yet the Holocaust, and the anti-Jewish sentiment in Europe upon which it was built, defined us, as it did so many other Jewish families in the United States. We had escaped the forces in Europe that eventually coalesced to form the system of genocide in the extermination camps. Did I, personally, flee Europe? No. Did I lie awake at night as a little kid and imagine, with terror, being rounded up by Nazis? All the time. It was part of who I was. Who I am.

One of my family's rules that was enforced as strictly as the religious prohibition against eating pork and shellfish was that we did not drive German cars. Everyone knew that German automakers, including the luxury brands BMW and Mercedes, had helped the Nazis carry out their work in the camps, so no matter how appealing their cars might have seemed to me as a little kid in the 1980s, I was committed to never admiring them, to never coveting them. Even riding in one was a horrifying prospect. My best friend when I was a preschooler in Miami Beach was also Jewish, but her family did not feel the same way we did, and they drove a white Mercedes sedan full of rich, tawny leather inside. She sometimes invited me to ride in the car, and even though I did not think my parents would have minded a simple ride here and there, I always held my breath for as long as possible while in the car and strenuously resisted every urge to acknowledge the comfort and splendor of its interior. As comical as this may seem now, it was a way for me to connect with my cultural identity and to feel that I had some small bit of control over a story of bewildering horror not lived by me personally but linked to me forever.

German companies have, at different times and in different ways, acknowledged the roles they played in the Holocaust. Some of the most terrifying revelations have come in response to lawsuits, such as the 1999 revelation by Deutsche Bank that it helped finance the construction of the Auschwitz concentration camp. These revelations are significant, not simply because they are the basis for seeking damages from the companies, but because the knowledge of these companies' dark histories *must* endure in the public consciousness. We cannot forget or bury the past if we want to be a healthy society.

The journey to accountability is not over, but when I thought about how Mike wishes that the American music industry would just *begin* to acknowledge its exploitation of Black musicians, and when I tried to think of what I casually knew about American companies' involvement in slavery itself—not to mention the gross mistreatment and abuse that followed after the Civil War ended—I realized that the American public consciousness in no way has in its store the same level of awareness of American companies' exploitation of Black people that Jews—and the world in general, I believe—have of German companies' evil acts during the Holocaust. It was a great benefit to my sense of freedom and pride and power and autonomy to be able to choose not to like German cars. Black people have not been given that choice.

DEADRIA'S WORK

The most recent iteration of the reparations discussion has not focused on this concept. Instead, it has taken another aspect of Germany's postwar amends as a model and has focused on the idea that the American government itself should try to make Black Americans whole.

This has not always been the case, as Deadria Farmer-Paellmann's story makes clear. Deadria, so moved by the scene at the African burial ground in Lower Manhattan, devoted the next ten years to trying to sue individual companies, including Bank of America, for reparations.

Working alongside a small group of lawyers and activists, some of whom had traced their own ancestries back to an enslaved person whose fate had been in the hands of a predecessor to an active

American corporation, Deadria sought to develop a case for making American companies pay for their involvement in the international and domestic slave trades. Using lawsuits filed against German companies after the Holocaust as a guide, the group devised a series of arguments for how damages should be sought against a company found to have a traceable involvement in slavery—and how to prove that the company was still liable for what its earlier leaders had done.

In 2002, Deadria sued Aetna, the railroad company CSX, and a bank, FleetBoston Financial, in Brooklyn federal court, one of nine lawsuits of its kind filed around the country brought by the descendants of slaves. Her lawsuit drew a line from the enslavement of 8 million Africans and their descendants in the United States from 1619 to 1865 to the conditions in which Black Americans were living in 2002: They had shorter life expectancies, they had a higher infant mortality rate, and, as she summarized it, they were behind in "every social yardstick." She also described part of the racial wealth gap: Roughly a quarter of the country's Black population was living in poverty, compared to just 8 percent of its white population. The lawsuit also pointed out that some of the slavery-linked business that the companies had engaged in was not just wrong in hindsight; it was illegal under state law in some northern states at the time it was conducted.

Deadria wanted to force the companies to disclose to the fullest extent possible their participation in slavery, including how much they earned from participating in the slave trade or financing activities linked to slavery, and to set up an independent historical commission that would become the keeper of all relevant corporate records. It also sought damages and the disgorgement of profits—the sum of which was to be determined at trial—for the wrongs each company helped perpetrate.

The companies summoned the most prestigious white-shoe law firms to defend themselves. By the time the cases had run their twisted courses through the federal legal system, some of the most prominent corporate law firms in the United States—Skadden, Arps; Jones Day; Kirkland & Ellis; Williams & Connolly; White & Case; O'Melveny & Meyers; and Fried, Frank—were all fighting to protect some of the largest American corporations from having to pay damages for their involvement in the slave trade.

Going up against these giants was a bold course of action, not least because, even though there were other people engaged in reparations lawsuits, Deadria was in many ways alone in her pursuit. The costs of seeing her case through its long road to a trial fell almost entirely on her.

"The reparations movement legally and intellectually was at a dead end. It was trash. And Deadria came in at a correct time and raised a possible strategic maneuver," Bob Brown, the cofounder of the Chicago chapter of the Black Panther Party movement, told me. "Deadria's contribution was that she came with new strategies."

(Brown had later filed his own lawsuits against a laundry list of giant companies and organizations over their ties to slavery, including financial firms like JPMorgan, Citi, Bank of America, and his work was based on the fruits of Deadria's.)

"Most of the leadership of the movement—of the so-called reparations movement in general, which I have contempt for—fault her," Brown told me. "Because she was a woman, because she was new, and because they did not have her theory in their legal expertise."

Deadria found that it was nearly impossible to raise money for the cause, she said, since most mainstream civil rights groups viewed her efforts to get big companies—rather than federal or state governments—to pay damages as radical and potentially harmful to their own interests.

The NAACP, for instance, would come around, at least briefly, to the idea of getting companies to pay reparations, but not until three years after Deadria filed her suit. The NAACP's interim CEO, Dennis

C. Hayes, announced at the group's annual convention in mid-July of 2005 that it would start going after private companies with ties to slavery. His comments drew strident public opposition, but their power was already diminished: Just one week earlier, a federal judge had dismissed Deadria's case along with the others that it mirrored.

She appealed the ruling. A federal appeals court upheld the lower court's dismissal of most of the arguments Deadria and the other plaintiffs had made, including that FleetBoston and the other companies had participated in human rights violations, that they had unjustly enriched themselves, and that they had failed to account for the value of the captive Africans' labor.

But the appeals court's ruling also granted the case a small but important victory, allowing one of Deadria's major claims to go forward: the assertion that the companies had committed consumer fraud by not revealing to the public that they had participated, directly or indirectly, in slavery and the slave trade.

Fifteen years later, Open Mike Eagle was saying the same thing.

THE FIGHT FOR DISCLOSURE

By the end of 2006, when the appeals court said that the consumer fraud claims against big companies that had hidden their ties to slavery could go forward, there was no money left to carry on, and Deadria said she was forced to abandon the effort. But her work in researching the companies' slavery links had sparked a nationwide movement to get companies to look into their pasts.

Tom Hayden, the anti-war activist who had been a California state senator since 1992, took up Deadria's cause and introduced a bill—which became a California law in 2000—that forced companies doing business with the state to disclose any connections they had to slavery before they could sign public contracts. Hayden's disclosure law echoed throughout the country as cities like Chicago, Philadelphia, and Milwaukee imposed similar requirements on companies seeking public contracts there. In Chicago, the effort to get the Slavery Era Disclosure Ordinance enacted was led by Dorothy Tillman, a civil rights leader who had been championing the idea of reparations for decades.

Most of the major banks found that one or more of their predecessors had had some kind of dealings involving enslaved people, whether it was selling insurance policies on them, accepting them as collateral for loans, or taking possession of them in foreclosures. Thanks to the disclosure laws, they had to share these findings with the public.

At least some of them did.

Fifteen years after American companies of all stripes were supposed to have come clean about their relationships to slavery, there was still very little common knowledge of it floating around. The cities with local ordinances requiring them to collect the companies' disclosures did not publish them on any kind of platform that casual consumers could easily access. When I wanted to see what banks had told the city of Chicago, for instance, I had to formally request the records from the mayor's office under a freedom of information law. It took weeks for officials there to do a records search, and when they sent me what they had, it turned out to be a hodgepodge of forms with, in several cases, no details attached. Some of the companies had simply checked a box saying they had found ties in their past to slavery without providing any account of their findings.

Chicago's rule, it turned out, had almost no teeth. The only way a company could be punished for not filling out a disclosure form was if the mayor's office decided either to void its contract or to sue the company for failing to file the form. Not long after the rule hit the books, Bob Brown had tried to get the city to do this, arguing that a long list of companies, as well as organizations like the local Democratic and Republican Parties and the Catholic Church, had failed to come clean about their pasts. He had a list of entities, originally 3,000 names long and eventually whittled to under two hundred, that he sued directly in Cook County Circuit Court. Banks like Citi and Bank of America were among them. They hired the most elite lawyers they could find, just as they had in Deadria's reparations case, while Brown, lacking any real funding for his effort, tried to handle most of the proceedings on his own. The cases were dismissed.

This is how things played out in other cities as well. In 2012, an editor for the Milwaukee newspaper the *Daily Reporter* found that, out of almost 4,000 separate filings companies had made about their past ties to slavery, only one—*one*—contained detailed information about *what* those ties were.

This was hardly the reckoning that Deadria was looking for, or that Mike and Leron felt was essential.

A recent Wells Fargo disclosure to Chicago, for instance, was a page-and-a-half summary of the work that a researcher hired by one of its predecessors, Wachovia, had done in 2005. At the top of the document was a note emphasizing that before Wells Fargo bought Wachovia in 2008 as part of a series of frenzied mergers precipitated by the financial crisis, it had no records showing that it or any of its predecessors had financed or profited from slavery. However, Wachovia, which was the fourth-largest U.S. bank when Wells Fargo took it over, had a heavily stained past.

Two of Wachovia's predecessors, the Bank of Charleston and the Georgia Railroad and Banking Company, had actually owned enslaved people. The records Wachovia's historian sifted through were incomplete, but they showed that the Georgia Railroad and Banking Company had either bought or intended to buy at least 162 people and had given work to contractors owning at least 400 more people. The Bank of Charleston had made loans to the owners of enslaved people who put at least 529 of those people up as collateral on the loans. In most

cases, the loan was paid on schedule, and the bank never took possession of slaves that were pledged as collateral on the loan. In several
documented instances, however, customers defaulted on their loans
and the Bank of Charleston took actual possession of slaves. "The total
number of slaves of whom the bank took possession cannot be accu-
rately tallied due to the lack of records," the disclosure read. Following
that was a list of eleven other banks Wachovia eventually bought
whose leaders either owned enslaved people, profited directly from
slavery, or directed the banks to invest in slave-owning institutions
like southern municipalities or the U.S. government itself before slavery was outlawed. The striking thing about the list was that only three
of the eleven institutions on it were from the South. The other eight
were from Philadelphia and parts of New Jersey, a reminder that the
entire U.S. financial system, and not just the defeated relics of the
Confederacy, is infused with the proceeds from the evil business of
slavery.

The original wave of disclosures by Wachovia and other big banks
has been distilled into snippets like this one, and the overall effect is
like that of a flat stone tossed into a pond that slips into the water
instead of smacking it. The splash ought to have been bigger to begin
with.

Wachovia's original report was 111 pages long. Each of its predecessor banks' histories with slavery was described in as much detail as
possible. In the case of the Philadelphia-based Bank of North America, for instance, researchers described the bank's founders' activities
importing captive Africans, selling them, and using others on a plantation they started near Baton Rouge. The researchers also provided a
list of area slave owners—186 names long—who may have had an account at the bank. They quoted advertisements, letters, and lists of
enslaved people that they had found among the bank's records.

Another section focused on the Bank of Baltimore, which was

founded by slave owners, and had a customer who owned 285 enslaved people. The *Baltimore Sun* picked up the details of its history
in a story about Wachovia's apology for these wrongs. The story
quoted Wachovia CEO G. Kennedy "Ken" Thompson saying, "I apologize to all Americans, and especially to African-Americans and people of African descent," and adding: "We know that we cannot change
the past, and we can't make up for the wrongs of slavery, but we can
learn from our past and begin a stronger dialogue about slavery and
the experience of African-Americans in our country."

According to the *Sun*, Wachovia pledged to "work with community groups to further education about African-American history," a
far cry from disgorging any ill-gotten gains. This was a part of the
non-splash, the non-event that the disclosures made up. Bankers in
that era were riding high, making billions in their mortgage businesses, and feeling that it was within their power to tell any malcon-
tents what they were and were not willing to give. As a Wachovia
spokesman, a man named Scott Silvestri who later went on to become
a "senior issues advisor" for Exxon, explained to the *Washington Post*
at the time: "We didn't want to have a donation or gift right out of a
gate. We wanted to think about what's the best way to address that."

At least Wachovia played ball with the city officials asking for
the disclosures; Bank of America at first tried to resist. In early 2005
the bank told the city of Chicago that none of its predecessors had
links to slavery, a declaration that Chicago alderman Dorothy Tillman, the architect of the city's disclosure ordinance, immediately
rejected. It was "incorrect," she said, and she would "bring evidence"
to prove it. That turned out not to be necessary. A few months later
Bank of America revised its disclosure to say that, yes, it had found
links to slavery in its past but that no predecessor had actually profited from it.

The bank's reasoning seemed especially tortured in light of the fact that—at the same time it was trying to insist that slave trading had never contributed to its coffers—an Ivy League university founded by a well-known merchant who had also founded a bank that would eventually be absorbed by the behemoth was undertaking what would later be called a "blueprint" for turning a history of slave trading into a calculation for reparations.

A significant portion of Bank of America's historical connections to slavery stemmed from its having bought banks in New England, including FleetBoston, an institution with roots dating back to the late 1700s in Providence, Rhode Island. Its founder, John Brown, was a prominent slave trader. As Bank of America was attempting to deny it had profited from slavery, Brown University, which John Brown also founded, was setting up a commission to figure out just how much of its existence could be attributed to the vile commerce.

The Bank of America report, which was done by a commercial research firm called the Heritage Research Center, emphasized that the bank that John Brown founded, Providence Bank, did not have any records showing loans to slave traders or other financing for the business and never owned slaves itself. But a note at the beginning of the report said that its researchers had deemed the sources of personal wealth of bank directors and investors irrelevant to the question of where a bank's profits came from. Therefore, the fact that Brown helped found the bank and infused it with some of the proceeds of his own business trading enslaved people was outside the scope of the report.

Deadria is still not satisfied with Bank of America's disclosure. She says that the researchers failed to mention the fact that Providence Bank was the U.S. Customs Service's bank in the port of Providence, meaning that all customs duties paid by traders moving goods through that port flowed through the bank, which collected fees from them. Records she gathered show that between 2,000 and 3,000 slaves were smuggled into Providence after the slave trade was officially banned in the United States. They would have come into port hidden, their presence disguised as other tradable goods on which their importers would have made sure to pay the proper duties in order to avoid arousing suspicion. The Heritage report made no mention of this. The researchers there concluded that, despite having been founded by a notorious slave trader, John Brown, Providence Bank did not own slaves or profit from slavery.

Here is another moment in the history of Bank of America that was determined to be outside the parameters of the bank's having profited from slavery: According to Heritage's research, in 1840, John Forsyth, the U.S. secretary of state at the time, approached the board of directors of Bank of the Metropolis, a Washington-based bank that was another of Bank of America's predecessors, and asked for a $10,000 loan collateralized by forty enslaved people. The board agreed to the deal but asked for more collateral: forty-three people instead of just forty. Its members also added a few extra conditions to the terms of the loan. Over the next several months, Forsyth's fulfillment of some of these conditions seemed to indicate that the agreement was being executed, but the records are incomplete, and Heritage's researchers decided they could not determine either way whether the bank had really gone through with the plan to mortgage Forsyth's slaves.

"The absence of early records for the bank and inaccessibility of property records limit the certainty with which Heritage can state that the Bank of the Metropolis did not profit from slavery, but available records in the public domain provide no information that such occurred," the researchers wrote.

A liminal connection to slavery is the sort that could be used to catapult the banks into another public position: that their predecessors are not particularly culpable because everyone in America shoulders part of the blame. It was a problem that another researcher who delved into the pasts of several major U.S. banks decided to deal with differently than Heritage had.

James Lide and a team of researchers at the company he worked for, History Associates, found himself contracted by several large banks, including JPMorgan, to look into their links to slavery and write reports that would fulfill the requirements in the disclosure laws. He began each journey by meeting with bank officials to settle one crucial question first: Which banks counted as predecessors? Lide said that he and his team had to make something that looked "like an inverted family tree" for each bank, many tiers of institutions "all funneling toward the present-day bank."

Each bank that hired Lide and his team had to sign off on its own genealogy before Lide dug into what its predecessors had done in the past. That way, a lineage was clear even if the line between what did and did not count as profiting from slavery looked blurred. Lide did not want to have to make that determination himself.

"What we tried to do was arrange that on the spectrum and not decide 'What is defined as connection to slavery?' but 'Here's what we have found,'" he said. "History can't tell you what it means to profit from slavery. That definition of profiting from slavery has changed and evolved over time. That is a political decision."

This was itself an imperfect solution, because it let banks choose to disown unsavory predecessors as long as they could find a lawyer willing to write a justification for it. This let some banks that had been formed from hastily made deals escape the spotlight. But it forced others to make a commitment to owning their pasts, whatever the outcome of the research.

JPMorgan eventually announced that two of its predecessors, banks that were both based in Louisiana, had owned enslaved people. Together, the two—Citizens' Bank and Canal Bank—had accepted

13,000 people as collateral on loans to nearby plantations. Some of those loans defaulted, which led the banks to take possession of 1,250 people.

From start to finish, JPMorgan's dive into its own past was handled by one of the bank's public relations specialists, who worked closely with Lide and planned out the timing and nature of JPMorgan's public announcement about Lide's findings. In a somber letter to employees signed by William B. Harrison, the company's CEO at the time, JPMorgan disclosed Lide's findings and announced it would be donating $5 million to cover Black college students' tuition expenses in Louisiana.

How JPMorgan got to that number isn't clear, but it was certainly a popular sum: Bank of America, in denying it had profited from slavery, also announced it was donating $5 million to a group of institutions, it said, that were dedicated to preserving African American history.

Perhaps the most significant outcome of the slavery era disclosure laws has been the silence from another big bank, Citigroup. Citi's recent history is a messy amalgam of other organizations, but its marketing materials and even its new CEO, Jane Fraser, often tout its two-hundred-year history going back to 1812, when it was City Bank of New York. Citi has boasted about how, during the Civil War, the bank's president, Moses Taylor, helped organize a $50 million loan to the Union forces and U.S. president Abraham Lincoln's war effort.

Taylor is without question the single most influential figure in Citi's past. After starting out as a wealthy customer, he joined its board in 1837 during a massive financial panic that caused many of City Bank's competitors to fail. The bank's other leaders thought having a man of Taylor's clout on its board would help nurture its customers' continued confidence.

Immediately after joining the board, Taylor began playing an outsized role on it. He served on a special committee to manage short-term debt that was being passed back and forth between various banks at the time, and City's president picked him alone to help deal with a bank in Albany that owed City a great deal of money. Just five years after joining the board, Taylor became president pro tempore of the bank himself and in 1855 was finally elected president, a job that gave him near-total control over its operations. He successfully steered it through another financial panic in 1857 and through its conversion to a national charter at the end of the Civil War.

No one would dispute the idea that Taylor was the de facto grandfather of Citi. But the bank has never acknowledged where Taylor got his money or how close he was to the transatlantic slave trade.

It has only recently, over the last few years, become widely fashionable for historians to closely examine the role the North played in continuing to transport kidnapped Africans across the ocean to the New World after the transatlantic slave trade was banned in 1808. But the latest scholarship shows that New York was a crucial hub in the operation. Spanish and Portuguese slave traders set up shop in Manhattan during the first half of the nineteenth century, their numbers growing especially strong after the 1830s, and organized the secret transport of kidnapped people from Africa and the sale of these people to plantation owners in Cuba, other parts of the Caribbean, and the southern United States.

The more focus there has been on New York's connection to the slave trade, the more Taylor's name has popped up thanks to his deep, lifelong connections to the Cuban sugar industry. Even if Taylor, who owned a fleet of six ships and chartered others, did not send any of them to pick up people from Africa and take them to Cuba (and no one knows for sure that he did not: He did import "machinery" from across the Atlantic for Cuban businessmen, and since the slave trade was outlawed, he would not have broadcast the addition of any human cargo to those voyages), the source of his great wealth—he would have been a billionaire in today's dollars—came from his business on that island. In fact, during the height of their operations, he and his son-in-law partner did a fifth of all the sugar trading business between the United States and Cuba. In Cuba, sugar production was booming due to planters' reliance on slave labor to raise and harvest their crops.

Taylor had intimate connections with Cuban sugar merchants that traded enslaved humans, including Drake Brothers, a firm that owned a plantation with four hundred slaves working on it. There is a record of the Drakes having paid $12,000 to a Portuguese agent "with no business in Cuba except the slave trade" that exists only because Moses Taylor preserved it in his personal papers. His son-in-law and partner Percy Pyne, a major benefactor of Princeton University, had even more intricate relationships with Cuban plantation families, going so far as to help wealthy plantation owners' children get jobs that would launch their careers and even advising some on the best marriages to make. In 2019, Princeton did an investigation into Pyne's and Taylor's links to slavery and found that Taylor, from the very start of his career, had "[no] aversion to carrying the produce harvested by the enslaved." One of Taylor's earliest and broadest relationships among the Cuban sugar merchants was with a man named Tomás Terry who got his start buying sick people who were enslaved and reselling them later, Princeton's investigation found.

The reliance by Cuban sugar planters on slaves and the horrific conditions in which the planters kept their enslaved people was no secret, either. According to the Princeton study, one abolitionist described Cuba as "more destructive to human life" than any other place in the world where slavery was still practiced.

It is far from clear, too, that Taylor's involvement in the trans-atlantic slave trade was limited to these secondary interactions with Cuban plantation families. Slave traders went to great lengths to conceal their cargo, their backers, and the payments they made and re-

ceived. No one like Taylor, if he had participated in the outlawed
activities that made up the slave trade, would have kept records to
show it.

There is also plenty of evidence that Taylor was at best a lukewarm supporter of anything remotely linked to anti-slavery causes,
including the Union side of the Civil War. In 1850 he was on a small
committee of wealthy New York businessmen formed to gin up support for the Fugitive Slave Law, part of the Compromise of 1850 that
was supposed to keep the South from seceding from the North by
making anyone who failed to arrest a Black person suspected of having escaped from slavery criminally responsible and subject to fines.
Taylor and these other rich men reasoned that completely outlawing
slavery would cause the collapse of the South, which was a disagreeable thing because it would hurt their financial interests.

Ten years later, in 1860, Taylor participated in a notorious meeting of Wall Street tycoons who gathered in downtown Manhattan, on
Pine Street, to lament the election of Abraham Lincoln and plan a
response that some at the meeting advocated should include getting
New York City to secede from the Union just as the South had done.

Only when it became clear that war could not be avoided did Wall
Street financiers, including Taylor, get together to raise money for the
effort. It seemed less like a conviction and more like a hedging operation. The historian David K. Thomson, who writes about U.S. Treasury bond sales during the Civil War, told me that Taylor's decisions
to underwrite U.S. debt amounted to "reading the political winds" and
were limited.

No one knows what kinds of records Citi might have in its archives that have never been examined by historians. But the bank has
certainly shied away from any mention of Taylor's odious antebellum
activities. In a coffee-table book it produced in 2011 to celebrate its
bicentennial, the bank described Taylor as "a commodities trader."

I asked Citi in 2021 whether this characterization of Taylor still stood. I heard back from Rob Runyan, a Citi spokesman, who summarized the bank's position like this:

In 2005 we conducted a review of our history with the help of an archives consulting company in search of evidence that Citi had historically profited from slavery. This review found no evidence of any business dealings or investments that profited from slavery or insurance on slaves. The research focused on the company's and predecessor companies' direct investments. Recent research conducted by third parties has demonstrated that Moses Taylor, who from 1837–1882 served on the board of City Bank of New York, one of our predecessor companies, had disturbing ties to slavery through other companies he ran. We believe it's important for our company and our country to acknowledge the realities of our collective history and how the ugly institution of slavery has led to various forms of institutionalized racism that still reverberate today, evident in the inequities Black Americans face in so many facets of life. Citi is committed to bringing our expertise to bear in addressing these inequities.

Runyan added that Citi had recently announced an "action" worth $1 billion, "aimed at closing the racial wealth gap in America," which he said was evidence of Citi's commitment.

Other than responding to my questions for this book, however, Citi has made no updates to its public statements about Taylor.

THE COST OF RECENT WRONGS

Most proponents of reparations don't think big companies should be the ones forced to make them. Rather, they think the federal government, via an act of Congress, is the right location for a program. But not everyone has been content to wait for Congress to act. In the summer of 2021, the city of Evanston, Illinois, near Chicago, began distributing payments to Black Evanston residents whose lives have been affected by Evanston's earlier redlining policies. Any Black Evanston resident who has lived in the city since 1969 or who is directly descended from someone who lived there between 1919 and 1969 qualifies for a $25,000 payment that can be used for home repairs or to buy a new home.

Evanston is the first municipality to adopt such a program, and its decision to structure its reparations as a response to its own segregation policies is illuminating. Large companies could focus on their specific wrongs, too. The hurt they caused did not end at the end of slavery. The hurt did not even stop after the Civil Rights Act technically made segregation illegal. It was not limited to a particular city or state or to a particular governing body, but the more responsible parties contributing to the damage, the greater the impact of the effort to repair it would be.

So far, the repairs banks have offered for specific wrongs have been incredibly small. For instance, in 2012, the five largest mortgage loan servicers at the time, JPMorgan, Bank of America, Wells Fargo, Citi, and Ally Financial (formerly called GMAC), agreed to pay a combined $25 billion to state and federal agencies that had been investigating them over their predatory home loan practices in the lead-up to the 2008 financial crisis. The investigation did not focus on the way the banks had exploited Black borrowers, specifically. Instead, they targeted a set of behaviors in which all the banks had engaged that were clearly, on their face, fraudulent, like faking borrowers' signatures on loan documents, ignoring requests for loan modifications, and lying to borrowers about what changes to their loan repayment plans they were really allowed to make.

This was a small subset of what the banks had really done, but it represented an enormous portion of the punishment they received. Only part of the money—albeit the larger share—went to the abused borrowers. The rest of the money had to be divided up between all fifty states as well as the federal government. The agreement obviously cost each bank billions of dollars in the long run, but in their 2012 annual reports they described how they had broken down the expenses associated with the settlement into various segments. Some of the money came from loss reserves they had been building up over years and held hundreds of millions of dollars that were just sitting there, waiting for something like this to happen.

JPMorgan, for instance, recorded expenses in 2012 related to the settlement of around $3.7 billion, but its businesses took in $97 billion for the year and left it with earnings of $21 billion. Citigroup was in worse shape all around. It spent something like $1 billion combined on adhering to the settlement terms that year, and many of its businesses lost money. But the firm still earned $7.5 billion overall. When compared to the idea at the core of the case for reparations—that businesses and the government have been taking everything they can from Black Americans in various ways for centuries—these numbers do not even begin to be responsive.

And that was not its purpose, anyway. The national mortgage settlement agreement forced banks to try to help borrowers who were still hanging on to their homes stabilize themselves and to pay out cash to others. But it had nothing to do with the way the banks had targeted some Black homeowners for refinancings into costlier mortgages or the way they had told other Black borrowers that they qualified only for subprime loans. What would the size of the payouts be if those damages and penalties were calculated? The settlements Wells Fargo reached with cities over its predatory practices were first and foremost concerned with the damages done to those cities in lost economic activity and tax revenue. They were only in the single-digit millions or tens of millions at the most. In the Justice Department's separate $175 million case, which the bank disposed of without ever having to admit wrongdoing, victims of its predatory practices got between $1,000 and $3,500 each if they had been overcharged in mortgage fees and $15,000 each if they had been steered into subprime mortgages when their credit should have justified conventional ones. These figures are pittances that do not account for the snowball effect of a predatory loan on a borrower's life. There was no calculation of the lasting impact on their credit scores or the other areas of their lives that were damaged as their homes slipped away from them.

TWELVE

MAKING PLEDGES

The air was mild on the day in December 2016 that Jesse Van Tol and John Taylor, the two top officials at the National Community Reinvestment Coalition, walked into the headquarters of BancorpSouth, a complex made up of two squat glass towers arranged in a slight V formation with a stone column in between them like a hearty, broadleafed weed jutting out next to the low-slung grid of downtown Tupelo, Mississippi. It had been six months since the bank had agreed to pay more than $10 million to settle the Justice Department's case over its redlining practices in Memphis, in which bank employees had been recorded making racist jokes and Black home buyers had been found to be routinely discouraged from trying to get mortgages.

Van Tol and Taylor were there to meet with BancorpSouth's CEO, James D. "Dan" Rollins III, to talk about what the bank could do to repair its wrongs and increase its activity in minority communities. This could be achieved through a variety of changes, from charitable donations to local community groups to more lending or branch activity in certain neighborhoods and cities. A certain amount of this sort of activity is required by law under the Community Reinvestment Act, which Congress passed in 1977 to try to counteract the forces of redlining. The issue was pressing for both sides of the meeting be-

253

tween the NCRC officials and BancorpSouth because BancorpSouth had just announced it was seeking to merge with two other banks in the region and the NCRC was poised to try to interfere with the mergers by calling regulators' attention back to BancorpSouth's bad behavior and its failure to meet its CRA requirements, and therefore recommending that they not approve the merger transactions.

When an assistant showed Taylor and Van Tol into a conference room, furnished in dark mahogany and astonishingly old-fashioned compared with the building's exterior, they met a surprise. Rollins was there, along with another bank executive Taylor and Van Tol had not expected to see: Alden J. McDonald Jr., the CEO of one of the largest Black-owned banks in the country, Liberty Bank and Trust Company, in New Orleans. His presence carried a huge symbolic weight. There were not many Black-owned banks left in the United States, thanks to a sustained policy by U.S. regulators and bankers of treating these banks with as much disregard, open contempt, and even aggressive hostility as laws of the land allowed in the early years following Emancipation, followed by decades of neglect after the end of the Jim Crow era.

The many debilitating drags on Black-owned banks are described in great detail by the University of California at Irvine law professor Mehrsa Baradaran in her book *The Color of Money: Black Banks and the Racial Wealth Gap*, where she notes that the federal government's unequal treatment of them endured right up to the 2008 financial crisis and its aftermath. Among other things, they were encouraged by regulators to hold outrageously large proportions of preferred shares in the government-sponsored entities Fannie Mae and Freddie Mac, which insured mortgage loans and which had to be taken into conservatorship, wiping out their stockholders, amid the deepening of the 2008 crisis. This destabilized several of the most prominent Black-owned banks. Liberty was one of the few left standing after the crisis,

and in 2016 there was only the slightest beginning of an acknowledgment by the wider public that this was a tragic state of affairs that
should not have come to be. Over the next five years a push would
develop for more investment in Black-owned banks, which included a
#BankBlack campaign on social media and a highly publicized startup
by the Atlanta-based musician Michael Santiago Render, whose stage
name was Killer Mike.

Rollins and McDonald stood up as Van Tol and Taylor entered the
room. Rollins was grinning. He told Taylor and Van Tol that Bancorp-
South had just announced an $8.5 million investment in Liberty Bank.
His message seemed to be: *See? Fixed it.*

("BancorpSouth and Dan Rollins have been very good partners to
Liberty Bank," McDonald told me in an email. He declined to discuss
the matter further.)

The NCRC representatives were not convinced. When Van Tol
and Taylor started to urge Rollins and the other BancorpSouth executives who had joined the meeting to do more, the bank executives
turned to McDonald, looking for support. He surprised them by saying he agreed that they ought to go further, not by investing in his
bank but by increasing—or initiating—their own activities in Black
communities.

The executives' faces drooped as Taylor and Van Tol detailed the
analysis they had done of BancorpSouth's lending in other communities, using records every bank has to publicly disclose about its mortgage lending activities. The NCRC had found that in the areas in
Mississippi, Arkansas, Texas, Alabama, and Louisiana where the bank
had branches, its lending to Black borrowers lagged by double-digit
percentage points compared to its lending to white borrowers. The air
in the room felt heavier and heavier. The bankers said they would have
to think about what else they could do.

BancorpSouth has since become Cadence Bank, thanks to a merger.

It is larger than it was, with $48 billion in assets as of the fall of 2021 and a branch network stretching across the U.S. Southeast and into Texas. Dan Rollins is still its CEO. He ignored my calls and emails seeking comment. His bank's gesture in 2016 was clumsy in the extreme, but it was not wholly unlike what some of the largest banks do whenever they feel the need to project to the public that they are trying to be good and help people. In 2020, after George Floyd was murdered, a slew of big banks announced new programs to combat racial inequality. The numbers attached to the largest banks' pledges were in the billions. They were expected to do a lot of symbolic work. When I asked Citi about Moses Taylor, for instance, its spokesman pointed to "our $1 billion action for racial equity" as "evidence" that Citi was "committed" to trying to fix racial inequality. It was the final word on Citi's admission that one of its founding figures had indeed had "disturbing ties" to slavery. The money was supposed to smooth that over.

But what did these massive pledges mean, exactly?

Big banks' pledges to "commit" money to fix racial inequality are not numbers conjured out of thin air, yet they also do not take the question of how much money is needed to actually solve a problem as a starting point. Instead, to create packages of financial activity that will be presented all bundled up to represent these pledges, the banks heap together a series of business decisions, regulatory obligations, tax write-off opportunities, and charitable donations to come up with as impressive a number as they can, then present it as a singular effort that is wholly driven by a do-gooder impulse.

It's not hard to look beyond those big numbers and see their components for what they really are: pieces of the bank's business. JPMorgan's pledge—the largest one, since it is the country's largest bank—includes making mortgages, small-business loans, and loans to big developers whose plans include affordable housing.

In his position at the NCRC, Van Tol often helps banks create these pledges, always urging them to do more than they initially think they need to. But he did not help with JPMorgan's and therefore felt he could provide an objective analysis of it.

"To be able to pass the bullshit test," he told me, "I look at: Is it one big number without a breakdown of what it's really for? Can you measure the dollars or units? Do you know what time period it's for? When the time period is done, can you go back and verify whether what was committed to it is done? Is it an increase? Is it new money? What is the baseline? Where is the bank starting?"

Of the $210 billion in similar community investment deals Van Tol struck with banks on behalf of the NCRC between 2015 and 2020, he said, each deal raised a bank's activities in poor and non-white neighborhoods by at least 25 percent, sometimes as much as 50 percent.

"When the public sees a big number, they may think that that is philanthropic money, but a major breakdown in a lot of these commitments is: What is debt and what is philanthropy or equity? What is something that's an actual expense for the bank and what is something that they make money doing?"

JPMorgan had come up with a sum of $30 billion for its commitment and had set up a web page that described various components. It would do 40,000 mortgages for Black and Latinx borrowers over five years. The bank's estimate for how much money it would lend out—"To do this, we are committing . . ." is how the website phrased it—was $8 billion. That's $8 billion lent out at a minimum interest rate of around 3 percent—as I write this in the summer of 2021, with mortgage rates at historic lows, 2.78 percent is a fair guess at the lowest rate a top-tier borrower could hope for—plus the fees and other earnings the bank stands to make from its home loans. It would also do $4 billion in mortgage refinancings in an effort to lower interest rates for 20,000 Black and Latinx borrowers as part of the pledge.

There is no question that making mortgage loans, whether they are for people who are buying a house or people who already have a mortgage but want to pay it off and take out a new one with better terms, can be good. But it is not charity. It's business. It's what banks do to make money.

In Van Tol's view, the most relevant question is how much more lending this would amount to than before. JPMorgan's racial equity pledge website did not specify what kind of an increase 40,000 loans over five years would be from its previous lending to those groups.

"It is all incremental—dollars and units," JPMorgan spokeswoman Patricia Wexler said when I asked her what the increase was. "We used the 2019 volume and origination dollars to establish a baseline for what we've lent to Black and Latinx families," she added, explaining that in 2019 interest rates were low enough to spark an increase in home buying, which meant lots of people got new mortgages. "It was among our highest volumes."

Next came a pledge without numbers, time frames, or any specifics: "Amplify education and counseling programs to prepare more Black and Latinx communities for sustainable homeownership."

This carried the implication that the reason many Black people couldn't get mortgages was that they really weren't qualified, that they didn't know how to handle money well enough, that if they were to get a loan and buy a home the situation would not be "sustainable." Focusing on education was something JPMorgan's CEO, Jamie Dimon, had turned to in his frequent public statements diagnosing America's ills. He mentioned it in his annual letter to shareholders a few months after JPMorgan made its pledge. "Many of our inner city schools don't graduate half of their students and often don't give our children an education that leads to a livelihood," he wrote in April of 2021.

"And, shockingly," he added, "life expectancy has gotten worse— particularly for poor and minority communities—nutrition and personal health aren't being taught at enough schools, and obesity, a main driver of diabetes, cancer, stroke, heart disease and depression, has become a national scourge."

When I asked Wexler whether Dimon had really meant that poor and non-white people's health problems were the result of no one having explained to them how to eat healthy foods, she said that what Dimon had really meant was that "access" to healthy foods was lacking.

"Underserved communities often lack access to everyday goods and services such as grocery stores that sell healthy foods or school lunch programs that offer healthy meals for students. JPM has been investing in places like Detroit and elsewhere to provide communities with greater access to the small businesses, neighborhood restaurants and grocery stores that offer healthy options," she said in an email that included a link to a *Fortune* article about JPMorgan's charitable donations and capital infusions in Detroit.

Wexler's response did not explain why Dimon's letter spoke not of access but of education, and she did not offer any further clarification when I asked. But I could see why she wanted to disavow the idea that "nutrition and personal health aren't being taught at enough schools" meant that poor people with health problems simply needed to have proper care of their bodies taught to them by an authority. If Dimon thought that the health problems of the poor could be fixed by simply training them in how they should eat, what foods to prepare, and how to brush their teeth, rather than acknowledging the fact that healthier food costs more and is less available to people in poor neighborhoods where there are few or no grocery stores—just to name one of many barriers they face to staying healthy—just imagine the kinds of financial hardships he'd blame on them.

There is a well-documented tradition of bankers and government officials blaming conditions they have created themselves on the hapless victims of racism. In *Race for Profit*, Keeanga-Yamahtta Taylor described in detail how bankers and government officials claimed that Black people were responsible for the squalid conditions in which they found themselves living thanks to redlining. They had been corralled into overcrowded neighborhoods and buildings, they were forced to pay *higher* rents than white tenants had to pay elsewhere in the same cities, and authorities refused to collect their trash, yet everyone got together and blamed them for the rats that terrorized their families, saying they did not know how to practice good hygiene. Mehrsa Baradaran illustrated something similar in *The Color of Money*. Black-owned banks somehow lacked "education" as well, as if an entire institution were somehow less astute than any other. Specifically, in 2007, the FDIC said it was trying to help Black-owned banks stay afloat by offering "technical assistance" and "training and educational programs" to Black bankers. Now here was JPMorgan saying it would "optimize existing financial education services" and "develop" new ones to bring about "homeowner readiness."

"We do not require people to go through education programs to qualify for a mortgage with us," Wexler informed me in an email. "However, there may be additional financial incentives if they do. For example, customers who qualify for the $5,000 down payment assistance grant can get an additional $500 if they take a first-time home-buyer course."

Another huge chunk of JPMorgan's pledge came from its plans to make construction loans to real estate developers. It would do $14 billion in loans and other capital infusions into projects that included affordable housing units, mostly apartment buildings, with the goal of financing—not creating, but financing, which is a broader activity that can include rehabbing older units—100,000 rentals. With that part of the pledge plus the $12 billion in mortgages, $26 billion of JPMorgan's pledge was instantly also capital that the bank could use to earn money. Loans to developers are quite lucrative for banks on their own, not just because they can be made at higher rates and traded, but also because some projects come with a tax credit designed by the federal government to sweeten the real estate deal and encourage wealthy developers to focus not just on high-end properties but on housing for poor people as well. There is still an overwhelming shortage of affordable housing in major American cities even as developers and banks continue to benefit from this tax credit.

"Win-win," Wexler explained. "It's good for affordable housing and the families that can benefit from it and good for the banks that finance the developers."

Yet another $2 billion in the bank's activity was also for profit. It pledged to do that volume in small-business loans to borrowers with businesses located in neighborhoods where the majority of the population was non-white. As we have seen, Black and Brown business owners do struggle to get bank loans, so this impulse made sense. But in some cities, including Detroit and Baltimore, businesses can lead the way to the gentrification of a neighborhood, a transformation that pushes non-white people away and locks them out of the newly created economic prosperity. A subsection of JPMorgan's business lending plan seemed to address that problem. The bank said it would create a new program that paired "technical assistance" with loans to borrowers without the credit history to qualify for a more conventional arrangement. The program would only be available in certain cities at first; then it would be expanded. The bank provided a list of the cities where it would begin in 2020 and 2021 and added that the education program would start first and the lending would come afterward.

Of JPMorgan's $30 billion pledge, $28 billion was made up of activities that were part of the bank's normal business and were now being counted as specifically good for closing the racial wealth gap. Another $750 million was straightforward business expenses. The bank said it would spend that much hiring minority-owned vendors to do things it could not do in-house.

That added up to almost $29 billion out of the $30 billion total. Almost. What about the other $1.25 billion? This was the margin in which real giving was to be found. The bank said it would give $75 million to community development financial institutions, those frequently not-for-profit organizations that made loans and grants to people who could not get normal ones from a for-profit bank. Another $250 million would be fed into the bank's existing philanthropic program, which made donations to many different charities but would presumably stick to a racial equity theme.

"There are other incremental investments and expenses that get us to, or beyond, the $30 billion commitment," Wexler said. She did not specify what they were, but the website for the bank's racial equity pledge mentioned that the bank would spend more to market its services to non-white people.

This revealed another significant belief: that Black and Brown people simply chose not to do their banking business at JPMorgan's retail bank, Chase, because they were somehow afraid of it. The bank's pledge to expand access to bank accounts for non-white people included a vow to "build awareness and trust in Chase Secure Banking to meet the needs of Black and Latinx unbanked and underbanked households."

"We are building trust and awareness because in some of the communities where there is a large minority presence and where we're trying to grow our customer base, we don't have enough local employees on the ground to establish those important relationships with non-profits and other community partners," Wexler said. "As such, we've hired hundreds of local community relationship advisors and community home lending advisors, many of whom are Spanish speaking in communities where that is the preferred language. Also, we've significantly increased our marketing spend in order to reach more customers in minority tracts across the country."

Research has shown, though, that trust is not the only major reason many poor people and a disproportionately large number of nonwhite Americans don't have bank accounts. Rather than fear, a keen understanding of the reliability of check cashing services, which charge fixed fees, as opposed to banks—which often surprise their customers with unpredictable service and overdraft fees (Chase says customers have the option to open an account that never charges overdraft fees)— often drives low-income people away from traditional banks.

Whether JPMorgan's activity would help close the racial wealth gap could only be determined in hindsight, once it was analyzed and compared with what they had been doing before. In October of 2021, a year after announcing the pledge, the bank released a high-level summary of its progress, reporting that it had already completed $13 billion of activity that counted toward its $30 billion goal. The report was fairly light on details; it touted the bank's $4 billion in mortgage refinancings as well as an expansion of its home buyer grant program. But Van Tol wanted to emphasize to me that we were looking at something comparatively good. JPMorgan, with its size, its willingness to specify *any numbers at all*, and its intended increase in philanthropic activity, was essentially the best of the best.

THIRTEEN

WHAT WALL STREET
SHOULD DO

Early on in my work on this book, in preparation for describing the model the Yale professor Roderick Ferguson laid out in his book *The Reorder of Things* to show how companies cannibalize minorities' demands for equal treatment and recognition, I got on a Zoom call with him. He has argued that capitalism itself may not survive a true effort to achieve equality among people. In his essay "On the Postracial Question," Ferguson quotes the founder of the Black Panther Party, Huey Newton, to establish a formula for the legitimate process of building equality: "We realize that this country became very rich upon slavery and that slavery is capitalism in the extreme. We have two evils to fight, capitalism and racism. We must destroy both racism and capitalism," Newton said.

Ferguson explains in the essay: "As a political organization, the Black Panther Party encouraged analyses that sought to illuminate the links between the histories of capitalism and the histories of racial exploitation." He seems to be saying that capitalism must be put on trial as part of any true reckoning with racism because its functioning has rested for centuries on the exploitation of certain groups. And he might be right.

"But I'm writing a book about banks," I told him. "Part of what I want to do in the book is make concrete suggestions for things that big financial companies can actually do to change things. The way you just phrased it, is there any capitalist system that would be able to actually accommodate this change and make it real?"

I asked, knowing that the most obvious answer was no, but Ferguson had a more interesting reply.

"You are trying to reach big banks," he said. "There are basic things that they could do that would be an improvement. Like stop discriminating against folks in loans. That's meaningful and deep, too. It's meaningful because it hasn't actually been done."

Representation alone isn't enough, either, Ferguson said. But it's a start. Just like lending hasn't been made fair, equal representation has not been brought about. "Hire more Black people," he said with a smile.

It's that simple. While reflecting on our conversation later, I realized that Ferguson himself has not completely abandoned the system he critiques in his work. The whole time he was dissecting universities' appropriation of movements to recognize minority difference, he was working for universities. His book is dedicated to the "memory of the FOCI (the Faculty of Color Initiative)," a movement at the University of Minnesota to increase the number of non-white faculty members there. He has worked "in" the system, too, and he continues to do so. His work and efforts show that there is no reason to throw up one's hands in the face of this problem. The beginnings of such a solution are simple enough. There are basic changes that have not been adequately made.

There are also things banks can do that fall into the realm of big ideas yet stop short of a wholesale critique of capitalism, like supporting the push for reparations.

There has been a concerted effort to convince Congress to create a new program to repay the descendants of slaves for the centuries of labor that the United States and its predecessor colonies stole from their ancestors. As I learned about the history of activists' efforts to get banks to acknowledge their connections to slavery, I began to wonder why none of the proponents of the latest reparations plan, which would call for a multitrillion-dollar program to distribute funds to Black Americans, were trying to get companies to participate alongside the federal government. So I asked one of the architects of the plan, Duke University professor William A. Darity Jr., what he thought banks could do to pitch in on the effort.

Darity's view is that the amount of money required to pay reparations is too large for the private sector to handle. And in light of the previous failures to use the courts to hold companies accountable for their links to slavery, it is not worth trying to get them to contribute. Furthermore, much of what they did before the Civil War was perfectly legal, so the responsibility really lies with the government that presided over the atrocities.

But that does not mean banks can't play an important role in the reparations movement, according to Darity. In his view, the most effective way for them to help the cause would be to use their considerable lobbying power in Washington to get reparations legislation enacted into law.

"That would be a terrific boost for the effort," he told me, adding that banks had a great deal more than their links to slavery for which they ought to make amends.

"The banks have an atrocious history beyond the period of slavery and quite dramatically in the context of the public-private partnership that established redlining," he said. "Another issue that needs to be examined is the banks' complicity in preserving discriminatory practices—practices that endure to this day. That's something else that needs to be put on the ledger. A number of these major banks find their origins in slavery and the slave trade, but the array of harms that they have inflicted on Black folks stretches far beyond the period of slavery."

From the post–Civil War period until now, banks have participated in the oppression of Black Americans. Yet, far from requiring them to do penance for an almost incalculable harm, Darity's idea would see them contributing to a specific lobbying effort that could fit into their already established operations in Washington.

Lobbying in favor of reparations could also be economically sound for the banks. If Black people had more money in general, they might do more banking business, more borrowing, more investing. They might be more lucrative customers. Talk about a win-win.

Supporting reparations could also help shift the general tone of discussions among elected officials toward a stronger consensus in general on what is needed to bring about racial justice. If banks supported reparations, the idea of congressional committees explicitly focusing on diversity in the U.S. private sector might not seem so alien. And the politicians who scorn calls for racial equity might feel a little lonelier than they do right now.

Having outwardly oriented positions in support of reparations could also go a long way toward helping financial firms change their internal cultures. Lower and middle managers, knowing that their institution's position was that the United States needed to right the wrongs it had done to Black people, would have more exposure to the general outlines of the wrongs perpetrated against them in the first place, the thousands of assaults on their liberties and opportunities for prosperity that have led to today's giant racial wealth gap. And, yes, they would be more likely to be aware of the racial wealth gap.

CHANGE COMES FROM WITHIN

American CEOs love to boast about how they can change the world. In early 2018, JPMorgan Chase CEO Jamie Dimon, Amazon CEO Jeff

Bezos, and the billionaire investor and Berkshire Hathaway founder Warren Buffett declared that they were teaming up to fix the American healthcare system. They would start by designing new healthcare delivery methods for their own employees, who together numbered more than a million people, and then scale up whichever new ideas proved successful so that all Americans could access them.

News coverage of the announcement suggested that lots of people really believed that these three men's initiative, which had yet to be named and which had no full-time leader and no specific plan of action, could have been the start of a revolution in healthcare. "Tuesday's announcement landed like a thunderclap," my *Times* colleagues wrote, citing an anonymous source who claimed that Buffett, in particular, believed that "the condition of the country's health care system is a root cause of economic inequality."

In January of 2021, three years after launching the project, JPMorgan, Amazon, and Berkshire Hathaway pulled the plug on it. It turned out that disrupting healthcare was hard! There were pesky roadblocks, like patient privacy laws and data-sharing restrictions. And there were even more basic difficulties, like finding top executives to devote their full attention to the joint effort and coming up with ideas for what to do to start the process of real change.

Despite its failure, the three big companies' collaboration demonstrated how American CEOs could wield power that extended far beyond the bounds of their day jobs. Millions of people appeared receptive to their influence. Imagine if this raw power were directed toward supporting reparations.

Imagine a big bank like JPMorgan redesigning its internal messaging so that all its employees knew where it stood on reparations and how forcefully it was willing to back up that position. This could transform individual employees' understanding of the historical and current barriers Black Americans confront every day. More than any set of gussied-up business goals packaged as a racial equality pledge, a company's embrace of reparations would orient its internal culture toward a better understanding of the history of slavery and racism in America. If banks and other financial firms had to spell out their support for a federally funded reparations program and defend their positions on it to hostile politicians and customers, other changes would naturally follow. Individual employees would get the message that the dominant values of their institutions included a commitment to racial justice based on an acknowledgment of how bad things really were in the past and how bad they still are. No more easy-to-ignore lip service. This could help improve day-to-day conditions for Black employees and customers. And it would radiate outward into American society, potentially reducing hysterical reactions to various scholars' and schoolteachers' attempts to teach a more accurate history of the United States and its treatment of Black people.

Yes, I'm talking about critical race theory. No, it's not some wild abomination of the facts of history. It's simply an explanation of how Black people were and are exploited in America and how that exploitation has been doggedly glossed over in the public narrative of the country's history. As the Harvard Kennedy School professor Khalil Gibran Muhammad put it, "The point is to socialize the basic idea that structural racism is not a fantasy of some cabal of radical academics."

Muhammad is not a stranger on Wall Street. He has visited banks like Goldman Sachs and Citigroup and delivered a much-polished lecture he created that gives a rundown of what could be called critical race theory. In a virtual appearance in July of 2020 as part of Goldman's lecture series "Talks at GS," for example, Muhammad described his research on how modern-day policing, characterized by ruthless treatment of Black people across the United States, had its roots in slavery, when law enforcement's main role was to protect production centers—plantations and industrial operations—from destruction by workers, including slave laborers. (Destruction could include escapes by those captive slaves, which would cause the production center to cease functioning.) Muhammad pointed out that the Thirteenth Amendment to the U.S. Constitution, which supposedly abolished slavery, allowed for a big exception: People could still be forced to do slave labor as punishment for a crime. This offered white capitalists a new way to maintain control over Black former slaves. By criminalizing a wide range of their everyday behaviors, from voting to owning land, they could keep some of the free labor they felt they needed. This in turn laid the groundwork for the mass incarceration of Black people that has continued in the United States up to the present time, as detailed in landmark work by scholars like Muhammad and Michelle Alexander, the author of *The New Jim Crow: Mass Incarceration in the Age of Colorblindness.*

Why is something like this important for bankers to understand? Because it shows how easily the origins of a present condition—in this case the massively lopsided demographics of U.S. prison populations—can be obscured or erased, with an alternative explanation, a false one, cropping up in its place.

This happens in the financial industry.

In March of 2021, a group of academics, regulators, and bankers dialed into a publicly broadcast Zoom call that was part of a series of discussions on racism in the economy arranged by leaders of the regional Federal Reserve banks. The day's topic was racism in housing. Scholars presented their work on the history of redlining and housing discrimination in the United States. Keeanga-Yamahtta Taylor was among them. Policy advocates proposed ideas for how to reverse some of the wrongs, including the persistent bias in home appraisals that research shows consistently leaves Black homeowners with less equity in their homes than white homeowners.

One of the participants was Bill Rogers, then the president and chief operating officer of a large regional bank, Truist. When Rogers (who later became Truist's CEO) was asked by a moderator to give his feedback on the proposal for overhauling home appraisals, he first praised the researchers generally, then trotted out a familiar financial industry talking point warning against overcorrecting for a problem. "My little note of caution, though, is: Let's not have unintended consequences with the appraisal process," he said. "Because we don't want the standards to become too loose. We saw what the impact of that was in 2006 and 2008, and those communities that we want to most help were the most negatively impacted by that."

Rogers was suggesting that the tidal wave of home foreclosures leading up to the 2008 financial crisis could be traced back to overly liberal mortgage lending caused by recklessly high home appraisals.

Taylor was having none of this. "The one thing that I would say, specifically, that Bill Rogers brought up, with the 2008 crisis and creating a link between loose or more liberal appraising and that crisis: I really reject that logic," she said.

"Black people, Black families—in 2005, 2006, 2007—were targeted by banks. This was not a question of a loosening of the rules and regulations. Black families were targeted with what some people described as 'ghetto loans for mud people,'" Taylor continued, referring to evidence that emerged in Baltimore's lawsuit against Wells Fargo, when loan officers used this description. "And then when the investigations and stories about why the subprime lending crisis was centered in Black communities came out, we realized that this was pervasive across the industry, targeting Black people so that in Chicago Black families that had six-figure incomes were more likely to receive a predatory loan than white families making $35,000 a year. We can't actually get beyond this crisis if we fail to come to grips with how we got here in the first place."

Bankers are so used to warning about "unintended consequences" and so quick to put forth explanations for crises in their industry like the one Bill Rogers offered, it's almost a reflex. And they're rarely if ever in a setting where they risk getting pushback like Taylor's. Usually these kinds of comments from bankers become the final word.

What's more, Wall Street's general worker population has recently shown resistance to ideas like the ones Muhammad, Taylor, and Alexander have shared about why such a huge disparity exists between Black and white prosperity in America. This became clear when one financial firm, American Express, tried to go just a step further than its peers in starting an internal discussion on the history of the United States' exploitation of Black people and the things individual employees could do to try to be fairer and more empathetic to their colleagues and to customers.

American Express's top leaders had invited Muhammad in early 2020—before George Floyd's murder made this sort of talk fashionable—to speak to them about his work detailing the foundational role that slavery and, later, the exploitation of Black Americans had played in developing the U.S. economy. It was not an out-of-the-ordinary experience for Muhammad, except for one thing: American Express hadn't asked him to give the talk to an auditorium full of employees who were voluntarily attending. Its executive committee—the top layer of its management, including its CEO, its general counsel, its chief financial officer, and a dozen or so top leaders—had specifically gathered in a private conference room to listen to Muhammad's lecture. The firm's chief diversity officer, Sonia Cargan, conferenced herself into the meeting from her office in London. These executives were *serious*. And they were impressed. Muhammad's visit, just before the coronavirus pandemic shut down in-person gatherings, was only the beginning of his engagement with American Express. As a result of what they learned from listening to him, the heads of three of the giant company's business lines invited Muhammad to return and give lectures to their employees separately.

No one was forced to attend or view these wider lectures, but the big bosses wanted to lead by example, so they expressed plenty of enthusiasm about Muhammad's appearances and his ideas. Each time he spoke to a group of American Express employees, Muhammad shared material that he had been talking about for years in his Harvard University lectures, his books, other public speeches. He described how redlining worked, how it kept Black communities in a state of instability and distress and poverty that justified further mistreatment of them by white authorities and businesses. He talked about the backlash in the South right after the Civil War ended that saw white farmers and plantation owners demolish attempts by Black leaders and workers to influence local politics and participate in the American economy on equal footing.

"In terms of the actual content, it's the same because the history doesn't change," Muhammad later explained on a podcast he cohosts in which he recounted what happened next.

In August of 2021, more than a year after Muhammad began giving lectures to American Express employees, an opinion piece appeared in the *New York Post* with the headline: "Lie of Credit—American Express Tells Its Workers Capitalism Is Racist."

The author of the piece claimed that American Express wanted its employees to "abandon capitalism" and wanted white employees specifically to feel guilty over their long-standing privilege. He quoted from anti-bias training materials a disgruntled employee had allegedly leaked, with slides explaining concepts like microaggressions. The *Post* author described these as part of the company's "race-based regulation."

It was all supposed to sound horrible and shocking, but the anti-bias training materials stood out to me as the best and most detailed attempt to explain how to be less racist that I had come across at a financial company. For instance, one slide offered an incredibly simple explanation of why it was problematic to embrace the idea that American society had achieved equality and that programs to protect Black people and other minorities from ongoing discrimination were unnecessary. According to the *Post*, the slide said that it was hurtful to say "I don't see color" or "Everyone can succeed in this society if they work hard enough." The *Post* author took it for granted that readers would be scandalized by this.

After the *Post* story came out, I did a little digging and got to see some of those materials myself. I saw that, in addition to advising against telling a Black person that all anyone needed to do to succeed was work hard, that same slide also contained an explanation for what the claim signified: "belief in the myth of meritocracy or that people of color are given extra unfair benefits because of their race, are lazy, incompetent, and need to work harder." The explanation about why it was bad to say "I don't see color" noted that, to a hearer, this would be a way of denying the hearer's experience—denying that there were any "barriers faced because of their race/ethnicity."

My reaction was: *Yes! This is all true! And more people need to understand this if the financial industry is truly going to start treating Black people equally.*

American Express was doing things right, but the *Post* article, made possible by an employee who thought anti-racism training had no place there, caused a scandal.

"This isn't even about one company," Muhammad said on his podcast, noting that the *Post* author had sought and identified other companies where Muhammad had lectured and had called them out, too. Muhammad began receiving death threats.

Corporate America has a long way to go.

FOURTEEN

ON THEIR OWN

Some of the people I met while working on this book decided to try to take their destinies out of the hands of large institutions. Their paths to independence were not easy. Black entrepreneurs struggle in bizarre ways to avoid getting snagged by bias in places that might offer funding. Even after they become their own bosses and start their own companies, they find their success depends on benevolence fickly displayed by white investors and incubator directors. White people still play powerful roles as the arbiters of their success.

MARCEAU'S STORY

It was supposed to be a working brunch.

Marceau Michel and his business partner, Himalaya Rao-Potlapally, had agreed to visit two would-be investors in October of 2020 for the fund they had just launched, one that would make early-stage capital infusions into startups owned by Black entrepreneurs. Their new venture capital firm, Black Founders Matter, was Marceau's idea, born from his own strife.

Just three years earlier he had developed a tech startup idea, a company called Werkhorse that was designed to connect skilled workers with businesses needing temporary contractors. It was a concept that was good enough to win awards in the competitive world of startups, as well as a coveted spot in an incubator in Portland, Oregon, where Marceau was living. But each time he tried to raise money to implement his business plan, Marceau was stymied. He suspected it had something to do with the fact that he was a young Black man. The white men he was pitching to kept rejecting him, sending him away from meetings empty-handed, with only vague directives to gather more evidence that his idea would actually work, to show them more proof that it would make a good investment. It happened over and over and over again, until Marceau was ready to give up.

Marceau's mentors at the incubator knew that something wasn't right, but they couldn't figure out how to help him. They watched as he struggled to find backing for Werkhorse, growing so frustrated that he eventually made a T-shirt bearing the phrase "Black Founders Matter." At first, he had no intention of reproducing the design, but as he wore it around Portland and then made one for a friend to wear to a tech conference in San Francisco, people started to ask where they could get their own "Black Founders Matter" T-shirts. Marceau set up an e-commerce site to let anyone who wanted a shirt order one as needed. Then he stopped thinking about the thing.

But the shirts took off on their own. The automated sales and production system Marceau had set up meant that there was no limit to the number of shirts people could order, and soon he had done more than $10,000 in sales. The "Black Founders Matter" T-shirts had attracted his mentors' notice. Lightbulb! Why not steer Marceau into a venture capital career? they thought. Why not encourage him to start his own fund?

One of the incubator's founders negotiated for Marceau a six-month residency at a Portland-based venture capital firm so he could learn the ropes. He was the only Black employee, and while the white and mostly male team initially embraced him and looped him in on deal activity while giving him space to come up with his own invest-ment ideas, his experience there soon soured, too. He tagged along with his colleagues to an after-work happy hour and suddenly found himself with a coworker who was snorting cocaine. When the co-worker offered him some and he declined, citing a big day at work the next day, the coworker turned icy. Marceau felt like the rest of the team shut him out, too, after that, and the managing partner sug-gested he leave the company early. He refused.

Despite the bitterness that infused the rest of his time at the ven-ture capital fund, Marceau absorbed everything he could about the business and then, with Himalaya's help, launched his fund. The two partners found quick success. Almost immediately, they raised $1 mil-lion to invest in a company called A Kids Book About, an online pub-lishing company that specialized in creating books for kids that gave parents a way to frame difficult discussions, such as talks about race, gender, and other social issues. (Its founder was a Black man.) The pair next set their sights on a $10 million fund and quickly began attract-ing buy-ins from public pensions and eager investors against the back-drop of the #BlackLivesMatter protests in 2020.

So Marceau had been through quite a lot already by the time, in the fall of 2020, he found himself standing in the lobby of a swanky Portland apartment building, waiting to be sent up to one of the building's spacious condos. The condo's owners, a husband and wife, had gushed about Black Founders Matter, promising to invest some of their own money in the company's first fund and offering to introduce Marceau and Himalaya to more well-heeled Portland denizens. Their proposal: that Marceau and Himalaya attend a brunch at their house to let them make the introductions.

Marceau's journey into the world of high finance had been long and unpredictable. Born in Queens to Haitian immigrants who were Jehovah's Witnesses, he had lived a sheltered middle-class childhood in New York. His family moved to Brooklyn and was deeply involved in church activities; Marceau did not drink or smoke or do drugs, and for a long time he could not admit, not even to himself, that he was gay. But in his early twenties he threw off the yoke of his family's expectations. He realized that to really have the space to be who he wanted to be, he'd have to leave Brooklyn. He headed west. He came out to his friends and started to live the life he felt was the best expression of his true identity, the energetic man with the brilliant smile and the uncanny ability to draw listeners to his bosom as though they were old friends and not strangers. Along the way, he'd come to realize more and more what he liked and did not like. He did not want to eat meat anymore; he became a vegetarian. He sampled the drugs everyone else was doing and found that weed was okay, but he never wanted to depend on it.

He seemed like a model of confidence and positive energy. Talking to him was its own source of succor. But the morning of the brunch, Marceau was not feeling energized and happy. As he looked at his reflection in the dark glass of the glossy elevator on the way to the investors' apartment, he was feeling small and afraid. Nervous. Eager to please.

He went down a long, dark hallway, tapping on a heavy white door. The door swung open.

A small party was already in full swing. Himalaya, the "numbers" half of Black Founders Matter, the right brain to Marceau's creative left, had arrived with her wife a few minutes earlier and both were mingling with the other guests, mimosas in their hands. The hosts' apartment was a cavernous space with fifteen-foot windows, sleek, yet somehow a little unnerving. Beyond the living room, the doors to a broad balcony were open and a table was lavishly set, dotted with bottles of wine.

The host, in jeans and with an apron tied around his waist, darted from guest to guest making sure their drinks were topped off. The hostess, dressed in black, was making introductions and laughing excitedly.

This was the first in-person fundraising opportunity Marceau and Himalaya had had since the coronavirus pandemic began, and they were determined to be perfectly charming. There were two couples there, the potential investors the hosts had promised to present to Marceau and Himalaya, along with a single woman whom the couple introduced as a close friend. Marceau unleashed his energy into the group while Himalaya and her wife, both shy by nature, felt themselves growing more relaxed and also more eager to please.

After another round of drinks, the party sat down to eat on the balcony. There was no sign of bagels or fruit, jam, cream cheese, pastries, toast, eggs, tomatoes, or any other typical brunch dishes. Instead, when Marceau and Himalaya and her wife sat down, they were served the only thing that their hosts had prepared: coq au vin.

It was an embarrassing mix-up on both sides. Marceau, Himalaya, and her wife were all vegetarians. The hostess had asked them about dietary restrictions when she'd extended the invitation, but Himalaya was used to solving her own food riddles no matter what was put in front of her, and she had wrongly guessed she'd be able to get by on whatever side dishes were on the menu. As it turned out, the only side dish that day was polenta made with dairy, also a no-go. The hostess was clearly pained, and apologized again and again. That was when Himalaya's wife raised her wineglass.

"It's true that we don't normally eat meat," she said, "but we do eat meals prepared with love, and it is so clear that this food was prepared with love. Thank you so much for welcoming us into your home." She toasted the host couple, and a sigh of relief passed around the table as the guests lifted their glasses and drank. The meal began.

Marceau, Himalaya, and Himalaya's wife each had seats among

the other guests, and they conducted their own conversations. Himalaya's wife chatted with the hostess while Himalaya focused on the couple closest to her. Marceau was at the other end of the table, laying out his vision for Black Founders Matter to the guests nearest to him. Over the course of the meal, Himalaya and her wife both had talks with the single woman at the brunch as well. From the start, the host couple had made it clear that she was not a potential investor. Now she shared more about her life with Himalaya and her wife, explaining that at times when she had had no home of her own she had actually lived with the host couple. The three of them were very close. *Extremely* close.

Overall, the meal seemed to be going well, and Himalaya thought privately what a relief it was to be among such nonthreatening people. There were no men at the brunch who acted like it was their right to touch her or lower their voices and proposition her or engage in any of the numerous forms of bad behavior to which she had been subjected while trying to raise money from rich people who were mostly white and who appeared to see Himalaya as an object available for their taking. Sure, it was tough to eat the prepared meal, but there had certainly been worse things to endure at other wealthy investors' homes, and Himalaya felt sorry for not being more up front about her dietary choices.

At the other end of the table, Marceau couldn't eat any more. He saw Himalaya get up. Softly, she asked for directions to the bathroom. She was gone for several minutes. Her wife went next. Marceau knew that the food was making them sick. His own stomach started to rumble, perhaps in sympathy, perhaps because of his own hiatus from meat. But he forced himself to stay positive.

Things actually appeared to be going okay from his perspective, despite the weird food and the stark décor. The hosts were wildly enthusiastic about Black Founders Matter, and their excitement appeared to be catching. It was midafternoon by the time everybody got up from the table, and the host couple began to clear things away. Himalaya's wife jumped in to help, first carrying plates to the kitchen out of sight, then helping disassemble the extending leaves that made up the long dining table and carrying the chairs back in from the balcony. The champagne and wine had made her heady with energy and goodwill.

Soon after that, Himalaya and her wife began saying their good-byes; they had a flight to catch, to Minneapolis, their home base. As they gathered their things and waited for an Uber to the airport, the host couple begged Marceau to stay a little longer, and he relented. He sat down on one end of the long white couch, trying to relax his agitated digestive system.

Someone pulled out a joint and started passing it around. Marceau took a couple of pulls. The hostess came and sat by him and started a new conversation. World affairs, the philosophy of governance. Heady stuff, and the pot was getting to him, but he was feeling all right.

Marceau noticed suddenly that the host had changed his clothes. His apron was gone. His jeans were gone. He was now wearing pajamas.

The single female guest walked into the living room from wherever she had been and Marceau saw that she, too, was now in some kind of nightclothes. She sat down at the host's feet and he began massaging her shoulders, caressing her hair. Marceau began to feel alarmed. He looked at the hostess. She was in the middle of a point that he didn't want to interrupt. But not long after that she asked whether it wouldn't be better if Marceau were to spend the night. The host jumped up and ducked out of the room again, returning seconds later holding another pair of pajamas. "These are for you," he said to Marceau. "It's too late to go home now. Just stay over—we even have a toothbrush for you."

It was barely six o'clock, barely dark outside.

Marceau jumped up.

These people were trying to have *sex* with him!

"I have to go," he said. "I'm gonna go."

"Don't go!" the host said.

"Don't leave yet!" said the hostess.

Marceau did not even wait to call an Uber. Trying to keep a smile on his face, trying to keep up some warmth, he peeled himself from their grasps and fled to the elevator. He learned a few weeks later that they had scrapped their plans to invest in Black Founders Matter.

• • •

Marceau came away from the sex-adjacent brunch feeling exploited and wondering whether the couple would have tried the same thing with a white venture capitalist.

His fund was built as a rejection of the discriminatory treatment he had experienced, but there seemed to be no end to the string of incidents in his professional life in which white people abused their power over him and reminded him of how he still lacked his own. But if his encounter at the Portland sex pad had potentially little to do with race, the next incident, which occurred just a few weeks later, seemed more centered on it. A white venture capitalist running a VC incubator appeared to be offering a helping hand to minorities, but little help was forthcoming. In fact, when I came on the scene months later to examine what had happened, after the dust had settled, the head of the incubator said that Marceau and I had, on top of everything else, misunderstood the intention of the incubator. It was not to give minorities a helping hand, he explained.

Here's the story: Marceau and his team had applied for and been admitted into a new venture capital fund accelerator program called VC Lab, which had set itself the goal in 2021 of launching 1,000 new

VC firms in the following five years, because, as its backers put it on the lab's home page, "we believe the venture capital industry needs more diversity and more innovation." This statement was what led Marceau and his team, as well as me, an observer, to believe that VC Lab was supposed to be a place where minority-owned VC firms might expect some special attention.

The program was supposed to last sixteen weeks and would be conducted entirely virtually. The groups admitted to it would collaborate on regular projects directed by its leaders and reviewed and graded by a combination of teachers and peers. Black Founders Matter was already up and running, but Marceau and Himalaya felt they could use all the networking opportunities they could get. Just being accepted into the accelerator was another accolade they could boast about to potential investors: "another logo we could add to our pitchbook," as Marceau put it. Plus, at the end of the program, there would be a "demo day" during which all the groups who had completed the sixteen-week course would get to present their funds to a captive audience, offering yet another opportunity to meet new investors.

The first thing Marceau noticed, after he and his team joined the accelerator, was that VC Lab was not 100 percent free. Even before they had delivered the first lecture session, the lab's leaders blasted out messages to the class offering "office hours" when team members could have one-on-one discussions with them for an "upgrade," meaning the groups would have to pay a fee to access them. Marceau had not anticipated these costs, but he reminded himself that having the VC Lab name on his fund's résumé and getting to the demo day at the end made the rest of the experience worthwhile. Plus, the weekly group assignments were interesting. They took time; Marceau estimated it was about a ten-to-fifteen-hour commitment per week, although when I spoke with VC Lab's creator, Adeo Ressi, he said the time commitment was more like thirty hours a week. The feedback was helpful, Marceau thought. The lab's leaders broke the big class down into groups comprising several funds each. The group members collaborated on each project, and the lab's teachers then rated the groups—rather than the individual funds—on a scale of 1 to 5. Marceau's group got the second-highest rating in the class after the first week's project, a 4. The highest rating that week was a 4.5.

Things did not go smoothly for long. During the second week's assignment, VC Lab's administrators blasted an email offering anyone in the class who wanted it an extension on the project deadline for the week. To accept the extension, just respond to the email, the leaders said. It was not clear why anyone particularly needed extra time, but most people, when offered, accepted it. One of the Black Founders Matter associates replied that the group would take the extension. Marceau also responded to the email and confirmed that his team would take the extra time that was offered. But Himalaya, his partner, did not respond at all. She assumed that since Marceau and the associate had each sent their own messages on behalf of the group, she would be covered. Later that day, Adeo, who is also the CEO of VC Lab's parent organization, the Founder Institute, emailed Himalaya and the other members of the class who had not responded to the deadline extension offer, warning them that anyone with incomplete work would be kicked out of the program. But Himalaya still thought that the deadline extension requests her colleagues had sent in would cover her.

They did not. Adeo emailed her the following day to tell her she was being expelled from the program for failing to turn in her assignment.

The Black Founders Matter team was stunned. Marceau's associate, Jordan Leopold, replied to Adeo, asking him to reconsider. Adeo responded by asking for more information on what went wrong. He did not say whether Himalaya could be reinstated. "What are your roles? Who is doing the work? Why did this communication breakdown happen?" he asked. He suggested that the other Black Founders Matter participants were on the verge of getting kicked out, too.

"My team also advised me to drop everyone, but I would like a little more data before making any decisions," he said.

By now, Marceau was fed up. He replied to Adeo himself and explained that Himalaya had thought that the team's extension request covered her. They were all learning a great deal and would be sad to leave, but if Adeo stuck to his position about Himalaya, they would all withdraw. "So many of us non-white professionals are constantly rejected and disposed of by the very same allies that have the intention of creating more opportunity and equity. I hope that is not the case here," he added.

That did not go over well. "Marceau," Adeo replied, "you are behind. The work has been mediocre, according to the team. Building a new VC firm is hard, so you must do the work, individually and together."

He added that he would consider letting Himalaya back in, but only if the group's next project proved exceptionally good.

"If the work is not among the best that I have seen in the program, then you can reapply for the July program," he wrote.

Marceau decided he would no longer put up with this particular white VC executive's treatment of him. His response nuked the team's chances at using VC Lab to promote their fund, but to him it was worthwhile. He was finally going to take a stand against the actual power structure that had, in so many specific forms, lorded over him and kept him down.

"Unfortunately, I don't accept ultimatums from power hungry white men using Diversity Equity Inclusion to continue to gatekeep and demean," he wrote in an email to Adeo.

He and his team were pulling out of the program "due to your poor leadership and lack of cultural competency," he said.

"Trying to make an example out of my Asian American Female business partner truly shows how little you value actual inclusion and cultural sensitivity. Followed by now threatening us and holding our work product to unreasonable standards in an act of retaliation, while assuming failure, is embarrassing and deeply unethical. I suggest that you and your team seek out DEI Training before your next cohort and make the mandatory improvements."

When I asked Adeo for his version of what happened, he denied that his decision had anything to do with race and said that VC Lab's administrators felt they needed to be strict.

"Starting a venture capital fund is challenging, and so it is not uncommon for participants to fall behind, especially with COVID illness and restrictions," he said. "VC Lab is designed to help talented and motivated people start world-class venture capital firms all around the world."

But why the nuclear response? I asked. And what about giving minority-owned funds an extra bit of help? Wasn't that part of VC Lab's mandate?

"VC Lab is not designed to give any race or gender special treatment," Adeo told me, explaining that I was mistaken in thinking its intention was to give minorities an extra boost. "The program is designed to give everyone equal and fair help to create a venture capital firm, regardless of race and gender."

Marceau and I had known each other for almost nine months when he shared this with me. Over the course of our conversations, he told me about the cocaine incident at the Portland VC fund but asked me at first not to write about it. He agonized over whether to let me describe the predatory investors' surprise sex party brunch. He finally decided that, whatever the consequences, he wanted to share these things with me, and I could feel, even over the phone, what a relief it was for him to share these experiences. He had been through so much already, but finally speaking out about it was animating him in a new way. Going public was its own source of power.

"I would rather go down speaking my truth than silently existing and being abused at every turn," he told me. He said that whatever the specifics of his work had been, a major part of his job had felt like it was all about "keeping your dignity and respect but not shattering white fragility in the process."

FROM BANKER TO STARTUP FOUNDER

Some of the people I first met because they were experiencing discrimination are now, through their own next steps, demonstrating ways victims of racism and bias can carve a path for themselves. Their examples might not work for everyone, but they offer some insight into what is possible when simply trying to go along with the flow of things, trying to work around the obstacles created by widespread racism, no longer works.

Kayode Odeleye knew he had to prepare for life after Standard Chartered. Before he quit, when he knew there was no way he would win in the struggle he was having with his racist boss, he began taking courses through an executive education program offered by the Massachusetts Institute of Technology. He earned business development certificates from MIT and began brainstorming ideas for his own company. At the beginning of 2021 he went to work creating a new technology company that would automate certain investment banking services and compete with big banks like Standard Chartered by offering companies a lower-cost option for putting together funding packages using automation. The global economy doesn't need as many investment bankers as it has right now, Kayode told me.

"You have all these guys running around, making millions of dollars doing nothing; they will be out of a job," he said as he described the company he was building.

His experience at Standard Chartered still haunts him. One evening in the spring of 2021 he read an opinion column in the *New York Times* by Ifeoma Ozoma, a former lobbyist for the social media platform Pinterest, describing how she suffered when, after filing a wage discrimination complaint against the company, she was forced to leave and, on the way out the door, required to sign a nondisclosure agreement that would prevent her from talking about the discrimination she had experienced there.

"For a long time, I hesitated to speak about the issues I experienced at Pinterest. I didn't want to be sued, and I hoped that the company would do the right thing and address the pay inequities and retaliation I faced. But it didn't," Ozoma wrote, arguing that companies should be barred from pressuring employees to stay silent about these sorts of behaviors.

The piece touched Kayode deeply. That night he lay in bed wide-awake, going over the details of what he had been through at Standard Chartered and mapping out a blog post he wanted to write about it, to get the word out. "I couldn't sleep," he told me in an email the next morning in which he described a powerful urge to talk about everything openly, to make sure that the bank couldn't bury it, that they didn't forget about him. Speaking publicly would also be a way for him to expel the trauma of the experience from his everyday life—to let other people help him deal with it so that he did not have to face the memories every day alone. As he put it: "I have been thinking of drawing a line and putting this whole torture behind me."

BECOMING AN ACTIVIST

Ricardo Peters is barred by the terms of a confidential settlement with JPMorgan from discussing the deal he finally worked out with the bank.

When I last spoke with him, before the settlement severed our communications, he had abandoned plans to start an independent financial advisory business and was mulling ways to devote his time to offering free financial literacy courses for people in his part of the country. He was thinking of starting his own nonprofit organization. Teaching people who did not grow up with wealth how to hang on to their money would be more fulfilling, he thought. He wanted to develop programs for children to provide them with some early information on wealth and finance, the kinds of things they did not learn in school. In a way, Ricardo was experiencing triumph, but it did not feel like that to him.

"I lost a lot of myself from that whole experience," he said. "They took something from me that I will never get back and that they never owned. It's lost forever."

He has ideas, too, about how banks should reshape their processes for responding to discrimination complaints. In his view, an independent body paid for by the banks should be formed—something akin to the FDIC, which is supported by banks' deposit insurance payments—and that body should have sole responsibility for investigating discrimination claims. The banks should not be able to do the investigations themselves in-house, in Ricardo's view, because they can never be neutral.

I ran this idea by a lawyer working on discrimination cases who gave it a lukewarm reception. There already *is* an independent investigative body, the Equal Employment Opportunity Commission, part of the federal government. A separate investigator would not likely be much help, in the lawyer's view. But the lawyer said Ricardo was certainly right about big companies' inability to handle in-house investigations fairly.

TAKING CHARGE OF THE MERITOCRACY

A year and a half after I met Jacqueline Campbell, JPMorgan Securities' diversity officer, at the Quad-A conference, I caught up with her.

She told me she had quit the bank just six weeks after speaking at the September 2019 conference, almost a year to the day after she had gotten her diversity job there. She was not like some of the other former JPMorgan employees I had met who expressed bitterness and fear when they spoke about their time at the bank. She said nothing negative.

Jaq, as she calls herself, had kept the inner light that blazed so brightly in her Quad-A presentation burning, and was determined to keep shining it wherever she went. She had a new idea, one that she thought would be more powerful than anything she could have implemented at a big bank.

Jaq's idea impressed me for its holistic approach to dealing with the ongoing discrimination Black financial advisors faced at big firms. She had decided to start her own independent advisory business— not, like some other people I had met, by striking out alone, but by founding a practice in which she acted more like an impresario, managing other advisors' careers and building a team that could handle larger and larger clients. To start things off, she immediately offered equity shares to other advisors willing to join her. Even in that basic first step she got creative: She specifically wanted to attract a group of advisors who were nearing the ends of their careers and wanted to slow down. She had to offer them real money—a cut of the revenue their clients generated well into the future, for instance—but it was for a good cause. Jaq wanted these older advisors to come over and retire with her so *she* could have a hand in deciding who would be given their books of business after they were gone.

It was genius. One of the biggest problems for Black financial advisors is still that, no matter how hard they work, they rarely get the benefit of being given established clients by older advisors. It's another vicious cycle: The older white advisors, who came up during a time when racism in the wealth management business was not something anyone even thought about addressing and thus never had any Black peers or mentees, still generally want to pass their business on to people who look like them when they decide to leave the industry. Still. Right now. As you read this.

Jaq wants to be the woman who breaks that vicious cycle, one end-of-career transfer at a time. Somewhere out there—in the Detroit area, actually—she is collecting older advisors. She calls them "sunsetters."·

She's also collecting young trainees, whom she calls "sunrisers." In her system, the older advisors bequeath their clients to the sunrisers, who finally get what white financial advisory trainees have gotten for generations: reliable revenue sources that they can use for momentum while they meet new people and build up their practices. She is looking for them at historically Black colleges and universities and at other colleges' and universities' multicultural business student groups, where non-white business students gather.

When I spoke with her, in April of 2021, she was just getting the business going, but she had already selected a group of thirty summer interns for an inaugural class. As for clients? The sky was the limit, as far as she was concerned. She wanted to bring in as many big accounts as possible while also making sure the practice could handle people whose finances looked more like those of an everyday saver, not a bigwig. She wanted part of the business to be focused on advising philanthropists. She wanted to make sure there were some big names among the clients.

She summed it up for me: "African American advisors are always taught to go after the small accounts, but, no, I'm going to shift that. I'm going to get us to go after the millionaires, because we deserve every millionaire that we didn't get."

ACKNOWLEDGMENTS

I would like to thank the leaders of the *New York Times*, with special thanks to Carolyn Ryan, Ellen Pollock, and Anupreeta Das, for graciously giving me the time and space to write this book. Without their support it would not have been possible. A hearty thanks to my colleague and first reader, David Enrich, and to colleagues Kate Kelly, Mary Williams Walsh, Andrew Ross Sorkin, and Rachel C. Abrams for their indispensable guidance.

Thanks also to my editor, Julia Cheiffetz, publisher at One Signal, and to Nicholas Ciani for their invaluable input and thoughtful, patient responses, and to Amara Balan for keeping everyone together and on track. To my agent, Betsy Lerner, for helping me craft this idea and get it out into the world. To fact-checkers Allison Deger and Chris Rickert. To Jessica Bruder, who helped brainstorm the book's title. To Lindsay Stern for a swift and useful German translation. To the people who helped me stay focused and balanced: Yasanthi Soans; Suki Kim; Mary Childs; Susanne Craig; my husband, Chris Reese; my sister Caroline Ehrlich, my two bird companions, Frankie and Friday. To my parents, Marc Flitter and Tobi Richman-Steinhardt, and stepparents David Steinhardt and Alice Flitter.

Thanks most of all to those who stood up to the many powerful and organized forces of oppression and shared their stories with me. I am in awe of your bravery.

NOTES

Introduction

2 A study published in 2015: Katherine V. W. Stone and Alexander J. S. Colvin, "The Arbitration Epidemic: Mandatory Arbitration Deprives Workers and Consumers of Their Rights," Economic Policy Institute, December 7, 2015, https://www.epi.org/publication/the-arbitration-epidemic/.

6 White Americans hold: Neil Bhutta, Andrew C. Chang, Lisa J. Dettling, and Joanne W. Hsu with assistance from Julia Hewitt, "Disparities in Wealth by Race and Ethnicity in the 2019 Survey of Consumer Finances," Federal Reserve Board of Governors, FEDS Notes, September 28, 2020, https://www.federalreserve.gov/econres/notes/feds-notes/disparities-in-wealth-by-race-and-ethnicity-in-the-2019-survey-of-consumer-finances-20200928.htm.

6 just as some of the civil rights era's: Heather Long and Andrew Van Dam, "The Black-White Economic Divide Is As Wide As It Was in 1968," *Washington Post*, June 4, 2020, https://www.washingtonpost.com/business/2020/06/04/economic-divide-black-households/.

6 it is also caused: Ibid.

7 more likely to have retirement savings: Ibid.

7 Put simply: Thomas M. Shapiro, *Toxic Inequality: How America's Wealth Gap Destroys Mobility, Deepens the Racial Divide, & Threatens Our Future* (New York: Basic Books, 2017), 120.

7 the racial wealth gap: Michael W. Kraus, Ivuoma N. Onyeador, Natalie M. Daumeyer, Julian M. Rucker, and Jennifer A. Richeson, "The Misperception of Racial Economic Inequality," *Perspectives on Psychological Science* 14, no. 6 (2019): 899–921.

7 it has actually grown: Bhutta et al., "Disparities in Wealth by Race and Ethnicity."

7 The crisis hurt Black families: Sarah Burd-Sharps and Rebecca-Rasch, *Impact*

of the U.S. Housing Crisis on the Racial Wealth Gap Across Generations, Social Science Research Council report, June 2015, https://www.aclu.org/sites /default/files/field_document/discrimlend_final.pdf.

8 "The observed gaps": Ibid.

9 If racism is "over": Sumi Cho, "Post-Racialism," *Iowa Law Review* 94, no. 5 (July 2009): 1589–1649.

12 In 1995 a federal appeals court: *Cato v. United States*, Nos. 94-17102, 94-17104 (U.S. Ct. App. 9th Cir. Dec. 4, 1995), https://caselaw.findlaw.com/us -9th-circuit/1160081.html.

1. Banking While Black

24 That was when he turned: Emily Flitter, "'Banking While Black': How Cashing a Check Can Be a Minefield," *New York Times*, June 18, 2020. https://www .nytimes.com/2020/06/18/business/banks-black-customers-racism.html.

29 "All right": Ibid.

30 a federal appeals court ruled: *Lopez v. Target Corp.*, 676 F.3d 1230 (11th Cir. 2012).

31 the Fair Access to Financial Services Act: "Fair Access to Financial Services Act: Combatting Discrimination in Banking," Senate Banking Committee, 2020, https://www.banking.senate.gov/imo/media/doc/The%20Fair%20Access %20to%20Financial%20Services%20Act_One%20Pager1.pdf.

33 "a victory for the privacy": State Staff, "Georgia's Legislative Wrap-Up," Concerned Women for America, Legislative Action Committee, April 5, 2016, https://concernedwomen.org/2016-georgias-legislative-wrap-up/.

33 The bank's leadership even apologized: Charles E. Ramirez, "Discriminated Against Once, Detroiter Sues When Bank Fails to Cash Settlement Check," *Detroit News*, January 24, 2020, https://www.detroitnews.com/story/news/local /wayne-county/2020/01/23/detroiter-sues-says-bank-refused-accept-checks -because-hes-black/4551849002/.

2. Mystery Shoppers

36 These officers routinely charged: Ben Lane, "BancorpSouth Fined $10.6 million for Discriminatory Lending, Redlining," HousingWire, June 29, 2016, https://www.housingwire.com/articles/37405-bancorpsouth-fined-106-million -for-discriminatory-lending-redlining/.

36 The room erupted in laughter: *USA and the Consumer Financial Protection Bureau v. BancorpSouth Bank*, Case No. 16-cv-00118-GHD_DAS (U.S. Dist. Ct. N.D. Miss. June 29, 2016), https://files.consumerfinance.gov/f/documents /201606_cfpb_bancorpsouth-joint-complaint.pdf.

37 the loan officer offered: Yuka Hayashi and Aruna Viswanatha, "'Mystery Shoppers' for Home Loans: CFPB Uses Undercover Techniques on Bank," *Wall Street Journal*, updated August 17, 2016, https://www.wsj.com/articles

/mystery-shoppers-for-home-loans-government-uses-undercover-techniques
-on-bank-1471464656.

38 Black people were less likely: Federal Deposit Insurance Corporation (FDIC),
    *How America Banks: Household Use of Banking and Financial Services, 2019
    FDIC Survey*, October 2020, https://www.fdic.gov/analysis/household-survey
    /2019report.pdf.

38 They received calls: Emily Flitter, "Wells Fargo Closed Their Accounts, but
    the Fees Continued to Mount," *New York Times*, August 16, 2019, https://www
    .nytimes.com/2019/08/16/business/wells-fargo-overdraft-fees.html.

39 Black and Hispanic account holders: Michelle Fox, "Black and Hispanic
    Americans Pay Twice As Much in Bank Fees As Whites, Survey Finds,"
    CNBC, January 13, 2021, https://www.cnbc.com/2021/01/13/black-and
    -hispanics-paying-twice-amount-banking-fees-than-whites-survey.html.

40 The difference was so large: Anneliese Lederer, Dedrick Asante-Muhammad,
    Jerome Williams, Sterling Bone, and Glenn Christensen, *Racial and Gender
    Mystery Shopping for Entrepreneurial Loans: Preliminary Overview*, National
    Community Reinvestment Coalition, 2020, https://ncrc.org/wp-content
    /uploads/2020/02/NCRC-Mytery-Shopping-Race-and-Gender-v8.pdf.

41 Black and Hispanic customers: Amber Lee, Bruce Mitchell, Anneliese Lederer,
    Jerome Williams, Sterling Bone, and Glenn Christensen, *Divestment, Dis-
    couragement and Inequity in Small Business Lending*, National Community
    Reinvestment Coalition, 2019, https://ncrc.org/wp-content/uploads/2019/09
    /NCRC-Small-Business-Research-FINAL.pdf.

44 "The white kids that are out there": Tanzina Vega, "It's Lonely in the Black 1%,"
    CNN, October 14, 2016, https://money.cnn.com/2016/10/14/news/economy
    /black-1-unstereotyped/index.html.

45 an audit found: Stacy Cowley, "The US Gave $3.7 Billion in Relief to Ineligible
    Businesses, Auditor Finds," *New York Times*, November 30, 2021, https://www
    .nytimes.com/2021/11/30/business/sba-eidl-pandemic-relief.html.

45 Bank of America was technically: Emily Flitter, "Black-Owned Businesses
    Could Face Hurdles in Federal Aid Program," *New York Times*, April 10, 2020,
    updated June 4, 2020, https://www.nytimes.com/2020/04/10/business/minority
    -business-coronavirus-loans.html.

46 30 percent of the total: Robert Fairlie, Alicia Robb, and David T. Robinson, *Black
    and White: Access to Capital Among Minority-Owned Startups*, Stanford Insti-
    tute for Economic Policy Discussion Paper No. 17-3, December 15, 2016, https:
    //drive.google.com/file/d/1QSX0bvF3ZgYd_XyIPNeIMI6_GYyMVQx5/view.

48 to make the study more conservative: Anneliese Lederer, Sara Oros, Jerome
    Williams, Sterling Bone, and Glenn Christensen, "Lending Discrimination
    Within the Paycheck Protection Program," National Community Reinvestment
    Coalition, 2020, https://ncrc.org/lending-discrimination-within-the-paycheck
    -protection-program/.

49 68 percent of the population: Emily Flitter, "Black Business Owners Had a Harder Time Getting Aid, a Study Finds," *New York Times*, July 15, 2020, https://www.nytimes.com/2020/07/15/business/paycheck-protection-program -bias.html.

49 They had struggled noticeably: Stacy Cowley, "Racial Bias Skewed Small-Business Relief Lending, Study Says," *New York Times*, October 11, 2021, https://www .nytimes.com/2021/10/11/business/ppp-loans-covid-racial-bias.html.

3. Ricardo and Jimmy

51 Dimon was one of the biggest hypocrites: This chapter is based largely on interviews and documents and recordings provided by Ricardo Peters and Jimmy Kennedy over a six-month period in 2019.

53 the bank operated about 5,000 branches: There were between 3,100 and 3,200 branches offering Chase Private Client Services in 2019, according to information provided by Patricia Wexler on December 17, 2019. Wexler said that three-quarters of the branches that lacked CPC services were within five miles of a branch that offered them.

55 a huge contingent of people: *Senegal et al. v. JPMorgan Chase Bank, N.A.*, 18-cv-06006 (U.S. Dist. Ct. N.D. Ill.).

4. The Truth About HR

79 sang a "decent" falsetto: Jane Lewis, "Bill Winters: Downfall of a Banking Hero," *MoneyWeek*, July 29, 2019, https://moneyweek.com/511835/the-downfall-of-a -banking-hero.

83 "Having a policy became a proxy": Lauren B. Edelman, "How HR and Judges Made It Almost Impossible for Victims of Sexual Harassment to Win In Court," *Harvard Business Review*, August 22, 2018, https://hbr.org/2018/08/how-hr -and-judges-made-it-almost-impossible-for-victims-of-sexual-harassment-to -win-in-court.

86 "doing God's work": Dealbook, "Blankfein Says He's Just Doing 'God's Work,'" *New York Times*, November 9, 2009, https://dealbook.nytimes.com/2009/11/09 /goldman-chief-says-he-is-just-doing-gods-work/.

87 "should be taught American history": Andy Serwer, "JPMorgan CEO Talks China, Trade and Immigration in His Annual Letter," Yahoo! Finance, April 5, 2018, https://finance.yahoo.com/news/jpmorgan-ceo-jamie-dimon-talks -china-trade-immigration-annual-letter-095554402.html.

87 "short-termism": Jamie Dimon, JPMorgan Chase CEO Letter to Shareholders, April 7, 2021, https://www.jpmorganchase.com/content/dam/jpmc/jpmorgan -chase-and-co/investor-relations/documents/ceo-letter-to-shareholders-2020.pdf.

88 WhiteRock: Aziza Kasumov, "BlackRock Under Pressure to Live Up to Its Promises on Diversity," *Financial Times*, March 21, 2021, https://www.ft.com /content/6476e681-4154-43a6-93e4-f5c86ae30dd9.

5. Unsafe at Any Level

98 The paper's 2015 story: Jenny Anderson, "In Tidjane Thiam, Credit Suisse Gets Risk Expertise," *New York Times*, March 10, 2015, https://www.nytimes.com/2015/03/11/business/dealbook/credit-suisse-brady-dougan-tidjane-thiam.html.

98 "I am very happy to interview": David Teather, "Very British Coup for an African Francophone," *Guardian*, May 4, 2007, https://www.theguardian.com/business/2007/may/04/insurance.money.

99 Thiam took the blame: Amie Tsang and Michael J. de la Merced, "Credit Suisse C.E.O. Tidjane Thiam Exits After Spying Scandal," *New York Times*, February 7, 2020, https://www.nytimes.com/2020/02/07/business/dealbook/credit-suisse-ceo.html.

99 "Whether it's labeled racism, xenophobia": Kate Kelly, "The Short Tenure and Abrupt Ouster of Banking's Sole Black C.E.O.," *New York Times*, October 3, 2020, https://www.nytimes.com/2020/10/03/business/tidjane-thiam-credit-suisse.html.

100 "The Karen Next Door": Allison P. Davis, "The Karen Next Door," *New York Magazine*, December 21, 2020, https://www.thecut.com/article/montclair-new-jersey-permit-karen.html.

101 he resigned on November 1, 2021: Michael J. de la Merced and Matthew Goldstein, "James Staley, Barclays's C.E.O., Steps Down After a Jeffrey Epstein Inquiry," *New York Times*, November 1, 2021, https://www.nytimes.com/2021/10/24/business/james-staley-barclays-jeffrey-epstein.html.

6. The Friendly Guy Next Door, Edward Jones

106 It counts on a constant stream: United States Securities and Exchange Commission, Form 10-K filing, The Jones Financial Companies, L.L.L.P., March 12, 2020, https://www.sec.gov/Archives/edgar/data/815917/000156459020010385/ck0000815917-10k_20191231.pdf.

135 "difficulties developing or expanding": United States Securities and Exchange Commission, Form 10-K filing, The Jones Financial Companies, L.L.L.P., March 14, 2019, https://www.sec.gov/Archives/edgar/data/815917/000156459019007788/ck0000815917-10k_20181231.pdf.

7. How Insurance Works if You're Black (It Doesn't)

142 in the previous decade: United States General Accounting Office, *Insurance Regulation: The Insurance Regulatory Information System Needs Improvement*, GAO/GGD 91-20, November 1990, 2, https://www.gao.gov/assets/ggd-91-20.pdf.

142 many regulators did not particularly care: Kenneth J. Meier, "The Politics of Insurance Regulation," *Journal of Risk and Insurance* 58, no. 4 (December 1991): 700–13.

142 "The commissions range in size": Ibid.

142 a combined total: Ibid.

146 the data had been available: Jonathan Weil and Janet Elliott, "Insurers' Trade Secrets May Not Be So Secret After All," *Wall Street Journal*, August 16, 2000.

151 The representative apologized: Emily Flitter, "Black Homeowners Struggle to Get Insurers to Pay Claims," *New York Times*, December 29, 2020, updated January 1, 2021, https://www.nytimes.com/2020/12/29/business/black -homeowners-insurance-claim.html.

154 it had not relied on the article: *Chaudhry v. Provident Life and Accident Insurance Company*, 12-cv-05838 (U.S. Dist. Ct. N.D. Ill. July 16, 2014), https: //casetext.com/case/chaudhry-v-provident-life-accident-ins-co.

156 44 percent of all Katrina victims: Thomas Gabe, Gene Falk, Maggie McCarty, and Virginia W. Mason, *Hurricane Katrina: Social-Demographic Characteristics of Impacted Areas*, Congressional Research Service Report for Congress, Order Code RL33141, November 4, 2005, https://www.tidegloballearning.net /sites/default/files/uploads/crsrept.pdf.

156 The judgment was upheld: Mark Sherman, Associated Press, "Justices Uphold Katrina Fraud Verdict Against State Farm," PBS News Hour, December 6, 2016, https://www.pbs.org/newshour/nation/justices-uphold-katrina-fraud -verdict-state-farm.

157 State Farm denied that she: Javonte Anderson, "State Farm Denied His Claims Because of Racial Discrimination, Lawsuit Alleges," *Chicago Tribune*, May 3, 2019, https://www.chicagotribune.com/news/ct-met-state-farm-lawsuit -racial-discrimination-20190503-story.html.

162 housing advocates won a round: Jean M. Zachariasiewicz, "Not Worth the Risk: The Legal Consequences of the Refusal to Insure Properties with Section 8 Tenants," *Banking & Financial Services Policy Report* 33, no. 11 (November 2014), https://boise-rentals.com/files/27.pdf.

8. The Problem with the Machines

166 Consumer advocates pounced: Andrew Kersley, "Couriers Say Uber's 'Racist' Facial Identification Tech Got Them Fired," *Wired UK*, March 1, 2021, https://www.wired.co.uk/article/uber-eats-couriers-facial-recognition.

166 "super creepy": Sara Morrison, "A Disturbing, Viral Twitter Thread Reveals How AI-Powered Insurance Can Go Wrong," Vox, May 27, 2021, https://www .vox.com/recode/22455140/lemonade-insurance-ai-twitter.

168 An alert would be sent: Stacy Cowley, "Banks and Retailers Are Tracking How You Type, Swipe and Tap," *New York Times*, August 13, 2018, https://www .nytimes.com/2018/08/13/business/behavioral-biometrics-banks-security .html.

172 in November of 2019, another big bank: U.S. Bank news release, "U.S. Bank Hires Dr. Tanushree Luke as Head of Artificial Intelligence," November 6,

2019, https://ir.usbank.com/news-releases/news-release-details/us-bank-hires-dr-tanushree-luke-head-artificial-intelligence.

172 This public image of AI: Cathy O'Neil, "Summers' Lending Club Makes Money by Bypassing the Equal Credit Opportunity Act," *Mathbabe* (blog), August 29, 2013, https://mathbabe.org/2013/08/29/summers-lending-club-makes-money-by-bypassing-the-equal-credit-opportunity-act/.

173 The specific example she picked: Cathy O'Neil, *Weapons of Math Destruction: How Big Data Increases Inequality and Threatens Democracy* (New York: Broadway Books, 2016), 141–60.

173 alternative data: Julapa Jagtiani and Catherine Lemieux, *The Roles of Alternative Data and Machine Learning in Fintech Lending: Evidence from the LendingClub Consumer Platform*, Federal Reserve Bank of Philadelphia, January 2019, https://www.philadelphiafed.org/-/media/frbp/assets/working-papers/2018/wp18-15r.pdf,

175 They remain the centerpieces: Michelle Singletary, "Credit Scores Are Supposed to Be Race-Neutral. That's Impossible," *Washington Post*, October 16, 2020, https://www.washingtonpost.com/business/2020/10/16/how-race-affects-your-credit-score/.

175 "It has striking effects": Natalie Campisi, "From Inherent Racial Bias to Incorrect Data—the Problems with Current Credit Scoring Models," *Forbes*, February 26, 2021, https://www.forbes.com/advisor/credit-cards/from-inherent-racial-bias-to-incorrect-data-the-problems-with-current-credit-scoring-models/.

176 "The cheating of Black communities": Keeanga-Yamahtta Taylor, *Race for Profit: How Banks and the Real Estate Industry Undermined Black Homeownership* (Chapel Hill: University of North Carolina Press, 2019), 23.

176 Even before the 2008 financial crisis: Paul S. Calem, Jonathan E. Hershaff, and Susan M. Wachter, "Neighborhood Patterns of Subprime Lending: Evidence from Disparate Cities," *Housing Policy Debate* 15, no. 3 (June 8, 2004): 603–22.

176 the bank had overcharged home loan fees: Charlie Savage, "Wells Fargo Will Settle Mortgage Bias Charges," *New York Times*, July 12, 2012, https://www.nytimes.com/2012/07/13/business/wells-fargo-to-settle-mortgage-discrimination-charges.html.

177 the city dropped the suits: Kevin Wack, "Big Banks Outlast City of Miami in Long Legal Battle," *American Banker*, February 3, 2020, https://www.americanbanker.com/news/big-banks-outlast-city-of-miami-in-long-legal-battle.

177 Wells Fargo settled: Caitlin McCabe, "Wells Fargo to Pay Philly $10 million to Resolve Lawsuit Alleging Lender Discrimination Against Minorities," *Philadelphia Inquirer*, December 16, 2019.

178 When Donald Trump became president: Kelsey Ramirez, "HMDA Enforcement Defanged by Trump-Led Regulators," HousingWire, December 22, 2017, https://www.housingwire.com/articles/42142-hmda-enforcement-defanged-by-trump-led-regulators/.

178 almost a quarter of all new home loans: Jason Dietrich, "Mortgage Applications with Missing Race Data and the Implications for Monitoring Fair Lending Compliance," *Journal of Housing Research* 13, no. 1 (2002).

178 only 11 percent of new mortgages: Ibid.

178 The OCC economist, Jason Dietrich: Ibid.

179 individual Black homeowners: Debra Kamin, "Black Homeowners Face Discrimination in Appraisals," *New York Times*, August 25, 2020, updated August 27, 2020, https://www.nytimes.com/2020/08/25/realestate/blacks-minorities -appraisals-discrimination.html.

179 "much of contemporary AI": Kristin Johnson, Frank Pasquale, and Jennifer Chapman, "Artificial Intelligence, Machine Learning and Bias in Finance: Toward Responsible Innovation," *Fordham Law Review* 88, no. 2 (2019), https://ir.lawnet.fordham.edu/cgi/viewcontent.cgi?article=5629&context=flr.

180 the idea that special programs: Safiya Umoja Noble and Sarah T. Roberts, "Technological Elites, the Meritocracy, and Postracial Myths in Silicon Valley," in *Racism Postrace*, ed. Roopali Mukherjee, Sarah Banet-Weiser, and Herman Gray (Durham, NC: Duke University Press, 2019), 114.

181 Damore's fellow Silicon Valley insiders: Dalvin Brown, "Ex–Google Engineer Who Alleged Discrimination Against Conservative White Men Asks Judge to Dismiss Lawsuit," *USA Today*, May 10, 2020, https://www.usatoday.com/story /tech/2020/05/10/google-james-damore-diversity-discrimination-lawsuit /3105662001/.

185 "star ethics researcher": Karen Hao, "We Read the Paper That Forced Timnit Gebru out of Google. Here's What It Says," *MIT Technology Review*, December 4, 2020, https://www.technologyreview.com/2020/12/04/1013294/google -ai-ethics-research-paper-forced-out-timnit-gebru/.

186 in an email to employees: Nitasha Tiku, "Google Hired Timnit Gebru to Be an Outspoken Critic of Unethical AI. Then She Was Fired for It," *Washington Post*, December 23, 2020, https://www.washingtonpost.com/technology /2020/12/23/google-timnit-gebru-ai-ethics/.

9. On the Diversity Circuit

195 The bankruptcy decimated the city's infrastructure: Monica Davey, "Financial Crisis Just a Symptom of Detroit's Woes," *New York Times*, July 8, 2013, https://www.nytimes.com/2013/07/09/us/financial-crisis-just-a-symptom-of -detroits-woes.html.

198 "a very limited pool of Black talent": Imani Moise, Jessica DiNapoli, and Ross Kerber, "Wells Fargo CEO Ruffles Feathers with Comments About Diverse Talent," Reuters, September 22, 2020, https://www.reuters.com/article/us -global-race-wells-fargo-exclusive/exclusive-wells-fargo-ceo-ruffles-feathers -with-comments-about-diverse-talent-idUSKCN26D2IU.

199 "I've tried to know every Dottie": Adam Bryant, "Walt Bettinger of Charles Schwab: You've Got to Open Up to Move Up," *New York Times*, February 4, 2016, https://www.nytimes.com/2016/02/07/business/walt-bettinger-of-charles -schwab-youve-got-to-open-up-to-move-up.html.

201 "fall under new and revised laws": Roderick A. Ferguson, *The Reorder of Things: The University and Its Pedagogies of Minority Difference* (Minneapolis: University of Minnesota Press, 2012), 12.

201 "State, capital, and the academy": Roderick A. Ferguson, "On the Postracial Question," in *Racism Postrace*, ed. Roopali Mukherjee, Sarah Banet-Weiser, and Herman Gray (Durham, NC: Duke University Press, 2019), 75.

202 fewer Black employees in senior roles: M. J. Lee and Anna Palmer, "Rocky Road for Financial Services?," *Politico*, September 27, 2012, https://www.politico .com/story/2012/09/house-financial-services-facing-rocky-road-ahead-081725.

202 than in 2007: Representative Maxine Waters (D-CA), "Waters Statement at Historic Diversity and Inclusion Subcommittee Hearing," U.S. House Committee on Financial Services, press release, February 28, 2019, https://financialservices .house.gov/news/documentsingle.aspx?DocumentID=402374.

204 "It is not the proper role": Senator Pat Toomey (R-PA), "Letter to Minneapolis Fed President Neel Kashkari," May 23, 2021, https://www.banking.senate.gov /imo/media/doc/toomey_to_minneapolis_fed.pdf.

204 "We Don't Need a Woke Fed": Editorial, "We Don't Need a Woke Fed," *Washington Examiner*, May 25, 2021, https://www.washingtonexaminer.com/opinion /editorials/we-dont-need-a-woke-fed.

205 "Our talk about whiteness": Sara Ahmed, *On Being Included: Racism and Diversity in Institutional Life* (Durham, NC: Duke University Press, 2012), 43.

11. Reparations and the Big Banks

229 "America was built": Ta-Nehisi Coates, "The Case for Reparations," *Atlantic*, June 2014, https://www.theatlantic.com/magazine/archive/2014/06/the-case -for-reparations/361631/.

230 "This scheme of getting money": Deadria C. Farmer-Paellmann, "Excerpt from *Black Exodus: The Ex-Slave Pension Movement Reader*," in *Should America Pay? Slavery and the Raging Debate on Reparations*, ed. Raymond A. Winbrush (New York: Amistad, 2003): 27–30.

232 the 1999 revelation by Deutsche: Edmund L. Andrews, "German Bank Opens Files on Financing of Auschwitz," *New York Times*, February 5, 1999, https: //www.nytimes.com/1999/02/05/world/german-bank-opens-files-on-financing -of-auschwitz.html.

236 it would start going after private companies: "NAACP to Target Private Business," *Washington Times*, July 12, 2005, https://www.washingtontimes.com/news /2005/jul/12/20050712-120944-7745r/.

238 out of almost 4,000: Jeff Cota, "Milwaukee's Anti-Slavery Ordinance Short on Discovery," *Milwaukee Daily Reporter*, October 19, 2012, https://dailyreporter.com/2012/10/19/milwaukees-anti-slavery-ordinance-short-on-discovery/.

240 "We know that we cannot change": Laura Smitherman, "Wachovia Apologizes for Ties to Slavery of Its Predecessors," *Baltimore Sun*, June 3, 2005, https://www.baltimoresun.com/news/bs-xpm-2005-06-03-0506030249-story.html.

240 "We didn't want to have a donation": Darryl Fears, "Seeking More Than Apologies for Slavery," *Washington Post*, June 20, 2005, https://www.washingtonpost.com/archive/politics/2005/06/20/seeking-more-than-apologies-for-slavery/cff95386-8fbf-417b-aae0-bdb85f1f1a97/.

240 Bank of America revised its disclosure: Gary Washburn and *Tribune* staff reporter, "Bank of America Insists It Did Not Profit Off Slavery," *Chicago Tribune*, August 25, 2005, https://www.chicagotribune.com/news/ct-xpm-2005-08-25-0508250237-story.html.

241 Brown University, which John Brown also founded: Deborah Barfield Berry, "The US Is Grappling with Its History of Slavery. The Blueprint for Dealing with It? Some Say Brown University," December 16, 2019, updated April 23, 2020, https://www.usatoday.com/in-depth/news/education/2019/12/16/slavery-reparations-brown-university-antigua-colleges-paying-up/4401725002/.

244 JPMorgan disclosed Lide's findings: Associated Press, "JPMorgan: Predecessors Linked to Slavery," NBC News, January 21, 2005, https://www.nbcnews.com/id/wbna6851727.

244 it was donating $5 million: Washburn, "Bank of America Insists It Did Not Profit Off Slavery."

244 the bank's president, Moses Taylor: "Citi Turns 200: City Bank Finances Union Cause," *Citi* (Citigroup corporate blog), April 6, 2012, https://blog.citigroup.com/2012/04/citi-turns-200-city-bank-finances-union-cause/.

244 The bank's other leaders: Daniel Hodas, *The Business Career of Moses Taylor* (New York: New York University Press, 1976), 51.

245 Taylor became president pro tempore: Ibid., 52.

245 slave traders set up shop in Manhattan: John Harris, *The Last Slave Ships* (New Haven, CT: Yale University Press, 2020), 42–47.

245 lifelong connections to the Cuban sugar industry: "An Old Merchant's Death," *New York Times*, May 24, 1882, https://timesmachine.nytimes.com/timesmachine/1882/05/24/96861473.pdf.

245 he would have been a billionaire: Roland T. Ely, "The Old Cuba Trade: Highlights and Case Studies of Cuban-American Interdependence in the Nineteenth Century," *Business History Review* 38, no. 4 (Winter 1964): 456–78, DOI: https://doi.org/10.2307/3112547.

246 sugar production was booming: Harris, *The Last Slave Ships*, 27.

246 "with no business in Cuba": Ibid., 88.

246 "[no] aversion to carrying the produce": Maeve Glass, "Moses Taylor Pyne and

the Sugar Plantations of the Americas," *Princeton & Slavery* (blog), Princeton University, n.d., https://slavery.princeton.edu/stories/moses-taylor-pyne.

247 a disagreeable thing: Jonathan Daniel Wells, *The Kidnapping Club: Wall Street, Slavery and Resistance on the Eve of the Civil War* (New York: Bold Type Books, 2020), 208–11.

247 to lament the election of Abraham Lincoln: Ibid., 272.

249 Any Black Evanston resident: Associated Press, "Evanston, Illinois, Becomes First U.S. City to Pay Reparations to Black Residents," NBC News, March 23, 2021, https://www.nbcnews.com/news/us-news/evanston-illinois-becomes -first-u-s-city-pay-reparations-blacks-n1261791.

251 There was no calculation: Philip A. Lehman, "Executive Summary of Multi-state/Federal Settlement of Foreclosure Misconduct Claims," National Mortgage Settlement, July 23, 2012, http://www.nationalmortgagesettlement.com /files/NMS_Executive_Summary-7-23-2012.pdf.

12. Making Pledges

260 "technical assistance": Mehrsa Baradaran, *The Color of Money: Black Banks and the Racial Wealth Gap* (Cambridge, MA: Harvard University Press, 2017), 264.

263 (Chase says customers): Lisa Servon, *The Unbanking of America* (Boston: Mariner Books, 2017).

13. What Wall Street Should Do

265 "As a political organization": Roderick A. Ferguson, "On the Postracial Question," in *Racism Postrace*, ed. Roopali Mukherjee, Sarah Banet-Weiser, and Herman Gray (Durham, NC: Duke University Press, 2019), 76.

269 "the condition of the country's health": Nick Wingfield, Katie Thomas, and Reed Abelson, "Amazon, Berkshire Hathaway and JPMorgan Team Up to Try to Disrupt Health Care," *New York Times*, January 30, 2018, https://www.nytimes .com/2018/01/30/technology/amazon-berkshire-hathaway-jpmorgan-health -care.html.

269 JPMorgan, Amazon, and Berkshire Hathaway: Emily Flitter and Karen Weise, "Amazon, Berkshire and JPMorgan Will End Joint Health Care Venture," *New York Times*, January 4, 2021, https://www.nytimes.com/2021/01/04/business /haven-amazon-berkshire-hathaway-jpmorgan.html.

272 "'ghetto loans for mud people'": Michael Powell, "Banks Accused of Pushing Mortgage Deals on Blacks," *New York Times*, June 6, 2009, https://www.nytimes .com/2009/06/07/us/07baltimore.html.

274 "In terms of the actual content": Khalil Gibran Muhammad and Ben Pushkin, "Critical Race Theory in the Classroom," *Some of My Best Friends Are . . .* (podcast), S.1, Ep. 4, September 30, 2021, https://podcasts.apple.com/au/podcast /back-to-school-backlash/id1578329459?i=1000536928820.

274 "Lie of credit": Christopher Rufo, "Lie of Credit—American Express Tells Its
     Workers Capitalism Is Racist," *New York Post*, August 11, 2021, https://nypost
     .com/2021/08/11/american-express-tells-its-workers-capitalism-is-racist/.

14. On Their Own

290 she was forced to leave: Ifeoma Ozoma, "An NDA Was Designed to Keep Me
     Quiet," *New York Times*, April 13, 2021, https://www.nytimes.com/2021/04/13
     /opinion/nda-work-discrimination.html.

INDEX

ABOUT THE AUTHOR

EMILY FLITTER is a *New York Times* reporter covering finance and Wall Street. Before joining the *Times* in 2017, she spent eight years at Reuters, where she wrote about financial crimes, campaign finance, the Trump campaign, and environmental issues. She graduated from Wellesley College and holds a master's degree in journalism and Near Eastern studies from New York University. She lives in New York with her husband and two parrots.